D1274826

LINCOLN
AND THE RUSSIANS

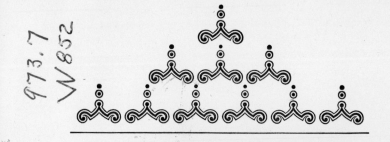

Lincoln and the Russians

ALBERT A. WOLDMAN

THE WORLD PUBLISHING COMPANY

CLEVELAND AND NEW YORK

FIRST EDITION

Library of Congress Catalog Card Number: 52-8436

CONTENTS

PREFACE

THE STORY of Lincoln and Russia is virtually an unknown chapter in the Lincoln saga. It needs retelling today not only because of the light it may shed upon current problems, but especially because Russia's real motives in befriending the United States during the Civil War, concealed even from Lincoln, have only recently been revealed as a result of diligent research among the dusty archives of the Russian government. Much of my source material is from the voluminous diplomatic correspondence between Edouard de Stoeckl, Russia's Minister to Washington during the Civil War, and Prince Gortchakov, the Czar's Minister for Foreign Affairs in St. Petersburg. This correspondence was written in French. Another source is the *Krasnyi Arkhiv*, the Red Archives, written in Russian. I have had these materials translated and many excerpts thereof appear in this text. Still another source—especially for new material on Cassius M. Clay—is the Lincoln Papers which became available in 1947.

Is a Russian-American war inevitable? Must the conflicting political systems of the democratic United States and communistic Russia lead them to the battlefield? Or can they—despite their clashing ideologies —co-exist in peace and work together for the salvation of the world?

The little-known story of American-Russian relations during the Civil War may help to furnish answers to these all-important questions. Abraham Lincoln, "the supreme American," who knew Russia as a "country where they make no pretense of loving liberty," and regarded her government as the exemplar of despotism, led our government into an informal yet firm alliance and working partnership with the realm of the Czars—despite the fact that our "government of the people, by the people, for the people" and Czar Alexander II's absolute autocracy were the very antithesis of each other.

This Russian-American *entente cordiale* was a political paradox without equal. To the ruling classes of Europe, the United States was then the world's most dangerous and extremist revolutionary government. We were the "Reds" of those days. On the other hand, Americans regarded Russia as the classic example of absolute power and despotism, and the foremost exponent of suppression of popular movements throughout the world. From the official Russian viewpoint this alliance was probably more difficult for Russia to swallow than for the United States. Lincoln as the head of a democratic nation fighting for survival could more easily justify the partnership than the Czar could justify it in the eyes of the autocrats, haters of democracy and champions of absolutism who surrounded him. As will be seen, the United States and Russia became international bedfellows because they had a common fear and a common enemy—Great Britain. Russian autocracy would have been pleased to see American democracy destroyed. Americans had nothing but contempt for Russia's absolutism. Yet, for mutual protection against a common foe, they forgot their ideological differences and formed a working partnership that kept the two governments firm friends for decades. This strange alliance was a potent factor in preventing European intervention in the American Civil War, and in stopping an Anglo-French alliance from attacking Russia over the turbulent Polish question.

If the analogy between Russian-American relations of Lincoln's day and those of the present period is not identical, the similarity is, nevertheless, substantial. Then as now the Russians as a people had never experienced real freedom. The territorial and other demands of the Soviets of today are not much different from those of their czaristic predecessors. Then, as now, the centuries-old desire of Russia to reach an ice-free port on the Black Sea, the Bosphorus or the Persian Gulf met with the unswerving opposition of the British and their allies. Then, as now, Russia was the most hated nation on the continent. The repressive despotism of the Czar's government was then as odious to democratic America as is Russia's communism today. But our Ministers to St. Petersburg were instructed to do all within their power "to confirm and strengthen" the traditional "relations of amity and friendship" between the two nations.

Lincoln found political collaboration (as distinguished from ideological rapprochement) between the world's most liberal democracy and the world's most repressive despotism not only feasible but imperative for the Republic's welfare.

He built this policy on confidence in America, not on distrust of Russia. He was moved by faith in democracy, not by fear of autocracy. He believed that only a strong, united nation with unchallengeable power and unquestioned supremacy over the States in the national domain could maintain for us a lasting peace. This mighty faith was but a reëmphasis of his expression of faith at Cooper Union, February 27, 1860: "Neither let us be slandered from our duty by false accusations against us, nor frightened from it by menaces of destruction to the government, nor dungeons to ourselves. Let us have faith that right makes might, and in that faith let us to the end dare to do our duty as we understand it."

1

Lincoln Denounces Russian Despotism

ON THE evening of January 8, 1852 Abraham Lincoln left his dingy law office in Springfield, Illinois, and walked briskly to the courthouse on the square. A meeting—a result of the "Kossuth craze" which was sweeping the Northern States—was about to take place there and he had been invited to address the gathering. It was to be a demonstration on behalf of Hungarian freedom and a protest against Russia's unwarranted intervention in Hungary's struggle to throw off the yoke of Austrian tyranny.

Across the Atlantic Ocean, some four thousand miles distant from Springfield, political convulsions were shaking European civilization to its very foundations. The dark year of 1848 had seen the barricades and battalions of revolution rise from Paris to Moscow and from Prussia in the north to Sicily in the south. A democratic revolution had broken out in France in February of that year. Soon men throughout Europe rose up in arms for liberty—for economic security and better standards of living. Even in England there was unrest in the shape of the Chartist movement. This spree year of liberty was the year when two clashing ideologies represented by France, liberal and republican, and Russia, reactionary and monarchical, were creating divided counsels and conflicting prophets, and keeping all Europe in a ferment. It was the year of Karl Marx's *Communist Manifesto*; the year when Czar Nicholas of Russia wrote to Victoria of England, "What remains standing in Europe?"

Awakened Hungary under the inspired leadership of Louis Kossuth had succeeded temporarily in winning her independence from the Austrian overlords. The only resource left to the thoroughly beaten Hapsburgs was to invite the willing intervention of Russia.

Like a tempest from the north, the huge armies of Czar Nicholas I swept down on the little land of the Danube. To the fighters behind the barricades the Emperor issued a manifesto which closed with the words from Isaiah, "Listen, ye heathen, and submit, for with us is God!" Kossuth's followers fought heroically against hopeless odds, but after a brief resistance were utterly crushed. Gloatingly the Russian general reported to the Czar, "Hungary is lying at Your Majesty's feet."

Terrible was the reaction throughout Europe when the workmen and peasants who had seized power briefly were shot down by superior guns, and their revolutions blown off the map. The ebbtide rushed back violently and swept away all that the liberal agitations had won. As the gales of 1848 blew themselves out completely, a funereal gloom settled upon Europe. Absolutism was restored in the lands from which it had been briefly banished. By the hundreds of thousands, homeless, land-less and property-less peasants and toilers, whose hopes of winning oft-promised rights and reforms had been shattered, now turned their faces longingly toward America. Soon tidal waves of hungry, discontented people began pouring across the Atlantic bringing with them har-rowing accounts of the plight of their countrymen who could not escape.

The heart of America went out to Europe's victims of oppression. This nation's sympathy manifested itself in various ways. Among them were public demonstrations on behalf of Hungarian independence. One such meeting had already taken place in Springfield, on September 6, 1849. Lincoln's good friend and predecessor in Congress from the Springfield district, Edward D. Baker, had been the principal speaker, and Judge David Davis, who presided over the Eighth Judicial Circuit, had been the chairman of the meeting. The judge appointed Lincoln, his frequent traveling companion, together with five other citizens of Springfield, to draft appropriate resolutions to be sent to the American Secretary of State. As spokesman for the committee, Lincoln submitted a group of resolutions which, after expressing admiration for the Hun-garians "in their present glorious struggle for liberty," urged the United States government to "acknowledge the independence of Hungary as a nation of freemen at the very earliest moment." This recognition, the resolutions recited, is due from American freemen to their struggling brethren in the general cause of republican liberty and does not violate the just rights of the government against which the Hungarians are contending.[1]

Now, more than two years later, another public demonstration on behalf of Hungarian freedom was being held in Lincoln's home town. Governor Kossuth, exiled leader of Hungary's revolt, was touring the United States, pleading the cause of his oppressed people. In Washington, Senator Stephen A. Douglas, Lincoln's illustrious fellow-townsman, had been eloquent in his advocacy of an official governmental welcome to Kossuth. Dramatically the Little Giant from Illinois had asked: "Shall it be said that democratic America is not to be permitted to grant a hearty welcome to an exile who has become the representative of liberal principles throughout the world lest despotic Austria and Russia shall be offended?" And he had answered, "The armed intervention of Russia to deprive Hungary of her constitutional rights, was such a violation of the laws of nations as authorized . . . the United States to interfere and prevent the consummation of the deed."[2]

Lincoln, who had apparently abandoned politics and was now to all intents and purposes completely immersed in the law, was glad to participate in the public remonstrance against tyranny, and to raise his voice on behalf of human freedom. Far away as Hungary and Russia were from the banks of the Sangamon, they represented something vitally significant to him as a free American. Russia stood as the exemplar of repressive despotism, while Hungary represented the helpless victim of oppression struggling to be free. Hating slavery in any form, Lincoln sympathized instinctively with the underdog.

The meeting had been well publicized and "a large concourse of people from different portions of the state" gathered in the courthouse for the occasion. John Calhoun, who presided, opened the meeting and explained the purpose of the gathering to the audience, which included a number of men who had been identified with the republican movement in Europe. He recited the dramatic details of Hungary's struggle to throw off the yoke of Austrian oppression. He recalled how the Russian despot had come to the aid of the Hapsburg despot with armies, guns and money, and had succeeded in suppressing the revolt and rendering all the sacrifices of the Magyars unavailing. Judge Lyman Trumbull and others then described Kossuth's flight to Turkey, his imprisonment there at Austria's instigation, his release through the influence of our government, which sent the navy frigate *Mississippi* to bring the exiled leader to the United States, and the wild enthusiasm with which this "apostle of world democracy" was being greeted wherever he appeared.

The speakers also called the gathering's attention to the sharp protest of the Austrian Chargé d'Affaires at Washington against our government's "intervention." The American eagle fairly screamed with the orator's reply that since our nation has given the world a successful example of free government which has stood as the natural inspiration of republican movements everywhere, we shall always cherish an interest in nations struggling for similar institutions, and shall continue ever to raise our voices in protest whenever tyranny attempts to deprive a free people of their independence. The principle of nonintervention, shouted one of the speakers, must never be construed so as to "prevent this nation at any time from interfering in favor of any people who may be struggling for liberty in any part of the world."[3]

After the speeches, the presiding officer appointed a committee composed of Lincoln, Judge Trumbull, Archibald Williams, William I. Ferguson, Anson G. Henry, Samuel S. Marshall and Ebenezer Peck to draft resolutions implementing the sentiments expressed at the gathering. The next evening Lincoln presented these resolutions:

> Whereas, in the opinion of this meeting, the arrival of Kossuth in our country, in connection with the recent events in Hungary, and with the appeal he is now making in behalf of his country, presents an occasion upon which we, the American people, cannot remain silent, without justifying an interference against our continued devotion to the principles of our free institutions, therefore,
>
> Resolved 1. That it is the right of any people, sufficiently numerous for national independence, to throw off, to revolutionize, their existing form of government, and to establish such other in its stead as they may choose.

What strange words to be coming from the mouth of the man whom destiny was preparing to wage America's great Civil War against secession!

And yet this was the second time within about three years that Lincoln had expressed his belief in the right of secession. In 1848, in a speech in Congress, he had declared:

Any people anywhere, being inclined and having the power, have the right to rise up and shake off the existing government, and form a new one that suits them better. That is a most valuable, a most sacred right—a right which we hope and believe is to liberate the world.

Nor is the right confined to cases in which the whole people of an existing government may choose to exercise it. Any portion of such people that can, may revolutionize and make their own so much of the territory as they inhabit.

This is what Lincoln believed in 1848 and as late as 1852. But in 1860 he would no longer hold to that belief—although the South did. But to get back to the resolutions he helped prepare in January 1852:

2. That it is the duty of our government to neither foment, nor assist, such revolutions in other governments.

3. That, as we may not legally or warrantably interfere abroad to aid, so no other government may interfere abroad, to suppress such revolutions; and that we should at once announce to the world our determination to insist upon this mutuality of non-intervention, as a sacred principle of the international law.

4. That the late interference of Russia in the Hungarian struggle was, in our opinion, such illegal and unwarrantable interference.

5. That to have resisted Russia in that case, or to resist any power in a like case, would be no violation of our own cherished principles of nonintervention, but, on the contrary, would be ever meritorious, in us, or any independent nation.

6. That whether we will, in fact, interfere in such case, is purely a question of policy, to be decided when the exigencies arise.

7. That we recognize in Governor Kossuth of Hungary, the most worthy and distinguished representative of the cause of civil and religious liberty on the continent of Europe. A cause for which he and his nation struggled until they were overwhelmed by the armed intervention of a foreign despot, in violation of the more sacred principles of the laws of nature and of nations— principles held dear by the friends of freedom everywhere and more especially by the people of these United States.

The audience was unanimous in its support of the points covered by the resolutions. "But what about Ireland?" asked a Mr. McConnell. If the resolutions would add an expression of sympathy with Ireland's struggle against Great Britain, and with all other people who were fighting for liberty, he could wholeheartedly support the entire series. Lincoln's committee saw no objection to doing this and so added two more resolutions:

> 8. That the sympathies of this country, and the benefits of its position, should be exerted in favor of the people of every nation struggling to be free; and whilst we meet to do honor to Kossuth and Hungary, we should not fail to pour out the tribute of our praise and approbation to the patriotic efforts of the Irish, the Germans and the French, who have unsuccessfully fought to establish in their several governments the supremacy of the people.
>
> 9. That there is nothing in the past history of the British government, or in its present expressed policy, to encourage the belief that she will aid, in any manner, in the delivery of continental Europe from the rope of despotism; and that her treatment of Ireland, of O'Brien, Mitchell and other worthy patriots, forces the conclusion that she will join her efforts to the despots of Europe in suppressing every effort of the people to establish free governments, based upon the principles of true religious and civil liberty.[4]

After more spread-eagle oratory, the resolutions were adopted, and the meeting adjourned with "three hearty cheers for Kossuth, Hungary and Ireland."

For befriending the fugitive Hungarian Kossuth and the Irish and German patriots, Lincoln gained a footing as a liberal which was to stand him in good stead in his political campaigns that lay ahead.

An unexpected result of Kossuth's visit to the United States was an extraordinary impetus to the growth of the movement from which was to spring that political phenomenon, the American or Know-Nothing Party. Kossuth's sojourn focused attention upon the flood of immigrants who were pouring into this country. The apprehensions, jealousies and bigotries that made up nativism came violently to the fore. The Know-Nothings constituted a secret fraternity whose cry was "America for Americans." The Party received its nickname from "I don't know," the ever-repeated reply of its members to questions about its purposes and activities. They denounced the alien liberalism of Kossuth, Garibaldi and Mazzini and the tendency to push democracy to extremes. They thundered that the "radical" ideas propagated by

"German infidels and Italian patriots" threatened to undermine American institutions. So they admonished, "Put none but Americans on guard," and proceeded to oppose politically all who were not native-born white, Protestant Americans. The Know-Nothings grew rapidly in membership and influence and soon became a political power of great importance throughout the country.

Know-Nothing zealots called on Lincoln in Springfield to join them in their antiforeign and anti-Catholic campaign. It was the expedient thing for politicians to do. With unfeigned disgust Lincoln gave his reply: "Who are the native Americans? Do they not wear the breech-clout and carry the tomahawk? We pushed them from their homes, and now turn on others not fortunate enough to come over so early as we or our forefathers."[5]

It was while denouncing the bigotry of the Know-Nothings that Lincoln found his second occasion to denounce Russia as the world's leading exemplar of despotism. In a letter to his friend Joshua Speed written on August 24, 1855, he declared:

> I am not a Know-Nothing; that is certain. How could I be? How can any one who abhors the oppression of Negroes be in favor of degrading classes of white people? Our progress in degeneracy appears to me to be pretty rapid. As a nation we began by declaring that "all men are created equal." We now practically read it "all men are created equal, except Negroes." When the Know-Nothings get control, it will read, "all men are created equal, except Negroes and foreigners and Catholics." When it comes to this, I shall prefer emigrating to some country where they make no pretense of loving liberty—to Russia, for instance, where despotism can be taken pure, and without the base alloy of hypocrisy.[6]

Lincoln made this reference to Russia as the outstanding example of despotism and repression at a time when the United States and Russia were the warmest of international friends. Notwithstanding the fact that Russia was then the stronghold of reaction and the most hated and despised nation in Europe, democratic America was openly and proudly proclaiming her friendship for the realm of the Czars.

During the first half of the nineteenth century Russia, like the United States, was constantly at odds with Great Britain, and as the years progressed the clash of European imperialisms made war between

Great Britain and Russia inevitable. The Crimean War broke out in 1853, nominally over a monkish issue between Russia and Turkey involving the guardianship of certain holy places in Jerusalem and the insistence of the Czar in exercising protection over the Greek Orthodox subjects of the Sultan. This quarrel proved a felicitous occasion for the French and British to draw the sword against the Czar. It was to develop into an epic struggle between the Lion and the Bear for the control of the route to India. The squadrons of the Allies entered the Black Sea and bottled up the Russian fleet, and laid siege to the heavily fortified city of Sebastopol, Russia's mighty arsenal in the Crimea and the military center from which she threatened the south.

Ties of blood and a common language and a common history should have made the United States rabidly pro-British in this war of imperialism. "England is our friend when the question is against Russia; for who does not see that Russia represents that spirit of life and government which is diametrically opposed to our own." This opinion expressed by *Harper's Magazine* was the feeling of many Americans. But the United States had become England's bitterest maritime rival. Decades of bickering over the rights of neutrals and clashing commercial interests now came to the fore to throw official American sympathy violently on the side of Russia as another great victim of British imperialism.

Edouard de Stoeckl, Russian Chargé d'Affaires at Washington, observed with pleasure the jealousy and bitterness existing between the governments of Great Britain and the United States as they quarreled constantly over commercial rivalries. Stoeckl tried ever so hard to drag America into the Crimean War as an ally of St. Petersburg. "Russia," he wrote, "must be ever watchful, must never lose an opportunity to fan the flames of hatred."[7] He played upon the bitter rivalries of the two English-speaking nations. In disregard of American neutrality, he proposed plans to engage American privateers to prey upon British commerce. He prevailed upon his government "to encourage the Yankees to trade with her, to offer them special inducements in the way of lower tariffs, especially on cotton and colonial goods which have until now been brought in English bottoms." He wrote, "The Americans will go after anything that has enough money in it. They have the ships, they have the men, and they have the daring spirit. The blockading fleet will think twice before firing on the Stars and Stripes.

When America was weak she refused to submit to England, and now that she is strong she is much less likely to do so."[8]

It was not Stoeckl's fault that the United States did not become an active belligerent in the Crimean War. His propaganda in Washington proved highly effective. The Russian Legation was flooded with requests for letters of marque from American citizens desiring to enter the service of the Czar. From Kentucky came the offer of three hundred riflemen who volunteered to go to Sebastopol to fight the British.

President Pierce rather expected a rupture with England over neutral rights. Complaining of British tactics, he said, "We desire most sincerely to remain neutral, but God alone knows whether it is possible." Secretary of State Marcy added bombastically that the United States would defend to the utmost her right as a neutral to carry on legitimate commerce, and that she would not recognize a paper blockade. He announced that orders were being dispatched to the American squadron then on its way to Japan to proceed instead to the Baltic to defend United States shipping.

In the spring of 1855, Jefferson Davis, Secretary of War in the Cabinet of President Pierce, sent a commission of three American army officers to Russia and other lands of Europe to study the organization of European armies and to observe the war in the Crimea. Among the observers was Captain George B. McClellan, then only twenty-eight years old and looking even younger. In France, the American officers were presented to Napoleon III and the Empress Eugenie. They were royally entertained in Russia, but were refused permission to visit the battlefront. Notwithstanding this refusal, Captain McClellan and his associates journeyed to Sebastopol where they studied the military developments firsthand.

American friendship for Russia manifested itself in numerous ways throughout the Crimean War. In an effort to prevent American maritime power from going to the aid of Russia, Great Britain strove avidly to avoid trouble with the United States. She yielded voluntarily, though sometimes sullenly, on practically every issue involving the blockade, and gave assurance to Washington that she and her allies would observe a strict conduct as to neutrals. America's insistence that England accept the principle that the flag protects the cargo proved tremendously helpful to Russian commerce. Fear of American power was largely responsible for the rejection by the allies of Spanish help against the

Czar. Some Russians expressed the belief that had not England humili-
ated herself by backing down on every controversy with the United
States, America would have actually taken up arms as an ally of Muscovy.

During friendly exchanges between Washington and St. Petersburg,
Secretary Marcy made it a point to ascertain how Russia would view
annexation of the Sandwich Islands by the United States—a move
which both England and France strongly opposed. The Czar's Foreign
Minister advised Marcy that anything which would antagonize her
enemies would meet with Russia's approval.[9]

One hand washes the other. So a few months after receiving this
friendly assurance, Marcy imparted to Stoeckl some highly important
secret information that had fallen into his hands. The United States
government had learned from sources regarded as reliable, Marcy
disclosed, that England was planning to attack and seize Alaska. Acting
on this information Stoeckl warned the Governor of Alaska to prepare
for eventualities. Officers of the Russian-American Company, fearful
that they were in no position to defend Alaska against a British raid,
made a frantic effort to insure the safety of their possessions by the
ruse of a fictitious sale to an American company. They thus hoped
that Alaska could be claimed to be American rather than Russian territory, in the event of its falling into the hands of the British. The
United States government refused to be a party to such a plot, and the
plan of a pretended sale was abandoned.[10]

But the United States undertook to display her good will in another
manner. Recalling that Russia had proposed to act as mediator in the
War of 1812, Marcy now offered the tender of a similar service by our
government in the Crimean War. The President, with the approval of
the Cabinet, stood ready to act as mediator, he advised Stoeckl.[11] The
Secretary of State was working on a plan to be submitted to the belligerents whereby the bloody struggle could be brought to a speedy
end. The Russian government neither accepted nor rejected America's
offer. Her Chancellor professed his faith in the impartiality of the
United States, but he doubted whether the enemy would agree. Baron
de Stoeckl expressed the belief that England would surely reject
Marcy's proposal because of "America's well-known partiality for
Russia." To which Marcy replied, "Let her do so. It will be one more
count against her in our eyes. You surely cannot object to that."[12] As
in the case of Russia's offer to mediate the War of 1812, so now Amer-

ica's proposal to act as mediator in the Crimean War likewise fell through.

Throughout the war Marcy repeatedly expressed his friendship for the Czar, while on numerous occasions Czar Nicholas I, and later his son Czar Alexander II, who succeeded to the throne when his father died in March 1855, sent thanks to President Pierce and Secretary Marcy for their kindly deeds and encouraging words on behalf of Russia.

As the allied operations against the great Sebastopol arsenal in the Crimea stretched out for almost a full year, and the ultimate defeat of Russia became more and more apparent, one European nation after another abandoned the ranks of neutrals and joined the enemies of the Czar. By the time the beleaguered Black Sea port finally fell into the hands of the allied conquerors, the United States was the only major government in the world that was neither ashamed nor afraid to acknowledge her friendship for the Muscovite Empire.

But back in Springfield Abraham Lincoln remained altogether unmoved by the pro-Russian propaganda with which the Czar's legation in Washington had flooded the land. Nor was he influenced by the gestures of mutual admiration which the heads of the two governments exchanged. He remembered Russia only as the "foreign despot" who "in violation of the most sacred principles of the laws of nature and of nations—principles held dear by the friends of freedom everywhere and more especially by the people of these United States—" had, through unwarranted armed intervention, overwhelmed little Hungary as she strove to throw off the yoke of Austrian tyranny. So when in August 1855 Lincoln desired to illustrate to Joshua Speed what happens when bigotry, reaction and suppression overwhelm a land, he instinctively pointed to "Russia . . . where despotism can be taken pure, and without the base alloy of hypocrisy."

Lincoln was still a stranger to the mysteries of world power politics which had made America so violently pro-Russian during the Crimean War. Idealist that he was, he still did not realize that altruistic friendship is a thing almost unknown among nations; that their relations toward each other are not necessarily determined by sentiment or gratitude, but first and foremost by self-interest; and that the absence or presence of conflicting interests or common animosities, fears, hatreds or enemies are the foundations upon which most alliances and ententes have been constructed. Nearly six years were still to come and go before Lincoln would be suddenly catapulted into the colossal responsibility of saving the Union from breaking into pieces, and of managing the nation's delicate foreign affairs while the United States trembled on the very brink of a foreign war. Then—irony of ironies— in these soul-stirring days, democratic America would be able to count on only one friend among the entire family of nations—democracy-hating, despotic Russia, where, as Lincoln so aptly phrased it, "they make no pretense of loving liberty."

The Divided House

EDOUARD DE STOECKL, who as Chargé d'Affaires had rendered extraordinary service in winning American sympathy for the Russian cause during the Crimean War, in 1857 became St. Petersburg's Minister Plenipotentiary to the United States.

He had first come to Washington in 1841 as attaché or secretary of legation. In 1854, upon the death of Alexander Bodisco who had served as the Czar's Minister to the United States for seventeen years, Stoeckl presented his credentials as Chargé d'Affaires. In this post he served with zeal and cunning and his elevation to ministerial rank was his reward. In Washington, Stoeckl made many friends, and there in 1856, at the age of forty-eight, he married Elizabeth Howard, "American, Protestant, without property"—so he reported to the Czar. She was a charming woman, "stately as a queen and beautiful as a Hebe." And she was a clever woman, too, who helped her diplomat husband win his way into the best society in Washington.

Edouard de Stoeckl was tall and aristocratic in bearing. He was frequently addressed as "Baron" although he had no title of nobility. His jovial face was bedecked with side whiskers and mustache. He moved on friendly terms with members of Congress, leading statesmen, and numerous other prominent persons of the Capital—wining and dining in their company and frequently relaxing with them over the gambling tables of Washington. As the representative of one of the greatest of the world powers he had ready entrée to the office of the

15

President of the United States, and was on many occasions a guest at the receptions in the White House. He conferred frequently with the Secretary of State and other members of the Cabinet. He exchanged observations with members of the foreign diplomatic corps stationed in Washington, and kept a close contact with army officers, newspaper correspondents and other sources of information.

From this favorable environment he was able to make shrewd observations of events and trends. He wrote to Prince Gortchakov, the Czar's Foreign Minister, frequently and at great length concerning what was going on in the United States. And Czar Alexander II and the Foreign Minister encouraged him to continue these detailed reports. Russia was greatly interested in what was happening in the United States—her one potential friend in the family of nations.

Moreover, the Russian serf problem had much in common with the American slavery question. When the disastrous outcome of the Crimean War made it crystal clear that reform could not be delayed much longer, Czar Alexander II had addressed these solemn words to the marshals of the noblesse of Moscow:

> As you yourselves know, the existing manner of possessing serfs cannot remain unchanged. It is better to abolish serfage from above, than to await the time when it will begin to abolish itself from below. I request you, gentlemen, to consider how this can be put into execution, and to submit my words to the noblesse for their consideration.

Feeling such concern over the miserable condition of the serfs of his own country, it was but natural that the Emperor should be keenly interested in the controversy raging with ever-increasing intensity in the United States over the kindred question of Negro slavery.

So Stoeckl had much to write about. While his dispatches from Washington during the years of the Crimean War dealt almost exclusively with diplomatic issues relating to the conflict, his correspondence to St. Petersburg after the termination of the war abounded with reports of the difficulties between the North and the South, and the growing sectional bitterness and misunderstanding.

From his vantage point in Washington, Stoeckl watched the passing of the giants of the old order—powerful personalities and influential statesmen—John C. Calhoun, the old nullifier, in whose eyes burned the implacable resentment and defiance of the South, who was convinced the Union must break up soon, and with virtually his last breath murmured "the South, the poor South"; and the great pacificators, Henry Clay and Daniel Webster, who had been holding the nation together by a series of compromises. Like modern Joshuas they had commanded the sun to stand still.

They left behind, when they passed on, a whirlpool of sectional rivalry and political hate so bitter that Stoeckl felt that the union between the North and the South had in reality become nonexistent since no two nations upon earth entertained feelings of more bitter rancor toward each other.

The Russian Minister saw, with the passing of the great compromisers, a new generation of political leaders come to the front to cope with the madness of the times. The statesmen of the Webster and Clay school, Stoeckl wrote in December 1860 to Prince Gortchakov,

> have been replaced in Congress and in the local legislatures by men undistinguished either by ability or reputation. Totally lacking in patriotism, they have but one purpose: the increase of the antislavery irritation. . . . They preach war against the South and demand the extirpation of slavery by iron and fire.[1]

Stoeckl saw the American skies grow dark with portentous clouds. He heard the halls of Congress ring with the angry debates between free-soil and slavery advocates clashing over the admission of the Territory of Kansas. Reports reached Washington of violence and disorder—men shot; towns sacked; constant deeds of brutality; men from the North and men from the South seemingly losing all sense of their common humanity. "Bleeding Kansas" became a new watchword in the North as people began to realize that the "Kansas War" was but a rehearsal for something bigger. Antagonists of the "popular sovereignty" doctrine pointed to this anarchy-ridden territory as a tragic example of the failure that resulted when the voters of a territory were allowed to choose between freedom and slavery.

In the exciting debates on the admission of Kansas in 1857, as Senator Seward bitterly denounced the use of federal troops for the enforcement of the laws in that territory, he boomed, "When you hear me justify the despotism of the Czar of Russia over the oppressed Poles . . . then you may expect me to vote supplies of men and money to the President that he may keep the army in Kansas."

The hidden fires of coming revolution were already smoldering at the Capital when James Buchanan took the oath of office as the fifteenth President of the United States on March 4, 1857. That evening Minister and Madame de Stoeckl with other members of the diplomatic corps and their elegantly attired ladies had attended the gala presidential inauguration ball. While greeting the Russian Minister Plenipotentiary, President Buchanan could recall that more than a quarter of a century back he had served as the United States envoy to St. Petersburg. Here he had attended a *Te Deum* with the Czar in the Church of St. Alexander Nevsky, and in 1832 he had written to President Andrew Jackson that he had talked with the Empress. "She observed," reported Buchanan on that occasion, that "we had troubles enough among ourselves at home and alluded to our difficulties in some of the Southern States. . . . God forbid that the Union should be in danger." Now Stoeckl, while dancing at the inauguration ball with Madame de Sartiges, wife of the French Minister, commented that the current crisis in Washington compared with the situation in Paris just before the revolution of 1830. Then, at a ball given by the crafty Louis Philippe in the Palais Royal, Talleyrand whispered to the monarch, "We are dancing on a volcano."

It was an apt comparison as only two days after the inauguration of President Buchanan came the epochal Dred Scott decision which fanned the all-consuming slavery question into a white flame. The Supreme Court of the United States speaking through Chief Justice Taney ruled that Negro slaves must be regarded as property in the same sense as cattle. Owners of slaves were entitled to protection of such property in every part of the Union. Consequently, the Missouri Compromise and all prohibitory acts against the free traffic in slaves were unconstitutional.

From every corner of the North enraged antislavery spokesmen assailed Chief Justice Taney's cruel pronouncement with unrestrained vehemence. The Supreme Court decision, thundered Horace Greeley in his *New York Tribune*, deserved no more respect than if made by a "majority of those congregated in any Washington barroom." A most sensational attack against the decision came from Senator Seward, when on the floor of the Senate he openly accused the Supreme Court with having entered a conspiracy with President Buchanan and the slave oligarchy to perpetualize slavery in the United States.

But of all the discussions of the Dred Scott decision, either in Congress or elsewhere, none were to have so powerful an effect upon the

people as the opinions uttered by the then little-known Abraham
Lincoln of Sangamon County, Illinois, and Senator Stephen A. Douglas
in their famous senatorial campaign of 1858. With invincible logic,
keen analysis and remorseless persistence Lincoln attacked the decision's inhuman doctrine that Negroes have no rights which white men
are bound to respect, and literally tore it to shreds.

His initial address in the canvass, his famous "house divided against
itself" speech, delivered at Springfield in June 1858, was an analysis of
"that almost complete legal combination—piece of machinery, so to
speak—compounded of the Nebraska doctrine and the Dred Scott
decision." In the speech's immortal opening paragraph, Lincoln said:

> A house divided against itself cannot stand. I believe this govern-
> ment cannot endure permanently half slave and half free. I do not
> expect the Union to be dissolved—I do not expect the house to
> fail—but I do expect it will cease to be divided. It will become all
> one thing or all the other.

In this most famous State campaign in all our history, Douglas won.
But a national reputation became Lincoln's reward for his brilliant
presentation of the burning issues of the day. The fire and logic of his
speeches echoed over the land. Observers like Stoeckl, whose business
it was to evaluate events, became faintly aware of a new rising star in
America's political firmament.

A peaceful political solution of the slavery problem having been
rendered impossible by the Supreme Court, the way was open for a
fanatic like John Brown to attempt to settle the issue by "direct action." With a Bible under his arm and a saber in his hand, this self-
willed abolitionist from Kansas on October 16, 1859 crossed the bridge
at Harpers Ferry at the confluence of the Potomac and Shenandoah
Rivers only fifty-three miles from Washington itself, and with a small
band of fanatical followers seized the United States arsenal and began
to execute his cherished dream of freeing the slaves. Like a shot in the
night this absurdly gallant exploit struck terror in the hearts of the
entire nation. Long had the South suspected that the real intent and
wish of the abolitionists was to rouse a slave insurrection and bring woe
and devastation to all slave-holding sections. Now, by a single stroke,
John Brown's raid solidified all their fears and gave body and awful
meaning to their suspicions.

Captured, convicted, sentenced to death and hung, John Brown became the symbol and standard-bearer of an inspired cause. His tragic death on December 2, 1859 gave the abolitionists a martyr to order. They now had a saint to hold up before the sentimental masses of the North. Literally tens of thousands dipped their handkerchiefs in his blood and paraded throughout the North spreading his gospel of freedom. His tragic death became one of the greatest blows struck against slavery. It solidified Northern sentiment. John Brown on the gallows made men search their hearts over the great moral issue. Soon inspired hosts in blue would be marching to the tune of the John Brown song— a mighty battle hymn, which was to deal not with his sword, but with his soul.

Stoeckl, in informing Prince Gortchakov about John Brown's dramatic exploit, placed the blame upon the agitation of the New England abolitionists.

> When the sad result of this foray became known, John Brown was proclaimed from the very roof tops as the equal of our Savior. I quote these facts to point out how far Puritan fanaticism can go. Little by little the extreme doctrines of New England have spread throughout the land.[2]

President Buchanan, the irresolute pilot, stood helpless and bewildered at the steering wheel while the ship of state was hurled upon one rock after another throughout his tragic administration. He asserted that the people of the North had no more right to interfere with the institution of slavery in the South than with the serf question in Russia. In a message to Congress, he stated:

> How easy would it be for the American people to settle the slavery question forever and restore peace and harmony to this distracted country. All that is necessary to accomplish the object, and all for which the slave States have ever contended, is to be let alone and permitted to manage their domestic institutions in their own way. As sovereign States, they, and they alone, are responsible before God and the world for the slavery existing among them. For this the people of the North are no more responsible and have no more right to interfere than with similar institutions in Russia or Brazil.

With everyone grimly discussing the "impending crisis," with Southern hotspurs shouting for State sovereignty or disunion—amid sectional

bitterness, bewilderment and confusion without parallel—the fateful
presidential election of 1860 got under way. Members of the European
diplomatic corps in Washington, looking on at the critical campaign,
saw in Senator Douglas, long the leading Democratic candidate, a
popular and experienced political leader of extraordinary talent and
capacity. In Senator Seward, the acknowledged head of the Republicans, they saw a brilliant and accomplished statesman of great ability
and high intellectual power who had performed historic services in
behalf of the antislavery cause, and who was well versed in international
affairs. In Jefferson Davis, Edward Everett—a scholar in politics, James
Buchanan, and others they saw statesmen of culture and cosmopolitan
experience. All of these they regarded as comparing favorably with
the foremost political leaders of Europe.

But Abraham Lincoln, the provincial lawyer whom events were soon
to make so famous, ranked very low in the estimation of Stoeckl and
other foreign observers. It was known that he possessed practically no
experience in statesmanship, and that his entire executive training was
limited to a term as a village postmaster.

When the Northern Democrats nominated Senator Douglas as their
party's standard-bearer, the Southern wing bolted the convention and
proceeded to nominate John C. Breckinridge of Kentucky to uphold
the cause of the slave owners. Another group, the Constitutional Union
Party, nominated Governor John Bell of Tennessee on an evasive
platform which called simply for loyalty to the Union and for silence
on the slavery question.

When the hour came for the Republicans to select their candidate,
they tried to be very careful. Though the Republicans repudiated
Douglas' doctrine of popular sovereignty and denounced the Dred
Scott decision, they were violently opposed to anything that looked
like abolition. Accordingly, the selection of a bitter and uncompro-
mising antagonist of slavery like Senator Seward was thought highly
unwise. His declaration that there is a higher law than the Constitution
governing the nation's stewardship of the public domain had associated
him in the public mind with extreme abolitionists who were accused
of openly flouting the Constitution. He could never carry the Midwest,
asserted his enemies. Horace Greeley despised him and was prepared to
go to any length to defeat him.

Other prominent candidates—Senator Salmon P. Chase, former Governor of Ohio; Justice John McLean of the United States Supreme

Court, competing with Chase for the Ohio delegation; Edward Bates of Missouri; and Simon Cameron, powerful machine politician from Pennsylvania—from one standpoint or another were equally as objectionable as Seward.

Since the opening of the year 1860, the name of Abraham Lincoln had been freely mentioned as a possibility for the Republican nomination. His strength lay not only in his rivals' weaknesses but in his own obscurity. This humble son of poor pioneer parents had received less than one year of actual schooling during his entire life. He had grown to young manhood amid the primitive wilds of the frontier. Each of his practical experiences as surveyor, legislator, lawyer, congressman and candidate for the Senate had contributed something essential to his unique mental makeup. He was a speaker and writer of unusual power, commanding by the use of clear and simple language the minds and hearts of those who heard him or read his printed words. Of his honesty and sincerity there could be no doubt.

Of Southern origin, he was, nevertheless, an outspoken opponent of slavery. But he was not an abolitionist. Though he was willing to leave slavery undisturbed in the South, he was unalterably opposed to its admittance into the Territories. He did not believe that Congress had any constitutional power to interfere with slavery in the States.

Comparatively unknown, he had fewer enemies than any of the more conspicuous candidates. Consequently he was in a better position to unite all the factions of the Republican Party. Moreover, he was strong in the doubtful Western States which had been carried by the Democrats in 1856. This high "availability" commended him strongly to the delegates.

But Seward, with more pledged delegates than any other candidate, felt so certain that the Republican convention in Chicago would tender him the nomination, that he bade farewell to his colleagues in the Senate and returned to his home in Auburn, N. Y., to write his acceptance message.

Seward led on the first two ballots, but Lincoln was a close second. His unexpected strength made such an impression on the convention that Seward's enemies soon combined on Lincoln, and on the third ballot, when Cameron transferred his fifty pledged delegates, it was all but a stampede for the self-educated lawyer from the wind-swept prairie of Illinois. Some of Seward's followers actually shed tears for their fallen idol, never dreaming that a greater man had risen.

No sooner did the campaign get under way when deep mutterings foretold the coming storm. "Elect Lincoln, and the South will secede!" cried the campaign orators of the South. While the cloud of the presidential election hung heavy over the Capital, Stoeckl hastened to report to St. Petersburg his grave fear "that the election of Lincoln and party passions might cause the people to lose their heads and lead them to disrupt the Union." In his opinion, "The man above all others who should be President of the United States" was Senator Seward. He regarded the New York political leader as "the ablest American statesman."[3]

For months preceding the outbreak of hostilities, Stoeckl's correspondence with St. Petersburg referred again and again to the threatened secession of the Southern States. But almost to the very end he expressed the hope that the conservative element in the American population and the material interests of the rival sections would yet avert the calamity. Although he was fearful that the election of Lincoln would cause the proslavery zealots to lose their heads and clamor for the disruption of the Union, he nevertheless believed that "the American people—that is, the conservative element—possessed too much common sense to allow this disaster." He was sure that

> a people, so absorbed in their material interests as Americans are, must realize that federation and not democracy was chiefly responsible for their prosperity. The industrial classes and farmers of the North and the agricultural class of the South were too dependent on each other to separate. The economic bonds that bind the North and the South were too strong to permit the destruction of the source of their prosperity. And even if these two sections should be so foolish as to encourage separation, the West would never allow it. The rapidly growing West realizes that its continued growth and development depend on the products of the North and the South and the sale of its products in the markets of both sections. The power of the West's large delegation in Congress is the best guarantee of the permanence of the Union.[4]

The election fell on November 6. The split in the Democratic Party made the result a foregone conclusion. When the tidings flashed over the land that Lincoln had been elected President by a vote of the North against the South, a howl of derision rose from the South. Of the nearly 2,000,000 votes he received, only 24,000 came from the slave States.

The wires had hardly ceased to thrill with the message of death to slavery extension when the South began to boil with activity. South Carolina, "the cradle of secession," where the spirit of the dead Calhoun still reigned, sounded a trumpet call to the South. Her legislature immediately called a State convention to decide whether the State should remain in the Union or not. The success of the "black Republicans" meant the doom of slavery, said the Southerners. They must now choose between abolition and secession. On December 20, the convention unanimously adopted an ordinance declaring, "The union now subsisting between South Carolina and other States under the name of the United States of America, is hereby dissolved."

Stoeckl hastened to impart to his Foreign Office in St. Petersburg a detailed account of South Carolina's secession from the Union. "The separation of a State numbering scarcely 300,000 white inhabitants would be insignificant were it not the prelude to the complete dissolution of the American Confederation." He described how provocative acts of New England antislavery leaders succeeded in inflaming the passions of the South to the point that the split became inevitable:

> Everything was thus prepared, and the leaders of the South were awaiting only the opportune time to put their plan for the dissolution of the Union into execution. The election of Mr. Lincoln furnished them with this opportunity. . . .
>
> Without any doubt the secession of South Carolina will be followed by other slave States. The dissolution of the Union from this day forward may be considered to be a *fait accompli*. It is a question now whether the States once separated, can ever be reunited. . . . It is not impossible. There is one circumstance which might react favorably for a course of conciliation. It is the distress which prevails from one end of the Union to the other, and which grows from day to day. This distress has already produced a certain reaction principally in the North, where the people are no less attached to their material interests than to their principles . . . and it is certain that Mr. Lincoln, if the election were being held today, would lose half of the votes he obtained in November. The people of the North would be disposed to make some concessions. . . . But events are moving too swiftly.[5]

In the same report Stoeckl went on to place the blame for the rupture
of the government on both sides:

> I had the occasion recently to speak with one of the Senators of
> the extremist party of the South, and I expressed to him the opinion
> that if the slave States would make a joint proposal to the free
> States, I believed that the North would not be averse to working
> out a compromise. He replied that that might be true, but that to
> start discussing compromises concerning a revolutionary move-
> ment was tantamount to putting it out of existence, and the South
> wanted the revolution at all costs. Thus the two sections are
> equally responsible for the rupture of the federal pact—the North
> for having provoked it, and the South for wanting to precipitate
> events with a speed which makes *rapprochement* impossible. . . .[6]
>
> The consequences will be horrible for all the parties of the
> Union. Politically America will cease to be a great nation. Once
> split in two, the separate sections will not fail to subdivide further.
> They will thus lose their importance, their present prosperity, and
> will not be able to avoid a civil war. . . .
>
> In my opinion all hopes of a reconciliation are not yet lost. Dur-
> ing my long stay in the United States I have had the opportunity
> to study American character, and as gloomy as things now appear,
> it is impossible for me to believe a people so practical and so de-
> voted to their own material interests and prosperity can permit
> their passions to drag them to the point of sacrificing everything...
> and it is not unlikely that at the last moment an unforeseen event
> might yet save the country. I wish it with all my heart because
> aside from political considerations, we shall deeply regret the
> downfall of a great nation with which our relations have always
> been friendly and intimate, and which at one memorable occasion
> was almost the only power which sympathized sincerely with
> our cause.[7]

In his next dispatch to the Russian Foreign Office, a few days later,
Baron de Stoeckl advised Prince Gortchakov that Francis W. Pickens
was the new Governor of the seceded State of South Carolina. The
Foreign Minister knew Governor Pickens well, as for two years past
the Southern politician had been serving in St. Petersburg as America's
Minister.

Governor Pickens, under instructions from the South Carolina secessionist convention, sent three commissioners to Washington to advise President Buchanan officially of South Carolina's withdrawal from the Union. "They arrived in the capital like envoys from a foreign power," Stoeckl observed, and presented demands for

> the transfer of three forts situated at the entrance of Charleston, the principal port of South Carolina. The garrisons of these three forts are composed of only a hundred men or so. Major Anderson, the commanding officer, has constantly asked for re-enforcements. The President refused them on the ground that sending troops to the coast of South Carolina would offend that State. But at the same time he ordered Major Anderson to defend the fort in case of attack. Placed in a position of peril by the irresolution of the government, this officer adopted the only measure which prudence dictated. He concentrated his men in a single fort and abandoned the others after burying the cannons in the ground and setting the gun carriages on fire.
>
> Angered over Anderson's skilful maneuver, South Carolina's convention ordered her militia to occupy the abandoned forts and to raise the State banner in place of the nation's flag. This incident has created a violent sensation. The President, whose subservience to the South is well known, disavowed the acts of Major Anderson, and it was feared that, influenced by Southern Senators, he would give that officer orders to evacuate the fort in which he was entrenched. This would be a shameful capitulation. If Mr. Buchanan would yield to the counsel of the plotters who surround him and commit such an act, the North, regardless of party distinctions, would arise as one to avenge the affront to the national flag.[8]

In his next dispatch to St. Petersburg, Stoeckl wrote of President Buchanan's proclamation setting aside a day for fasting and prayer to invoke Divine Power to save the American nation from the perils which threatened it.

> It seems that only the intervention of heaven can stop the onrushing events and avoid the civil war which now appears imminent and almost inevitable.
>
> The representatives South Carolina sent to Washington to discuss the peaceful transfer of the ports have returned to Charleston after delivering what amounted practically to an ultimatum. South Carolina has already seized the arsenal at Charleston, and other

Southern States have seized federal property—even while they are still members of the Union and their representatives still sit in Congress.

Some hope was attached to the deliberations of a committee appointed by the Senate in 1860 which had presented a plan of compromise submitted by Senator J. J. Crittenden, an ardent pro-Union man from the border State of Kentucky. One of Crittenden's proposals provided for a Constitutional Amendment which would prohibit slavery "in all territory of the United States, now held or hereafter acquired, north of latitude 36° 30'," while in all territory now held or thereafter acquired south of that line, it should be permitted. To appease the slaveholders they were to be guaranteed by Constitutional Amendment the right of holding human beings in involuntary servitude, and the North was to acquiesce in their bondage.

Stoeckl advised Prince Gortchakov that "the two committees named by the Senate and the House to effect a compromise have accomplished nothing. The situation is so menacing that it seems impossible to avoid a civil war. To all intents and purposes it has already broken out." He reported the treasury of the United States empty and payments suspended, and American capital refusing to underwrite a government treasury bond issue except at a discount of twenty per cent.[9]

After Mississippi cast her lot with secession on January 9, 1861, followed one and two days later by Florida and Alabama, Baron de Stoeckl predicted that "the other States of the South would not be long in following them." In Georgia, Alexander H. Stephens, one of the South's ablest statesmen, pleaded for remaining in the Union. Before that State's legislature he urged: "The election of no man, constitutionally chosen to the presidency, is sufficient cause for any State to separate from the Union. Let the fanatics of the North break the Constitution. . . . Let not the South, let not us, be the ones to commit the aggression." Nevertheless, Georgia followed South Carolina's example and on January 19 became the fifth State to withdraw. Louisiana became the sixth on January 26, and Texas the seventh on February 1. "If Virginia secedes she will take with her the other border States," the Russian Minister wrote, "and disunion will be complete." Of Charleston, he added,

A troublesome incident occurred to aggravate the situation. After hesitating for a long time, the government finally decided to send reinforcements to Major Anderson who is commanding the federal port. At the entry of the Port of Charleston a commercial steamer loaded with supplies was fired upon as it approached the coast of South Carolina, and was compelled to seek the open sea. Fortunately, there were no casualties.

In Congress the event of the week was the communication to Congress of a presidential message. The President reports that the country is headed into full rebellion; that in several States the forts and the federal arsenals are invaded and that the acts of aggression against the federal government are growing every day; that danger is imminent and that it is necessary to act without delay. The President adds that it is his function to execute the laws and not to make them; that it is consequently the Congress' duty to seek means of re-establishing peace by any possible act of conciliation. Mr. Buchanan concludes by saying that the only choice is between compromise and civil war.

This message occasioned heated discussions in the Senate. The most noteworthy speech was made during yesterday's session by Mr. Seward. He is the head of the Republican Party, and he is designated for the post of Secretary of State under Mr. Lincoln. His speech which may be considered the program of the new administration was listened to with the most rapt attention.[10]

The entire nation had eagerly awaited the scheduled address by Senator Seward. Not that he was noted for his eloquence. As a matter of fact, he was an indifferent, perfunctory speaker. But it was known that this bland, cynical, complex, equivocating and temporizing intimate of Thurlow Weed, New York's astute political boss, was to become the head of Lincoln's cabinet—President in all but name. He was to speak for that unknown quantity in Springfield who throughout these days of painful suspense sat like a sphinx, silently and inactively watching the Union slowly fall to pieces.

When on January 12, 1861, Seward, clad in a gray frock coat, arose in the crowded Senate chamber to deliver his long-awaited address, he appeared to be the only calm person present. Stoeckl, who sat in the section reserved for members of the diplomatic corps, after listening attentively, wrote to the Foreign Office in St. Petersburg that Seward's effort was a disappointment. "No one was satisfied by this speech. Both the abolitionists and secessionists concluded they could expect nothing from the Republicans."

In the opinion of Stoeckl, the address, though vague, conciliatory and temporizing, nevertheless constituted a strong plea for the preservation of the Union—"the soul of the nation and the source of her prosperity and greatness": The Russian Minister wrote,

> With frankness he [Seward] predicted that dissolution of the Union would be disastrous. It would relegate the separate, rival sections to the status of the small states of Central and South America—constantly in danger of becoming victims of the ambitious great powers of Europe. "My party and I are prepared to make all sacrifices to preserve the Federal pact. We offer conciliation, concessions and the open hand of peace."

Stoeckl thought that Seward, who regarded the proposed Crittenden compromise as "unconstitutional and ineffectual, hesitates and contradicts himself at every step. In a word, he has made a number of slight concessions but not what the situation demands. . . . With this speech practically all hope of reconciliation disappeared."[11] The same dispatch contains a long analysis of the situation:

> Mr. Seward hesitated a long time before accepting Mr. Lincoln's offer to become the head of his Cabinet. In finally accepting this post, he believed himself strong enough to silence the storm and pacify the country.
>
> From what I heard from Seward's intimate friends and what I understood from my own conversations with him, his plan was to break away from the abolitionists and align himself with the moderate factions of the Republicans and Democrats and thus form a strong conservative party to bring the South back into the Union by granting the concessions she desires. This is unquestionably a statesmanlike program, and if executed vigorously would prove successful.
>
> It was the moment to act but Seward lacked the courage and by his hesitation lost the opportunity of rendering an eminent service to his country.
>
> The present administration will last only a few weeks longer. . . . It will then devolve upon Lincoln and his Cabinet to direct affairs

and face eventualities. Mr. Lincoln's administration will be faced
with two alternatives: recognition of Southern demands or submitting corrective measures.

The North will not permit dissolution of the Union. The Democrats would preserve it by compromise, the Republicans by force.
Mr. Lincoln, elected by the latter, will naturally be obliged to
follow their desire. This raises a question whether the Northern
States have the right and the means of compelling the secessionists
to remain in the Union by force. The American nation was born
in revolution. Since winning her independence she has regarded it
as political dogma that a people has the right of self-government.
The United States has applauded all the revolutions which have
broken out in Europe and Spanish America. All the agitators of
the old and new continents have been acclaimed here, and only a
few years ago the President and Senate of the United States welcomed Kossuth, who according to them was the very personification of human liberty. Now the very States which participated in
these demonstrations would subjugate by force of arms a third of
their fellow Americans who desire to leave them and live under a
government of their own. The right of State secession from the
Union is a question which has never been decided, and even in the
North public opinion is divided on this point.

On the other hand, the free States although more numerous than
the slave States hardly possess the material means necessary for an
aggressive war. The forts and arsenals which stretch out along the
coast from South Carolina to the Gulf of Mexico, are in the hands
of the secessionists. It would be necessary to recapture them and
occupy all points where the rebel flag has displaced the federal
flag. Where are the necessary troops and naval forces? A country
of such vast area with 9,000,000 inhabitants inspired with courage
and endowed with energy, will not readily yield to the North.
Moreover, the Southern States will have the advantage of fighting
on their own soil and will not have to send large forces of men
great distances. They can await the attack and prepare to repulse
it. The chances of the two sections are thus balanced, and the
struggle will be all the more bitter and prolonged because of the
very fact that neither side has much advantage over the other.

There is no doubt that religion and humanity condemn slavery,
but the government must have time to uproot so great an evil. To

accomplish this end it is necessary to combine with intelligence adequate legal measures, proper timing, and a willingness to give up some private property rights.

The number of slaves in the United States has increased to 4,000,000, representing a capital of more than three billion dollars, without counting the losses which would be suffered by those sections which would become impoverished by the freeing of the slaves, since whites cannot labor in the hot climate of the Mississippi valley and the coast of the Gulf of Mexico. The figures I have cited prove the impracticality of emancipating the slaves by indemnifying the slaveholders as England did in her colonies. Abolition of slavery will be accomplished only by a gradual process.[12]

In Stoeckl's opinion, the violent measures preached by the abolitionists have succeeded only in "arousing the passions of the South, throwing the nation into a turmoil and perhaps destroying its very existence." He wrote thus on the need of each section for the other:

The downfall of the great American Republic will not be the least important event of our epoch, and one wonders what will become of these States when once separated. While united by a federal pact they formed a power of the first order. But who can predict what a civil war will lead to? . . . The struggle must stop some day. The mutual hates must subside and the hardships which are inseparable from a civil war must necessarily produce a reaction. If at this time the American people have not lost their common interests, they will realize that their only salvation is a restored Union. The North needs the South, exploits its commerce and finds there a market for its manufactured goods. The $180,000,000 brought in annually by the sale of cotton passes through the hands of the bankers of New York and some other large commercial cities of the free States, which earn large profits therefrom. Strictly speaking the North can exist without the South, but it will lose the principal source of its wealth and prosperity. The South, from its standpoint, ought to realize that it will find no security for the institution of slavery except in the guarantees granted it by the Constitution.[13]

Stoeckl was appalled by "the demagoguery, confusion and corruption" which he believed were undermining the very foundations of the government. He placed much of the blame for the deplorable state of affairs upon the Constitution itself, and he predicted that the United States could not long continue unless the American people made some drastic changes in their Constitution. He had a suggestion that might save the nation:

> In order to consolidate the federal pact it would be indispensable to remodel the Constitution by giving the government more extensive power to restrict universal suffrage; to hold elections less frequently since elections create disorders and anarchy; to enact laws capable of preventing corruption; and to put an end, if possible, to the propagation of the revolutionary and socialist spirit— that plague from the old world which European immigration has transplanted to this country during the last ten years.[14]

Having thus analyzed the situation in the United States, the Russian Minister in another dispatch to St. Petersburg expressed the opinion that if the Crittenden compromise "had been submitted to the people as Senator Crittenden of Kentucky had urged, it would have been approved by a large majority. The representatives of the South have accepted this compromise, but the Republicans have rejected it on the ground that it was in conflict with the principles of their party." This contention Stoeckl regarded as "nothing but hypocrisy."[15]

The Southern States, Stoeckl thought, at least had the courage of their convictions. They claimed the legal right of secession—a right once claimed by their forefathers who shook off the yoke of English tyranny by revolution. The reply of the North, he maintained, constituted poor legal argument. "They have neither the forthrightness to accept a plan of reconciliation nor the courage to propose measures needed to save the country."

No doubt the Emperor was interested in knowing what Lincoln was doing while the United States government trembled on the brink of disaster.

> The President-elect remains at Springfield, Illinois. He scrupulously avoids issuing any opinion regarding the events of the day. To all questions addressed to him, he answers invariably that he still is an ordinary common citizen and not until his inauguration will he announce the program of his administration. His position

is hardly to be envied, and the rivalries and jealousies of the heads of his party do not make his task any lighter.[16]

Actually, Lincoln was leaving no doubt in the minds of his adherents as to where he stood on the question of the extension of slavery. On December 10, 1860 he wrote to Lyman Trumbull, "Let there be no compromise on the question of extending slavery. If there be, all our labor is lost, and ere long, must be done again. . . . The tug has.come, and better now than at any time hereafter."[17] In response to a letter from William Kellogg of the House Committee on the crisis, the President-elect wrote again, "Entertain no proposition in regard to the extension of slavery. The instant you do they have us under again: all our labor is lost, and sooner or later must be done over." He sent a similar letter on December 13 to Elihu B. Washburne urging that "on 'slavery extension' . . . hold firm, as with a chain of steel."[18]

Nine days after Seward's disappointing speech, Stoeckl witnessed another tragic drama in the Senate chamber as Senator after Senator arose and solemnly announced his resignation from his seat and his renunciation of allegiance to the United States. As Senators Jefferson Davis, Yulee, Mallory, Clay and Fitzpatrick marched out, women grew hysterical and men wept. Not a person present failed to understand the awful significance of the hour. It was as if an invisible Samson were pulling down the pillars of the temple and the whole government structure was about to topple down.

Events were moving with an inexorable speed. In a dispatch dated February 2, 1861, Stoeckl reported:

> The rebellion continues to spread in the South. Louisiana has seceded from the Union. On February 4 the delegates of the secessionist States are to meet at Montgomery, Alabama, to organize a provisional government to elect a President and a Vice President and to form an independent State.
>
> In the border States partisans of the Union and of the secession movement are practically equally divided. The legislature of Virginia requested the other States to send delegates to Washington to endeavor to work out a compromise. The seceded States and the extremists of the North have refused, but about fifteen States of the Midwest have replied to this appeal and their delegates are scheduled to meet. However, it is doubtful whether they will

achieve any satisfactory result. This conference has no legal standing, whatever its decision may be. It will have to be sanctioned by
the Congress and the latter is not inclined toward compromise.
Public opinion prevailing in the North has found no response in
the Capital. Numerous petitions are addressed daily to Congress
and the City of New York recently sent a petition signed by
38,000 merchants and industrialists who urgently request the
adoption of measures calculated to pacify the country. These expressions of public opinion have no effect on the Republicans in
Congress. Senator Seward is the only one who manifests any conciliatory attitude. Unfortunately, he has not succeeded in winning
over the other members of his Party, who refuse to yield on a
single point.

Even though the Republicans persist in this unyielding policy,
at least they are doing nothing to aggravate the situation. The
agitators of the South on the other hand are overlooking no opportunity to precipitate the civil war. They are preparing to attack
the two forts of Charleston and Pensacola, the only points still
occupied by the federal troops on the coast of the secessionist
States. Their goal is to hasten the winning over of the still waver-
ing border States. It appears, however, that the States of the South
do not possess the means of seizing these forts. On the other hand,
Mr. Buchanan has issued the order to the commanding officers to
exercise the greatest vigilance and to remain on the defensive. If a
conflict can thus be avoided, conditions will remain unchanged for
the four weeks still remaining before the inauguration of the new
President.[19]

In a report dated February 12 the Russian Minister continued his
account of the crisis:

The conference of the delegates of the border States and of the
North met this week in Washington under relatively favorable
auspices. There is no one, however, who dares to predict any
favorable results from this meeting.

Congress during last week concerned itself with the tariff question and with a loan of $45,000,000 intended to cover the expenses
of the new administration which, coming into power, will find the
federal treasury literally empty. It is easier to vote money than to
raise it. The last loan was negotiated at a discount of 12½ per cent.

But the government cannot procure its needs even at these burdensome rates. The leading financiers of New York have come to Washington, and have declared to Congress that if a settlement were made they would be ready to advance the funds at the ordinary rates of 6 per cent. Otherwise, the government was not to depend on them.

The army and navy have not escaped this general demoralization. Among the officers, a majority of whom are residents of the South, resignations and absences from duty are very prevalent. The commander of the American squadron in the Gulf of Mexico has had to forbid, under threat of extremely severe penalties, any political discussions. Even though suffering a lack of provisions, he sailed to Havana in order to get away from the coast of the United States.

We have just received the news by telegraph that the Congress of the Secessionist States, meeting in Montgomery, Alabama, has named Mr. Jefferson Davis, former Senator of Mississippi, the Provisional President of the Confederation of the South.[20]

On the day Lincoln began his eventful eleven-day journey from Springfield to Washington, Stoeckl conferred with Senator Seward to discuss the critical situation which confronted the President-elect, and thus reported the meeting:

Mr. Seward said to me that the first duty of Mr. Lincoln in taking up the reins of government will be to save his country with his friends if he can, if not, with his enemies. If the influential men of the Republican Party persist in refusing to make concessions, Mr. Lincoln will have to break from them and appeal to all the conservatives who will stand by him.

I asked him if he were sure that the new President shared his views. To that he replied: "I am not well acquainted with Mr. Lincoln. However, if he is a man of courage and ability, as I believe him to be, he will quickly realize that it is the only way of saving us from the dangers which surround us. If on the contrary he wishes to adopt extreme measures, all will be lost. I shall not associate myself with such policies, and the responsibility for eventualities will fall on those whose advice he has followed."

Mr. Seward realizes that in the light of the events of the times the program of the Republican Party is impracticable, and with characteristic wisdom, he feels the necessity of modifying it. By adopting that policy he has created implacable enemies for himself. Among the twenty-six Republicans who sit in the Senate, he can count on the support of scarcely three fourths. The others have openly declared themselves as opposed to him. These men, distinguished only for their violent fanaticism, are demanding a blockade of all the ports of the South, and the use of force to subdue the seceded States. They know that Mr. Seward is opposed to these extreme measures. And so they seek to discredit him in the estimation of Mr. Lincoln, and to stop him from participating in the new administration.

Mr. Lincoln left his residence in Springfield and is en route to the National Capital. Since his election he has kept absolute silence about events and about policies which he intends to follow, but during a recent stop in Cincinnati, he delivered a speech in reply to the greetings of the local authorities. The tenor of this speech could hardly be considered conservative, and produced a bad impression on the public. On his arrival here a bitter struggle will arise between the moderates headed by Mr. Seward, and their opponents to determine who will have the upper hand in the new administration. If the former prevail, there will still remain a chance for peace. With the other eventuality nothing can stop the storm which threatens to break the Union into pieces.[21]

Writing to Prince Gortchakov a few days later, under date of February 28, Baron de Stoeckl reported that Lincoln had arrived in Washington two days before:

> During his trip through the Western States, where thanks to the abundant harvest of last year the population was able to escape the disastrous effect of the political crisis, Mr. Lincoln was received with acclaim and not a word was addressed to him regarding the agitations which prevailed in the country.
>
> But it wasn't the same when he passed through the principal commercial cities of New York and Philadelphia. The greeting which he received from the people of these great cities was appropriate enough for an incoming President, but nothing more. In his welcoming speech the Mayor of New York did not mince words about the deplorable state into which business has fallen and the hardships which a civil war would bring to the commercial metropolis of the Union. The Mayor of Philadelphia went even

further: "I regret," said he, "that you are not going to stay longer with us, and see for yourself the misery among the working classes ... due to the greed and to the evil motives of the politicians of all parties. Beware of their advice and count on the people. They will rise up and help you save the country."

Mr. Lincoln showed some embarrassment at the frankness of these two mayors, and he replied that he was not less attached to the Union than they were, and that all his efforts would be devoted to preserving it. It was feared that his trip through Baltimore would give rise to disorder, so he passed through this city during the night without stopping there.[22]

3

Stoeckl Attempts Mediation

FEARS for the security of the nation's Capital grew alarmingly as Lincoln's inauguration day approached. Washington's nextdoor neighbors —the States of Virginia and Maryland—rocked with secessionist agitation, and debated excitedly whether to remain in the Union or to throw in their lot with the new Southern Confederacy. Wild rumors filled the air to the effect that secessionist leaders were plotting the seizure of Washington for the purpose of making it the seat of the Confederate government. Senator Iverson of Georgia had made just such a declaration in a speech on the floor of the Senate. And on Christmas day the *Richmond Examiner* defiantly called for citizens of Maryland to join with Virginians in seizing the Capitol.

In Washington, people spoke in fearful whispers of rumored secret secessionist organizations prepared to capture the city and the public archives, and take control of the government. So widespread became the reports of a conspiracy, that Senator Seward, surely not an alarmist, decided that President-elect Lincoln in Springfield ought to know about the situation. Accordingly, Seward wrote to him: "A plot is forming to seize the Capitol on or before the 4th of March, and has its accomplices in the public councils. You must not imagine that I am giving you suspicions and rumor. Believe me that I know what I write."

Extra guards were placed at the entrances of the Capitol, and a nightly search was made in the basement of the structure for hidden

38

explosives. The anxiety spread to the foreign legations in Washington. It was clear to Stoeckl that should the conspiracy succeed, Lincoln would have to establish his seat of government elsewhere. So nearly two months before Lincoln's scheduled inaugural, Stoeckl posed the question to the Czar's Foreign Minister—what should his legation do, in that eventuality?

We can anticipate two possible situations which might affect our legation's policy. First, there is the possibility that President-elect Lincoln will be inaugurated and then establish his headquarters in a city other than Washington. Then there is the possibility that the Confederates will make overtures for the establishment of diplomatic relations with Russia. It is evident that we must consider Mr. Lincoln as the legally elected President. If he remains in Washington, the diplomatic corps will reside there also. But it is possible that the secession movement will embrace Virginia and Maryland. In that event Washington would find itself an enclave in disunionist States. There is talk among the leaders of the South of launching a campaign to take possession of the city by force for the purpose of establishing the Capital of the new Confederation there. If this occurs, the diplomatic corps must, it seems to me, if only temporarily, leave Washington and accompany Mr. Lincoln to his new seat of government. The situation has not yet advanced to the point where we must form a decision relative to the establishment of diplomatic relations with the Confederacy.

It appears to me that the policy which would best conform to our own interests and dignity is this: We should recognize the independence of the Confederacy only after it has settled its own permanent relations with the North.

It is important to us not to take sides with the secessionists prematurely, as the preservation of the Union is for our own best interests. But, on the other hand, it is for our benefit to make friends everywhere and not to antagonize any State regarding matters which do not involve our interests. . . . My proposal, it seems to me, combines these two advantages: it retains our Union friends, and at the same time does not offend the secessionists.[1]

The dire predictions of the seizure of the Capitol before Lincoln's arrival did not materialize. The President-elect reached Washington nine days before his inaugural—"like a thief in the night," according to the report of Rudolph Schleiden, Minister from the Hanseatic Republic and the Free City of Bremen. Now all Washington was gossiping about Lincoln's secret night trip from Harrisburg to the National Capital. His advisors had persuaded him to cancel a scheduled stop at Baltimore to outwit would-be assassins who awaited him in that hot-bed of secession.

Stoeckl hastened to report to the Russian Foreign Office that the President-elect had arrived safely in Washington. "According to established custom, the Foreign Ministers left a visiting card with the new President, and it is not until after the inauguration that the diplomatic corps is officially presented to him":[2]

> Upon Mr. Lincoln's arrival here a furious struggle ensued between the moderates led by Mr. Seward, and their radical opponents in the Republican Party, to determine who will have the upper hand in the new administration. If the former triumph, there still remains a chance of saving the Union. In the other event nothing can save the nation from splitting up.
>
> It is now definite that Mr. Seward will be Lincoln's Secretary of State. The extremists of the Republican Party gave up their opposition to his selection. Realizing that the situation is growing more critical day by day, they prefer to leave the responsibility to Mr. Seward, while standing by, ready to attack him, should he deviate too greatly from their program.[3]

Though the Russian envoy had not yet seen or met the incoming Chief Executive, he did not hesitate to give official credence to the rumors prevalent throughout the Capital that the ungainly Westerner was a statesman of mediocre ability, and possessed of no knowledge beyond provincial politics:

> Mr. Lincoln has just one week to form his Cabinet and to decide on the direction his administration will take. I had the opportunity recently of speaking with one of the most influential leaders of the Republican Party. He said, "We want to preserve the Union, but we cannot make concessions to the South without abandoning our principles." I asked him what measures the new administration would adopt to maintain the principles of the Party and at the same time avoid hostilities with the seceded States. He admitted

that this was a dilemma and that neither he nor his colleagues knew how to cope with this difficulty.

This indecision is even more dangerous in that Mr. Lincoln does not appear to possess the talents and the energy which his Party attributed to him when they nominated him as their candidate for the Presidency. Even his partisans admit today that he is a man of irreproachable honesty but of mediocre ability.[4]

This opinion of Lincoln's mediocrity was shared generally by the Washington diplomatic corps, closely watching the course of events. Rudolph Schleiden compared his election with a lottery. "It is possible that the United States has drawn the first prize, on the other hand the gain may only have been a small one. But unfortunately the possibility is not excluded that it may have been merely a blank."[5] Most of them predicted that Seward would determine the policy of the new administration.

In marked contrast to Stoeckl's low opinion of Abraham Lincoln was his very high regard for Jefferson Davis, whom the Russian diplomat had known intimately for a number of years. Contrasting the procrastination prevailing in Washington with the vigorous action taking place in the South, Stoeckl added in his report to St. Petersburg:

Mr. Jefferson Davis, who has been named "Provisional President," is one of the most remarkable men in the United States. He began his career as a military man and distinguished himself in the Mexican War, in which he commanded a brigade. Since then he has been Senator and Secretary of War in the administration of President Pierce. He occupied the post during the Crimean War, and showed himself an ardent friend of our cause. This circumstance put me in intimate relations with him, and gave me the opportunity to know him well. He is one of those cold and energetic characters who never draw back from any obstacle. Mr. Seward himself told me that the secessionists could not have selected a more capable leader.

Mr. Davis' inaugural address was most temperate. He declared that his greatest desire is to have the seceded States live in peace with the nation of which they were once a part. However, should the attempt be made to subdue them by force they would accept the challenge and defend themselves to the bitter end.[6]

A few months later Stoeckl added: "So far he [Davis] has fully justified the reputation of an able and energetic man which he has always enjoyed. He has gained the confidence of his fellow citizens to the point of exercising absolute power, and this gives no small advantage to the people of the South over their adversaries in the North where everyone commands and no one wishes to obey."

The arrival of Lincoln to take over the reins of government caused Stoeckl to conclude that it now appears

> almost impossible that conflict can be averted. Until now a sort of armistice existed between the seceded States and President Buchanan, but the advent of the new administration alters this temporary state of affairs. Once in power, the new administration must move in one of two directions: either accept secession as a *fait accompli*, and evacuate Southern forts still occupied by federal troops, or propose an amicable settlement to the Confederacy as required by the circumstances. This would be the best policy one could recommend to the new administration. . . . True, it is a bold program, and, in view of their party principles can hardly be acceptable to Republican leaders, just coming into power. . . . Reconciliation, if at all possible, will be achieved not by force of arms but by favorable public opinion.[7]

Stoeckl caught his first glimpse of Abraham Lincoln at the inauguration ceremonies on the steps beneath the unfinished dome of the spreading structure of the Capitol. The Russian Minister rode in his barouche in the procession headed by the carriage bearing President James Buchanan and his successor. Down cobblestoned Pennsylvania Avenue the long procession proceeded toward the unfinished Capitol dome still encased in ugly scaffolding. Stoeckl was amazed at the presence of so many troops. "The principal thoroughfares," he wrote to his Foreign Minister, "were occupied by two thousand militiamen and by two batteries of artillery. Hostile demonstrations on the part of Southern sympathizers were feared. But there were no disorders and all went off peacefully."[8] Only faint occasional cheers greeted the incoming President as he rode along. Washington in many respects was a Southern city and its residents for the most part sympathized with the South.

Amid the pall of impending national tragedy, Abraham Lincoln took the oath of office as President of the United States. In his resonant, high-pitched voice trained in open-air meetings of the West, Abraham

Lincoln gave assurance to the nation that he had no intention of interfering with slavery where it already existed. Argument, persuasion, entreaty followed as he made it crystal clear that the Union must be preserved at all costs.

> Physically speaking, we cannot separate; we cannot remove our respective sections from each other, nor build an impassable wall between them. . . . In your hands, my dissatisfied fellow countrymen, and not in mine, is the momentous issue of civil war. The government will not assail you. You can have no conflict without being yourselves the aggressors. You have no oath registered in Heaven to destroy the government; while I shall have the most solemn one to preserve, protect, and defend it.

And then that impressive ending touched with haunting beauty: "I am loath to close. We are not enemies but friends. We must not be enemies. Though passion may have strained, it must not break our bonds of affection. The mystic chords of memory stretching from every battlefield and patriot grave to every living heart and hearthstone all over this broad land, will yet swell the chorus of the Union when again touched, as surely they will be, by the better angels of our nature."

It was an address "filled with contradictions," Stoeckl wrote to Prince Gortchakov. In his judgment, Lincoln's declaration that

> his duty was to execute the federal laws in all the States, that is, to occupy the forts and arsenals and to collect the duties, indicates rather well the intention of the new administration to have recourse to coercive measures; but . . . probably with the intention of softening the effect, Mr. Lincoln announced that he would strive to avoid civil conflict and that he would devote all his efforts to bring back the seceded States through conciliatory measures.
>
> The only interpretation one can give to this speech, so filled with contradictions, is that Mr. Lincoln came into office without having a fixed program. It even appears that he does not realize what the actual situation of the country is, and the imminence of the civil conflict which threatens it. He maintains that the nation is intact at the very moment when seven States have seceded from the Union, and have organized a separate independent government. On the one hand he speaks of coercive measures, on the other of

moderation. But he is silent as to the measures he expects to adopt to compel the seceded States to return to the Union, and as to the guarantees he will grant in order to placate them. The nation which awaited with such anticipation the announcement of the new administration's policies so it might resolve its hopes and its fears, knows no more today than it did on the eve of inauguration.

The same vacillating spirit which one observes in Mr. Lincoln's address, shows itself in the organization of his Cabinet. It wasn't until a day after his inauguration that he succeeded in completing his Cabinet.

All the attempts to form a homogeneous Cabinet have failed. Mr. Lincoln was forced to accept both conservatives and radicals, the former as represented by Mr. Seward, and the latter as represented by Mr. Chase. Though he does not possess the talents or capabilities of Mr. Seward, Mr. Chase is a man of great energy, and his political skill will, doubtless, enable him to gain ascendancy over the other counsellors of the new President. Friends of Mr. Seward, foreseeing this difficulty, advised him against entering the new administration unless he is given the opportunity of selecting his Cabinet associates. However, he has not taken their advice, stating that he cannot in good grace withdraw at a time when the aid of all influential men of the party is so essential for the salvation of the country.

In the present circumstances Mr. Seward is the indispensable man, and his withdrawal would have been fatal to the administration, and if only he had insisted Mr. Lincoln would have been obliged to yield to all of his demands. But Mr. Seward was not firm enough on this point, and it is more than probable that he will find it necessary either to comply with the policies of the radicals or leave the Cabinet.

The first question with which the new administration will have to concern itself will be to deal with a deputation sent to Washington by the seceded States to demand the surrender of the arsenals and the two or three forts which are still held by federal troops. It was decided not to receive these delegates officially. But an informal conference for the purpose of giving some sort of answer to their demands cannot be evaded. Should that take place, we shall probably learn what attitude the President will assume toward the seceded States.[9]

Stoeckl, who was very grateful to Buchanan for "the care he took to maintain friendly relations" with imperial Russia, and "for the kindnesses with which he had personally honored" him, felt a keen pity for the vain and helpless old man whose term of office had come to a close:

> Mr. Buchanan has passed nearly all of his life in the service of his country. He has occupied the high posts of Ambassador, Senator and Secretary of State with marked distinction. But once ensconced in the presidency, he revealed a glaring lack of the qualities necessary for a Chief Executive of a great nation. Even keeping in mind the extraordinarily difficult situation in which he was placed, it cannot be disputed that his own vacillation and the ineptness and frequently the lack of integrity on the part of his advisors, have at least in part hastened, if not actually brought about, the present crisis. The outset of his administration found the affairs of the nation in excellent condition. Business and industry were never more flourishing. All classes of the population, without exception, enjoyed a prosperity without parallel. And the public treasury had a surplus of $20,000,000. He is leaving to his successor an empty treasury, with government credit ruined. The Union is about to dissolve and civil conflict ready to break out.

Then Stoeckl went on to describe Buchanan's failures in foreign affairs; and his shortcomings as a party leader which resulted in quarrels with former President Pierce, Senator Douglas and others, the virtual wrecking of the Democratic Party, and the inevitable victory of the Republicans.

> The failures of Mr. Buchanan are due to the weakness of his character aggravated by his advanced age. An excessive egotism always caused him to show an obvious preference for anyone who flattered his vanity. Thus he was always surrounded by worthless men of questionable reputations. . . . Of course Mr. Buchanan is not alone responsible for the present crisis, but in any event, his will be the rather dubious honor of having his name irrevocably linked with it. . . .
>
> Immediately after the inauguration of the new President, Mr. Buchanan left Washington to return to his residence in Pennsylvania. The night before his departure the diplomatic corps went to his home to bid him farewell. I took advantage of the occasion

to tell Mr. Buchanan how much my government appreciated the care he took to maintain friendly relations with us, and I thanked him for the kindnesses with which he had honored me.[10]

Three days after the inauguration ceremonies President Lincoln received the diplomatic corps officially at a reception given in its honor by Mrs. Lincoln and himself in the Executive Mansion. It was there that Baron de Stoeckl formally met Lincoln for the first time.

The President wore his inauguration suit and fresh white kid gloves. In obvious discomfort, he stood for a long time shaking hands with his callers. The Foreign Ministers, bedecked with the ribbons and medals of their offices, extended the greetings of their sovereigns. Practically all possessed the average European aristocrat's contempt for republicanism, and had a morbid curiosity about the self-made product of Western democracy.

Lincoln listened gravely to Senhor de Lisboa, envoy from Portugal, who as dean of the diplomatic corps in Washington had been selected by his colleagues to speak on their behalf. De Lisboa, noted for his wit and humor, expressed the happiness of the assembled diplomats over the President's advent to power and wished him a most successful regime. In a brief response, the President thanked the envoys for their good wishes and assured them that he would leave nothing undone to maintain the friendliest relations with their respective governments.

Lincoln knew that the good will of these men who exercised such great influence upon the thought of Europe was of great importance to the United States. In greeting each of them warmly he fixed their faces and foreign-sounding names indelibly in his mind, knowing that in the coming months his administration would have to deal with them again and again. Aristocrats all, they considered the Southern slaveholders to be gentlefolk. Washington's most aristocratic society had been the wealthy slaveholders or sympathizers sojourning in the National Capital as members of Congress or the President's Cabinet. The diplomatic corps had been brought in close social contact with the men and women of this class who had vied with one another in extravagant entertainment. The representatives of the foreign governments in turn received extremely pro-Southern impressions and influenced their governments accordingly. This, in a measure, was to account for the reason that European powers were to take so favorable a view of the power and prospects of the Confederacy.

At his first opportunity after the reception, the Russian Minister recorded his impression of President Lincoln. In his dispatch to St. Petersburg of March 12, 1861 Stoeckl wrote: "Without having a remarkable face, Mr. Lincoln has an agreeable and honest expression. His manners are those of a man who has spent all his life in a small Western town, but he was polite and engaging toward all, and in general the diplomatic corps has only praise for the reception which was given it."[11]

During the epoch-making four years of the Civil War the Russian Minister was to see Lincoln more or less frequently. Seldom could he find anything complimentary to report about the American statesman. He could see only the agreeable and well-meaning provincial politician —weak, undecided, inexperienced, the slave of unscrupulous political intriguers and office seekers who had supported his candidacy only because his weakness and inexperience would make him their ready tool.

On the day the Lincoln administration was only three weeks old— which was time enough, according to Stoeckl, "to realize the full gravity of the situation"—the Russian Minister in his report to St. Petersburg, described the President's indecision and vacillation regarding the Fort Sumter difficulty:

> In his inaugural address, Mr. Lincoln had hastily asserted his determination not to give up the forts and arsenals of the United States located in the South. He has not been long in realizing that the execution of this program is impossible. . . . Major Anderson in command of Fort Sumter, situated in Charleston Bay, South Carolina, has provisions for only a few days. He has warned the Secretary of War that the entrance of the port has been so fortified as to require from eight to ten thousand men to force a landing. Unable to prepare this force, the government has no alternative but to evacuate Fort Sumter.
>
> But the President hesitates to give such an order as he knows full well what effect the abandonment of the fort will have upon the country. In the North even his rabid partisans will regard it as a humiliating defeat. The South will seize upon it as proof of the government's impotency. The administration will find itself in an even greater predicament if, in conformity with the program of the Republican Party, it determines to repossess the forts already taken over by the seceded States. Such operations will require

rather substantial military forces, and the government does not possess them. The active army of the United States is fixed at 17,000 men but the ranks are never complete. The strongest division was stationed in Texas and was comprised of almost 4,000 men. It was under the command of General Twiggs, a native of the seceded State of Georgia. This officer disbanded his army and placed the arms and material in the custody of the authorities of the Southern Confederacy. This corps no longer exists. The same has happened regarding several other detachments commanded by Southern officers who have offered their services to their respective States.

True, the government is preparing a small squadron sufficient to blockade the ports of the South, but blockade is an act of war, and the President would be violating one of the fundamental laws of the Constitution in initiating an attack without first receiving authority from Congress which possesses the exclusive power of declaring war.

This anomalous situation is further complicated by the discord which prevails in the Cabinet, and the indecision of the President who is occasionally influenced by individuals who counsel peace and moderation, but who more frequently is influenced by men who advocate violence and extreme measures. As a result, one day he is for peace, and the next, for war.

The Russian Minister sensed an intense desire for peace in the ranks of conservatives both in the North and the South. This circumstance, he believed, was a sublime opportunity for a mutually trusted mediator to perform a historic service. Who better than he could fill the role of go-between? He had intimate friends among the leaders of both sections. So without being asked by anyone to do so, he decided to undertake the onerous task of peacemaker.

However, Stoeckl advised his Foreign Office that because of the vacillating policy of Lincoln's administration, the President has not yet made up his mind whether it would be advisable for him to

consult . . . with representatives sent here by the seceded States . . . to present their demands, which Mr. Seward himself admits are reasonable. As yet the President has not replied to them. Like many other matters, it remains suspended in the air. . . .

In the border States the factions for and against secession are equally balanced, but the first aggressive act on the part of the federal government will drive them out of the Union. The breaking up of the Union is causing consternation in California, and already there is discussion whether it would not be in the best interests of the Pacific Coast States to form an independent republic. It is not altogether unlikely that this will occur in the future. . . .

Though we find ourselves in the midst of a widespread rebellion which threatens to convulse the nation, all of this is taking place without violence. Commerce and industry are at a standstill. The working classes are in more or less distress. But as yet there are no disorders. The Americans seem to look at the disruption of their political and social system with indifference. This can be explained only by the confidence which they have in their national destiny. Peace and tranquility prevail, but is this calm an indication of a return toward reconciliation, or rather a precursor of civil war and anarchy? Only the future will tell.[12]

Early in April, the Russian Minister, "following established custom," gave a dinner for the members of Lincoln's Cabinet. As Stoeckl wrote in giving his report of the affair:

When everyone had left, Mr. Seward expressed the desire of speaking to me privately. He asked me if I had any opinion as to what impression American events were producing in Europe. I replied that our government regretted exceedingly the dissension in the United States and would regard the dissolution of the Union as a real catastrophe. In so far as France and England are concerned, it appears to me that these powers are so concerned with their own commercial interests that it is not probable that they will do anything unless the Washington government takes measures that would seriously affect their commerce.

"In that event," continued Mr. Seward, "our relations with the powers of Europe will undergo no change for there will be neither an attack upon nor blockade of the South. We will leave the Southern States alone. . . . Abandoned to themselves these States cannot exist as a separate entity and will end up sooner or later by returning to the Union."[13]

As Stoeckl had already reported, three commissioners of Jefferson Davis' government—Martin J. Crawford, John Forsyth, and A. B. Roman—were then in Washington to obtain recognition of the independence of the new Confederate States of America. They were seeking to adjust upon terms of amity and good will all questions of the political separation of the two sections of the United States, by negotiating the surrender of the forts within the Southern States and adjusting monetary losses to the federal government resulting from the surrender of federal property in the South. The Russian envoy offered his services as mediator or go-between:

> I told Mr. Seward that I had seen Mr. Roman, one of the Southern commissioners, who assured me that he and his colleagues were in a most conciliatory state of mind, and that they were prepared to make all reasonable concessions to avoid the conflict which would inevitably result in civil war.
>
> Mr. Seward seized this occasion to tell me that he did not personally know Mr. Roman, but that he was familiar with his reputation for being a temperate-minded man. He regretted that because of his official position he could neither visit Roman nor have Roman come to his office. He then asked me if I would have any objection to arranging a secret meeting in my residence where they could meet as if by chance. I hastened to assure the Secretary of State that I would be happy to serve in any way I possibly can to bring about a reconciliation.

Accordingly, Stoeckl communicated with Commissioner Roman, suggesting an informal meeting at the Russian Embassy over a cup of tea two days later. Roman was highly pleased with the suggestion and readily accepted the invitation. But the next day Seward changed his mind and sent his regrets. Having thought the matter over carefully, he had come to the conclusion that it would be wiser not to keep the appointment as he had agreed. Horace Greeley, the New York editor and Seward's arch enemy, had just arrived in Washington, and Stoeckl concluded that the Secretary of State feared the meeting might become known to the press.[14]

> Several days later, I met Mr. Seward at the home of Lord Lyons. His attitude had entirely changed; he spoke only of the blockade and coercive measures. A rather lively discussion took place be-

tween him and the English Minister in my presence and that of the French Minister. Mr. Seward said to me, "I wish to inform you gentlemen that if civil war breaks out all commercial relations with the South would have to stop." Lord Lyons argued that such measures would be ruinous to English trade. "We regret it," said Mr. Seward, "but you will have to forego cotton for a while." Abandoning his customary reserve, Lord Lyons answered that England could not get along without cotton and that she would obtain it in one way or another. Although Mr. Seward made no reply, there no longer remained any question what England would do in the event of a blockade of the cotton States.[15]

The agents of the Confederacy, waiting patiently in Washington to see the President or the Secretary of State, were shocked to hear that, contrary to assurances, an expedition was on its way to succor the federal forts in the South. On April 9, Stoeckl informed St. Petersburg:

> For several days there has been great activity in the port and arsenals of New York. A frigate and several other vessels loaded with provisions and munitions and carrying troops have left this port. . . . The administration . . . has decided on coercive measures toward the seceded States. On the other hand I have learned from the representatives of the Southern Confederacy that Mr. Seward has given them the most formal assurances that the federal government was not contemplating any attack on the Southern ports and that the preparations being made in New York . . . are only for the purpose of appeasing the radicals of the Republican Party who have been excoriating the administration for its inaction. One cannot explain the apparent contradiction existing between the overt acts of the government and the assurances of peace of the Secretary of State unless one considers the indecision of the President and the disagreements which prevail in the Cabinet. Mr. Seward . . . is for conciliation, but he is influenced by his quarrelsome colleagues in the Cabinet so that he leans first toward one side, then toward the other.[16]

When on April 8 ships for the relief of Fort Sumter began their journey from New York, the commissioners sent a protest to Seward through Justice Campbell of the Supreme Court, who had been acting as intermediary. The Secretary replied, "Faith as to Sumter fully kept;

wait and see." Outraged at being betrayed, the commissioners broke off negotiations. Jefferson Davis took up the challenge and demanded the evacuation of Fort Sumter. Lincoln had the choice of vindicating the power of the government or making an unconditional surrender. On April 12, the fort was bombarded and after thirty-six hours the unprovisioned garrison capitulated. The Confederate flag was raised. The long-dreaded Civil War had begun.

The expedition which was being prepared at New York left this port on April 8: it was composed of four frigates, as many ships of smaller dimensions and several transports; roughly 3,000 men of the regular troops were on board. This expedition was intended to reprovision Fort Sumter in South Carolina and Fort Picken in Florida and then to go along the coast of Texas, which has seceded from the Union but which has not as yet joined the other insurgent States.

The government at Washington has announced to Mr. Jefferson Davis, the provisional head of the Southern Confederacy, that the forces of the United States will not commit any hostile act unless resistance is met while reprovisioning the federal forts. But Mr. Davis regarded the sending of such a strong expedition to the coasts of the South tantamount to a declaration of war; and considering it dangerous to permit forces of the North to enter to fortify strategic points on the territory of the seceded States, gave to General Beauregard, commander of the troops which the Confederates had assembled at Charleston, the order to attack Fort Sumter immediately. The bombardment started the day before yesterday and lasted almost 36 hours, at the end of which the fort surrendered. The news arrived here last night. Since newspapers are not published on Sundays and since the telegraph office is closed, we have not been able to obtain any details today concerning the attack on Fort Sumter, and the reasons for the inactivity of the squadron which was on hand during the bombardment without making the slightest attempt to meet force with force.[17]

A blaze of fury passed over the North as the news of the firing on the nation's flag spread like wildfire. Overnight the shock of the conflict united all factions. "There can be no neutrals now, only patriots and traitors," declared Senator Stephen A. Douglas, lately Lincoln's bitterest political antagonist. From every city, town and hamlet of the North came the patriotic cry, "The Union must be preserved!" President Lincoln issued a call for 75,000 volunteers to serve for three months.[18] Typical of the responses was the one from Iowa: "Ten days ago we had two parties in this State; today we have but one, and that one is for the Constitution and the Union unconditionally."

Seward had not intended to deceive anyone. He had given assurances about Sumter on his own responsibility, without warrant from Lincoln. He was certain his "policy" would be approved by the President.

Still smarting over his defeat at the Republican convention, Seward had accepted the most important office in Lincoln's Cabinet fully expecting to rule Lincoln and the country. But he learned quickly that Lincoln meant to be a real President and that under no circumstances would he permit anyone else to assume his responsibility of preserving the Union. It was he who gave the order to succor Fort Sumter, notwithstanding Seward's assurances to the contrary. The authority of the Union must be asserted at all hazards. This was President Lincoln's first major decision during the bewildering first month in office while he was vacillating in his policy—or lack of policy—regarding the forts.

According to Frederick W. Seward, assistant to his father in the Department of State, the Russian Minister in Washington "went to the very verge of diplomatic prudence in his efforts to bring them [the Southern representatives] into a good understanding with the Lincoln administration." Of course, these efforts were made with a view of keeping them in the Union. Equally, of course, perhaps, the secessionists chose in their published correspondence and in the press, to claim that these were intimations on the part of Russia of a design to manifest "sympathy with the South" and to "recognize" and "open diplomatic relations with the Confederacy."[19]

The intercourse between the Russian Minister and the Southern Senators came to an abrupt end when the first gun was fired at Sumter. Stoeckl reported that Secretary Seward's fickleness, lack of resoluteness and "posing as a great man" disgusted him. His earlier opinion of the Cabinet officer as "the ablest American statesman" changed as soon as Seward displayed his irresoluteness over the Fort Sumter issue. In the eyes of the Russian diplomat his conduct was tantamount to bad faith. Thereafter he relegated the Secretary of State to a class of "small politicians" without strong convictions and grossly ignorant of international affairs.[20]

Stoeckl's over-zealous efforts to act as go-between during the frantic days before the fall of Fort Sumter were misunderstood by the Secretary of State and in part became responsible for his amazing memorandum, *Some Thoughts for the President's Consideration,* which he sent to President Lincoln on April 1, 1861. Seward, an avowed expansionist and apostle of manifest destiny, believed that nothing would so readily unite the warring sections of the United States as a common war against a foreign foe.

Reports reached Washington that Spain had reasserted her authority over Santo Domingo. As a result of a revolution the Dominican Republic was overthrown and the flag of Spain was again flying over that island of the West Indies. "The reoccupation of Santo Domingo by Spain," wrote Stoeckl, "has created a sensation in Washington. A demand has been made of M. Tassara, Minister of Spain, what the intentions of his government are. The United States will resist this move as a violation of the Monroe Doctrine."[21] From neighboring Mexico came even more startling rumors. Great Britain, France and Spain, it was reported, were threatening intervention in Mexico in order to redress the wrongs their subjects were suffering from the anarchy and violence there, and to collect their debts.

Here was a great opportunity for the egotistical Secretary of State. Believing that President Lincoln was utterly incapable of formulating policies and that it was up to him to take over the real leadership of the government and to save the country, Seward decided to act. Losing all sense of reality he proposed the fantastic scheme of reuniting the North and the South by deliberately fomenting a foreign war—preferably with France and Spain and perhaps also with Russia and England.

"We are at the end of a month's administration, and yet without a policy either domestic or foreign" began the statement. Then Seward proceeded to offer suggestions for both. For the "policy at home" he proposed as the ruling idea: "Change the question before the public from one upon slavery, or about slavery, for a question upon Union or Disunion."

His plan "For Foreign Nations" was even more breath-taking. He would demand explanations from Spain and France categorically at once:

I would seek explanations from Great Britain and Russia, and send agents into Canada, Mexico, and Central America, to rouse a vigorous spirit of independence on this continent against European intervention. And, if satisfactory explanations are not received from Spain and France, would convene Congress and declare war against them.

But whatever policy we adopt there must be an energetic prosecution of it.

For this purpose it must be somebody's business to pursue and direct it incessantly.

Either the President must do it himself, and be all the while active in it, or

Devolve it on some member of his Cabinet.

Once adopted, debates on it must end, and all agree and abide.

Modestly Secretary Seward closed with the statement:

"It is not my especial province; but I neither seek to evade nor assume responsibility."[22]

Putting on his strangely small glasses President Lincoln read his Secretary's wild proposal for plunging the United States into an utterly unjustifiable predatory foreign war. The "thought" which virtually suggested that he abdicate his powers as President to his worldly-wise Secretary made him wince. But if it was galling to him, he did not make his feelings known to anyone. His lips showing taut, he penned a reply which answered Seward's contentions point by point. Calmly but firmly and with lofty dignity he ended with: "If this must be done, I must do it. When a general line of policy is adopted . . . upon points arising in its progress I wish, and I suppose I am entitled to have, the advice of all the Cabinet."[23]

Then he pigeonholed Seward's amazing document and kept it concealed so that no word of its contents became public as long as either of the two men was still alive.

Seward now acquired a genuine respect for his chief and drew closer to him. To his wife he wrote soon after receiving Lincoln's reply, "Executive force and vigor are rare qualities; the President is the best of us." Thereafter he settled down under Lincoln's leadership and throughout the rest of the Civil War conducted America's foreign affairs with great ability.

As soon as Prince Gortchakov learned that Southern newspapers were construing Stoeckl's conferences with leaders of the slave States as a forerunner of Russia's opening diplomatic relations with the Confederacy, he gave "the unequivocal assurance of Russia's sympathy with the Union."[24]

Thereafter the Russian envoy had no further dealings with the government of Jefferson Davis. The failure of his efforts at mediation and the outbreak of hostilities filled Stoeckl with sorrow. He believed the Union permanently destroyed. And although he regretted the fact very much, he nevertheless hoped that the North would soon accept the inevitable and seek close co-operation with the South in commerce and foreign relations.

Following Stoeckl's failure at conciliation, the Washington foreign diplomatic corps as a body, headed by England's Lord Lyons and France's Henri Mercier, planned mediation with their respective governments acting as umpires of the American dispute. But they quickly dropped this program when Secretary Seward, in a statement to the Governor of Maryland on April 23, made it crystal clear that under no circumstances would the differences between the federal government and the seceded States be submitted to foreign arbitrament. The Anglo-French mediation proposal was but masked intervention, he declared, and would be treated accordingly. In consequence, Lord Lyons wrote to Lord Russell, Britain's Foreign Minister, that Seward was a pernicious and dangerous person in Lincoln's government.

Bremen's Minister, Schleiden, then proposed to the President and the Secretary of State that he be permitted to hold confidential discussions with Vice President Stephens of the Confederacy, in an attempt to prevent bloodshed. Lincoln advised Schleiden that the federal government could not authorize negotiations nor invite proposals, but intimated that there could be no objection if he negotiated with Stephens without special authorization. Seward handed the diplomat a pass through the Union lines, and the next day Schleiden met with Stephens behind closed doors in Richmond. The Confederacy's Vice President believed that all attempts at peace would be useless as the South suspected the acts of Lincoln and Seward. Their objective, he pointed out, was the "subjugation of the Southern people." Unless these objectives were changed, "no power on earth can arrest or prevent a most bloody conflict." When Secretary Seward received Schleiden's report, he replied by an unofficial and confidential communication that the President was of the opinion that a continuance of the negotiations would be without beneficial results.

The dispute would have to be left to the arbitrament of the battlefield.

4

The Gloomy Year 1861

THE OUTBREAK of hostilities between the North and the South deeply affected Edouard de Stoeckl. He had intimate friends in both sections of the United States. It grieved him, he wrote to Prince Gortchakov shortly after the fall of Fort Sumter,

> to see the two sections of the country, called by nature herself into the most intimate alliance, engaging in a war without rhyme or reason and without any other possible termination than mutual ruin and destruction. Eighty years of prosperity without equal in history are due to this Union. It has been broken in the name of an abstract principle and converted into mutual hate and hostility. It appears that in all human nature there lurks a lust for blood that must be satisfied from time to time.[1]

Within a few days Stoeckl was advising his government:

> Washington is in a state of blockade. Mail is interrupted, telegraph wires cut, railroads out of commission by the partial destruction of the roads or of several bridges. For eight days we have received no mail or newspapers.
> Confusion reigns supreme. Men by the thousands are leaving their shops, stores or professions and volunteering for military duty. Massachusetts troops have arrived in Washington. More

than 20,000 militia will soon be concentrated in the National Capital.

Stoeckl also pointed out that President Lincoln's proclamation for 75,000 men, though successful in raising troops for the federal army, served also to consolidate the South. "The legislature of Virginia has declared for secession. Maryland mobs attacked United States troops as they passed through Baltimore." The Russian Minister predicted that Maryland, too, would soon secede. More and more officers were resigning their commissions in the federal army and navy and joining the Confederates. Most noteworthy were Colonels Robert E. Lee and Joseph E. Johnston. Few if any experienced military leaders were left in the federal forces.

On assuming the powers of his office, the President was compelled to make the choice between two courses: the use of conciliation or the use of force. By his proclamation he adopted the medium of force. With a single stroke of his pen he divided the Union into two hostile camps without hope of reconciliation. The border States which up to now have served somewhat as intermediaries between the North and the South have been practically expelled by force from the Union. Ostensibly the purpose of the proclamation was the defense of the Capital, but unfortunately it had to entail as a necessary and inevitable consequence the secession of Virginia and Maryland, and the placing of the Capital within enemy territory. At this moment the White House, the residence of the President, is almost within cannon shot of Virginia on the opposite bank of the Potomac River. It had been rumored for several days that an attack by the forces of the South is imminent. The White House is defended by a guard of one hundred men. The federal treasury has been converted into a fortress, and the Capital into a barracks. This state of affairs cannot continue. It will be necessary either to abandon the Capital and destroy the public buildings to prevent them from falling into the hands of the enemy, or to seize Maryland and Virginia by force of arms and govern them as conquered provinces—which would indeed be an anomaly in a republic.

Cassius M. Clay, the Kentucky abolitionist who stumped his State for Lincoln and as a reward was to be appointed Minister to Russia, delayed his journey to St. Petersburg to organize and captain a volunteer White House guard. He expected the war to come momentarily to Washington. Armed with three pistols and an "Arkansas tooth pick," he was prepared for a last-ditch battle at the doors of the Executive Mansion.

The danger and predicament in which the nation's Capital found itself, Stoeckl believed, was due to President Lincoln's "gross inexperience in the management of the more important affairs of state as well as of military affairs." He wrote, "Several thousand troops are stationed here and no measures have been adopted to provision them. Washington obtains its provisions from Virginia and Maryland. . . . Indignation is so great in Baltimore that any relations with Washington are regarded as high treason."

Stoeckl reported that the federal government, realizing its inability to hold the arsenals at Harpers Ferry and Norfolk, Virginia, had ordered the buildings burned and the supply of arms and ammunition destroyed. "The value of the destroyed property at the Norfolk naval arsenal is estimated at $27,000,000. Several fine naval vessels which were not quite ready to take to sea have been burned and sunk."

In addition to these troubles, Lincoln was beset with a quarrelsome Cabinet of divided counsels. The President, wrote the Russian Minister, was being influenced too strongly by

> Mr. Blair, the Attorney General, and his father, an old man of remarkable intelligence, both violent abolitionists. They will attempt by hook or crook to impose . . . their extreme views of the slavery question. The President's policies which have alienated the border States have resulted in still another critical loss—all the military and naval personnel of these States have resigned and have offered their services to Jefferson Davis.
>
> In the meantime Jefferson Davis is organizing an army of 50,000 which he can double if need be. He counteracted Lincoln's proclamation for 75,000 men by issuing a call to shipowners to arm themselves as privateers to prey upon the merchant ships of the North. Mr. Davis, wielding almost dictatorial powers, is enthusiastically supported by the people of the South who manifest great confidence in him. . . . Though his policies have not been made public, all feel they will be intelligently thought out. Up to this point there is no indication that the single serious danger which

the Southern Confederacy has fear of—an insurrection of the Negro slaves—will ever take place."[2]

The rumors of a huge army of rebels marching from Baltimore to sack Washington, and of Confederate gunboats sailing up the Potomac to shell the Capitol, did not materialize, and Washington's residents breathed easier. So on May 6 Stoeckl wrote, "Now that the danger to Washington is over the people demand the carrying of the war to the South to force the seceded States to return to the Union."

Stoeckl pointed out that Lincoln had plenty of troops. However, they first had to be trained and properly equipped for a war of invasion.

Mr. Lincoln should not delude himself that a conquest of the South—even should he achieve it—will succeed in re-establishing the Union. Moreover, he should know that by invading the South during the months of June and July, he would be risking the destruction of his armies because of the terrible heat of the South. But his position is such that he cannot withdraw. He is entirely under the influence of the demagogues of his Party and cannot do otherwise than to obey them. These violent men are masters of the situation and are trying to take advantage of the enthusiasm displayed by the general public of the North by agitating their own radical doctrines.

Under their direction committees are being organized everywhere which claim the right to deal with the government and which almost daily send deputations to the President to dictate to him the course of action he should follow. Senator Wilson, noted for his radical views, arrived here with a group of extremists and called upon the President. In their conversation Senator Wilson said to the President, "We saved you from an attack by the secessionists. But you are now threatened by an even greater danger— one from the North. One backward step or even one false step will result in your downfall."

The principal newspapers of the large cities have become the mouthpiece of the extremists. Their fanaticism spares neither Lincoln nor his Cabinet. Mr. Seward especially is the object of their attacks. They are regarded as being too moderate under the present conditions. They no longer demand conquest alone, but also the extermination of the Southern States. One of these newspapers

declared: "The people will not wait. They will not hesitate to
choose a new leader should Lincoln fail them." The spread of such
subversive propaganda by an unbridled press must necessarily lead
to complete anarchy. Already disorders are taking place in the
large cities. In New York, mobs are marching through the streets
and engaging in all kinds of violence. Citizens have been compelled
to organize and arm themselves to defend their persons and
property.[3]

The struggle, Stoeckl predicted, would be one of the fiercest ever.
At first he thought it would be over by winter. Then he changed his
mind and predicted it would last until the end of the year or possibly
until spring. The apparent advantage which the North held in the
matter of numbers and resources would be counterbalanced by the fact
that the Confederates would be fighting on their own soil, in defense
of their homes. If by spring the federal government could not suppress
the insurrection, it would have to give up from sheer exhaustion. He
was to change his predictions again and again as the conflict raged on
with ever-increasing intensity. "The end of the conflict is not yet in
sight," he was to write on one occasion. And on another, "The conquest
of the South is still an open question."

Early in May Stoeckl had occasion to confer with Secretary Seward.
"He assured me," Stoeckl reported, "that Union sentiment in the South
is widespread and awaits only the presence of federal troops to assert
itself. . . . I have reason to believe that the Secretary of State is deluding
himself on this point. According to the reports we have of the South,
public opinion is unanimous for secession, and their hatred for the
North grows daily. It is doubtful, despite what Mr. Seward says, that
these sentiments would disappear under the humiliation of a defeat."[4]

Stoeckl concluded that the Secretary of State, up to now "moder-
ately disposed, has like Lincoln, succumbed to the pressure from the
extremists." "On to Richmond" had become the battle cry of the
North. It rang constantly in Lincoln's ears. It confronted him daily in
the flaring headlines of the *New York Tribune* and other journals
which demanded that Richmond must be taken before the Confederate
Congress could meet there. It was becoming more and more apparent
that a forward movement would have to be made as an absolute
political necessity.

General Winfield Scott, old and infirm, but viewing the war as a soldier, not as a politician, declared that it was impossible to weld a mass of raw recruits into an efficient army overnight. From sixty years' experience he knew it takes a long time to make an army, and that it is impossible to organize, train, march and fight all at the same time.

From the Russian Embassy in Washington, Stoeckl kept watching developments and reporting in detail to St. Petersburg. On May 13 he informed Prince Gortchakov:

> More than 50,000 troops are in Washington and Maryland. These contingents are composed of militias who have enlisted for only three months. They will be replaced by 64,000 enlisted volunteers as soon as their training is completed.
>
> A campaign was to have been launched on the third of this month. It is proposed that Virginia be invaded at three points: at Norfolk near the coast, at Alexandria located seven miles from Washington on the right bank of the Potomac, and at Harpers Ferry on the west. From these three points the federal troops are to advance towards Richmond, the Capital of Virginia, and take possession of the State. But up to this moment no movement has taken place and the army is in the same position that it was one week ago.
>
> This delay is due to the disturbing news received from the West. Tennessee declared it has seceded from the Union; Kentucky is still undecided, but everything appears to indicate that she will follow the example of Tennessee. These two States could furnish, in case of need, 80,000 men who are accustomed to the privations of Western life and who, when it comes to handling firearms, have no equals in the Union.
>
> General Scott, who commands military operations, hesitates to enter upon a war of invasion with an army composed of untrained and badly organized militias. These troops have neither wagons nor field hospitals; they lack the most rudimentary needs of an army. . . . There are no commissaries. The regiments which arrived here procured provisions as best they could and paid for them in gold. At New York and at Philadelphia and also here in Washington, several regiments have been lodged in hotels where each soldier is costing the public treasury one to two dollars a day.
>
> In the South preparations are being made for a desperate resistance of the Northern invasion, but we know absolutely nothing of

the campaign plans of Jefferson Davis. It is on this point that the government at Montgomery has an immense advantage over the Washington government whose every strategic movement is immediately known and often publicized in advance by the press.

There is a great divergence of opinion between Mr. Lincoln and General Scott. The former is subject to the pressure of the Northern States, which, as the price of their sacrifices, demand that the government act without delay. Mr. Lincoln cannot escape the exigencies of public opinion; he must act, no matter what the risk. General Scott sees the question only from the military standpoint and refuses to undertake an expedition without reasonable assurance in advance of success. As to the members of the Cabinet, some share the President's opinion, others General Scott's; and the result of this discord will be the adoption of half-measures which will satisfy no one and which will serve only to increase the administration's predicament.[5]

Stoeckl then discussed Lincoln's contention that no State possesses an inherent right to secede from the Union.

To permit the principle of secession, that is to say, the right of a State to break the federal pact when it decides that it is appropriate to do so, is to render absurd the very idea of a confederation. A government thus constituted would be an utter fallacy. If a State may secede at will, why, under the same principle, could not a county or a city withdraw? Secession could continue indefinitely and all power, all authority, would become but a meaningless phrase. The supremacy of the federal government finds its authority in public opinion. It is only necessary that this opinion be expressed by constitutional means. The Constitution left wide latitude to future reforms through the amending process. This means was open to the Southern States. They failed to avail themselves of it.

To give legal sanction to secession "would be to pronounce the doom of all governments present and future," he asserted. "Vigorous action on the part of the government will have the wholesome effect in the loyal States of a reassertion of national supremacy. It is essential that the secessionists be either vanquished or taught a bitter lesson."

Stoeckl pointed out that Lincoln's and Seward's declarations that the

United States is one nation inseparable and indivisible, though correct
in theory, was altogether false in fact. In their view,

> The Union has not ceased to exist. The secessionists are merely
> insurrectionists. The United States is one and will continue to
> remain one single nation. In theory this view is incontestable. Un-
> fortunately . . . in actuality . . . Mr. Seward is mistaken when he
> says the United States is one nation.
>
> From the very beginning of the federal government the North
> and the South have been different. Under the influence of different
> local institutions, and perhaps also of diverse climatic conditions,
> two nationalities, mutually antipathetic, have developed. The fed-
> eral pact, during recent years, tended more and more to become
> only an artificial bond between two sections which instinctively
> found each other repulsive. The question of slavery is the principal
> incident in this phenomenon. However, it is but one incident. The
> rupture of the Union was the explosion of a long-smoldering
> national antipathy.
>
> Thus the question of nationality, which is so important in
> Europe, is found also in the United States, and is complicated fur-
> ther by the race question. In the present crisis involving abstract
> principles of authority and legality, the federal government is
> being conducted along the lines of European governments.
>
> It now flagrantly contradicts its own declarations made during
> the Hungarian revolution and its actions in the hasty recognition
> of the Italian kingdom; it finds itself constrained now to recognize
> in America what it wanted to deny in Europe: that a government
> cannot exist without authority and that, in order to maintain this
> authority, even if that authority exists in principle, a display of
> power is at times indispensable.
>
> The war which has broken out here is essentially a war of prin-
> ciples. The government's case is a difficult one. On the one hand,
> it is a question of safeguarding the integrity of the principle of
> supreme authority; on the other, it is a question of yielding to the
> exigencies imposed by circumstances. Sooner or later a compromise
> is inevitable. The skill of the government will lie in its ability to
> act at the right time. If it does not recognize its true function and
> if, yielding to the pressure of the extremists, it tries to conquer and
> subjugate the South, then instead of restoring the Union it will

only succeed in bringing about its destruction and undermining the principles which form the basis of its existence.[6]

Stoeckl was amazed at the patriotic fervor with which the people of the North responded to President Lincoln's proclamation for troops:

> If Mr. Lincoln's administration only knew how to take advantage of this outburst of patriotism, great benefits would result. But to attain this, it will be necessary to act with skill and vigor. But none of the administration heads possess these qualities. Each new difficulty frightens them. They temporize, evidently waiting for July 4, the day set for the convening of Congress, so that Congress, rather than they, can assume full responsibility.

Then the Russian Minister again voiced his low opinion of the capabilities of Lincoln, whom he regarded as "President only in name." He believed the President to be completely under the domination of the extremists who surround him and actually control the government:

> The more complicated the situation becomes the more feeble and undecided he [Lincoln] appears. He admits that his task is beyond his powers. Fatigue and anxiety have broken him down morally and physically.
>
> As for Mr. Seward, his services in the office of Secretary of State hardly justify the high reputation he formerly enjoyed. He is completely ignorant of international affairs. At the same time his vanity is so great that he will not listen to anyone's advice. His arrogance harms the administration more than does the mediocrity of his colleagues.

Having thus disposed of President Lincoln and his chief Cabinet officer as mediocrities and failures, the Russian Minister now reported to his government:

> Mr. Chase, Secretary of the Treasury, is the only one who possesses real ability. A confirmed abolitionist, he has been consistently opposed to making concessions or offering compromises to the South. But he does not advocate the use of force as a means of restoring the Union.
>
> Besides the official advisors of the President there are sinister influences which unfortunately exercise great power over the vacillating Chief Executive. Mr. Greeley and Mr. Blair, experts in

the art of partisan intrigues and scheming, are at the head of a secret coalition of Senators and Members of the House of Representatives. Mr. Greeley is in New York where he influences public opinion through the medium of the press. Mr. Blair is here and acts directly upon the President.

This group imposes pressure upon the President to use extreme measures, and hostilities would have started already were it not for the opposition of General Scott who has said again and again to the President that launching an invasion with an army composed of raw recruits badly trained and without proper equipment would result in certain defeat. . . . In consequence General Scott has been violently attacked by Greeley and Blair. He would have already been replaced were it not for the difficulty of finding a commander who would consent to obey their dictates more or less blindly.[7]

A few days later Stoeckl learned that "the federal government has given up the plan of launching an invasion of the South. . . . General Scott has succeeded in demonstrating the dangers of such a move. He has prevailed in his proposal of occupying strategic points in Virginia and Missouri and waiting in this position until autumn, and then to advance into the South if necessary. It is hoped that in the interim, the Confederate States, surrounded on land along their entire borders and blocked by sea, will be forced into submission."[8]

On July 3, 1861, the day before Congress assembled for its extraordinary session, while President Lincoln was putting the finishing touches on his message, Stoeckl wrote to Prince Gortchakov:

I have had opportunity of talking with several leaders. If I can judge from their comments they have decided to adopt the most violent measures and to undertake a war to the bitter end, and to denounce as traitors all who dare to speak of compromise. As happens in all political convulsions men of peace and moderation are howled down, and events are directed by a noisy minority who resort to extremes.

The administration itself will not exercise much leadership. The extremists of the Republican Party have not forgotten that the President has been inclined to negotiate with the Confederates. They are trying to maneuver him so as to prevent him from attempting such a step.

But the scheming in Congress will be directed chiefly against the commanding general of the federal army. He is criticized for his inaction and failure to invade the South with the 200,000 men under his command. They do not dare to attack him openly because he is too popular throughout the country. But they endeavor to undermine him secretly. The extremists in Congress who fear the moderate policies of General Scott and his influence upon the President will overlook no opportunity to oust him and replace him with someone who will comply with their views.

General Scott has not been intimidated by these threats and continues to act with prudence and circumspection. Although he has an army of from 200,000 to 250,000 men, they are untrained. The stagnation of business and industry threw thousands of persons onto the streets who found relief only in the army. The large cities furnished the vast majority of these men. They are a strange conglomeration of all nationalities. Several regiments are composed entirely of Germans. Others contain only Irish. There are still others in which you find Spaniards, Italians, Belgians and French. There are even a number of Russians and Serbians. The generals are men who only yesterday were lawyers and merchants, and are entirely ignorant even of the elementary principles of their new offices. Officers of the regiments are chosen by the soldiers, so how can they issue orders to men to whom they owe their positions and who have the right to dismiss them at will?

Some 50,000 to 60,000 troops are bivouacking in the environs of Washington. It is difficult to name a form of disorder or rowdyism they do not commit, and under the very eyes of the President and the high command. Is it any wonder then that General Scott hesitates to undertake an invasion with an army composed of such elements, particularly with the season of bad weather approaching? This able American army veteran does not underestimate his adversaries, who though not superior in organization or size have the advantage of fighting on their own soil and of being able to convert the fighting into guerrilla warfare. They have already started this form of attack. The outposts of the federal troops cannot venture beyond their lines without falling into some ambush of the Virginia guerrillas.

There is still another motive contributing to General Scott's policy of moderation: it is his desire to avoid bloodshed as far as possible. He told me recently, "If the objective of this war is the reconstruction of the Union, if our enemies of today are again to become our compatriots, it is unwise to antagonize them unduly."

However, the present state of inaction cannot long continue. Public opinion, inspired by demagogues, demands action, and General Scott will be compelled to move and attack the secessionists. The latter, blocked by sea and lacking financial and material resources, will be on the defensive.

The President of the Confederacy has changed the seat of government to Richmond, Va., whence he directs military operations. . . .

Up to this point Jefferson Davis has completely justified the reputation he has always enjoyed of being a skilful and energetic leader. He has won the confidence of his people to the point of being able to assume dictatorial power. This is not a small advantage which the South has on her adversaries of the North where everyone wishes to command and no one to obey.

Whereas the army of the North costs (and I have this from the Secretary of the Treasury himself) a million dollars a day, Mr. Davis, without any resources other than a loan of $15,000,000, has succeeded in raising an army of an estimated 100,000 men who are fairly well armed and ardently resolved to defend every inch of their territory.

The unrestrained threats of conquest and extermination hurled constantly against the seceded States by the press, government officials and even the pulpit of the North have convinced the South that only in a desperate resistance lies any hope for them. Therefore, the separation which at the beginning of the crisis appeared to be sheerly political, has become in the eyes of the people of the South, a matter of life or death. And if it is difficult to predict all the phases through which the American revolution is destined to pass, there is at least one thing that seems certain, and that is that the reconstruction of the Union has become an impossible task.[9]

On July 4, 1861, the eighty-fifth anniversary of the Declaration of Independence, Congress assembled in special session in pursuance to Lincoln's call. From March 4 until July 4, the momentous issues of the Civil War had been decided by Lincoln alone. By his own fiat he had suspended the writ of habeas corpus, first in a limited area and then generally over the country. He had issued a proclamation of blockade in all the ports of the seceded States. He had declared martial law. By a proclamation he had ordered the regular army increased by 22,714 officers and men and the navy by 18,000, and had called for volunteers to serve for three years. Public money was spent without congressional appropriation.

As a congressman, Lincoln had once bitterly denounced President Polk for his alleged usurpation of power in prosecuting the Mexican War. Now Lincoln as President was going infinitely beyond Polk.

Stoeckl, sitting with Mercier and other diplomats in the dimly lit gallery of the House of Representatives, listened intently as a clerk with droning voice read the message of President Lincoln on this extremely hot day of July 4. Lincoln reported what had been done to meet the emergency and asked for approval.

> This issue embraces more than the fate of these United States. It presents to the whole family of man the question whether a constitutional republic or democracy—a government of the people, by the same people—can or cannot retain its territorial integrity against its own domestic foes. It presents the question whether discontented individuals, too few in numbers to control administration according to organic law in any case, can always, upon the pretenses made in this case, or any other pretenses, or arbitrarily without any pretense, break up their government, and thus practically put an end to free government upon the earth. It forces us to ask: "Is there, in all republics, this inherent and fatal weakness? Must a government of necessity be too strong for the liberties of its own people, or too weak to maintain its own existence?"

Toward the end of the message Lincoln said: "This is essentially a people's contest. On the side of the Union it is a struggle for maintaining in the world that form and substance of government whose leading object is to elevate the condition of men—to lift artificial weights from all shoulders." Lincoln then requested an appropriation of $400,000,000 to make the contest "short and decisive."[10]

What could Congress do but approve? Six days after receiving Lincoln's message, a joint resolution was offered in the Senate, which after reciting the President's "extraordinary acts, proclamations and orders," approved and declared them to be "in all respects legal and valid, to the same intent, and with the same effect, as if they had been issued and done under the previous express authority and direction of the Congress of the United States."

The President was authorized to raise the army to 500,000 men, to borrow $200,000,000, and to issue $50,000,000 in treasury notes. Only four months earlier the country seemed to prefer disunion to war. But Lincoln by his tactful and forceful measures had resolved the issue; the rebellion must be crushed and the Union restored. His war policy received approval in the House with only five dissenting votes.

While Congress was voting approval of the President's conduct of the conflict and granting him men and money to crush the rebellion, the cry rang throughout the North, "On to Richmond!" As long as he could, General Scott had resisted the demands for immediate action. But the political pressure and the newspaper clamor became too powerful, and at last he gave way. Reluctantly he gave the order for an advance upon Richmond, the Confederate Capital.

General McDowell, in command of 35,000 men, was ordered to strike a Confederate force and drive the Southerners back from Manassas near a little stream called Bull Run. Another Union commander, General Patterson, was to advance up the Shenandoah Valley to prevent the Confederates there from going to the aid of their comrades at Manassas Junction. On July 16, McDowell led his citizen soldiers across the bridges spanning the Potomac and began the long-awaited advance. By the 19th he was at the Bull Run stream behind which the Confederates, led by General Beauregard, lay.

Members of Congress, confident of a victory and anxious to see the Confederate rebels receive a whipping they would never forget, took horses or hired vehicles and accompanied by their ladies drove southward from Washington to watch the spectacle of real war across the Potomac. On the field of Bull Run, less than a day's horseback ride southwest of Washington, the green federal army fought courageously for many hours. Lincoln waited anxiously in the White House for reports of the battle. The first accounts were regarded as favorable. But what should have been a victory turned into horrible disaster chiefly because of the inexcusable failure of General Patterson to stop Confederate General Johnston from coming to the aid of Beauregard. Johnston, uninterrupted and unfollowed by Patterson, united his forces with those of Beauregard and attacked the green federal army, which crumpled up and was driven from the field. Panic-stricken the raw recruits turned into a mere mob of individuals and fled in terror.

In his next reports to the Russian Foreign Office, Stoeckl gave practically an eyewitness report of the Union disaster:[11]

> At about 4 o'clock . . . General Beauregard hurled 2,000 cavalrymen, who had not up to this time taken part in the action, against the federal army. . . . The effect of this maneuver was instantaneous. All troops without exception took to their heels and soon the entire army was one mad stampede in the woods and on the highway. The officers of the militia were the first to take flight, and the soldiers ran after them, throwing away their haversacks and rifles. It was thus that the federal army returned to Washington only four days after taking to the field.

Stoeckl stated that the official government bulletin of July 21 concerning the disaster appeared to be carefully censored. It admitted Union casualties of only 50 killed and 200 wounded, whereas a foreign correspondent who had been on the scene estimated the casualties at 5,000. Although the official bulletin stated that "the enemy was superior in number," Stoeckl reported:

> The armies must have been almost equal in numerical strength. General McDowell had more than 60,000 men. The Southern army was composed of between 40,000 to 45,000 men, but was eventually re-enforced by 15,000 of General Johnston's men.
>
> Manassas Gap was the important point and McDowell sent half of his forces there. But Patterson, instead of pursuing Johnston, retraced his steps and permitted him to go by forced marches to Manassas Gap, where he arrived with the rest of his troops the night before the battle. This contributed to the success of the Southern army. The brilliant maneuver of General Johnston, and the bungling retreat of General Patterson can be explained by the fact that the former is one of the most capable officers of the army, whereas the latter is a Philadelphia stockbroker. Patterson offers as the excuse for his retreat that he had no means of transportation, that he lacked provisions, and that his troops had refused to advance. It is probably the truth, for with untrained volunteers and a commissary which was entirely disorganized, nothing is impossible. He was stripped of his command, but apparently they have

not profited from their mistake as they replaced him by Mr. Banks, a Boston lawyer.

The federal army's losses have been enormous. Everything was abandoned: seventy cannons, thirty to forty thousand rifles, a considerable quantity of ammunition, wagons and medical supplies have fallen into the hands of the Southern army. The loss of men is terrific. The government published nothing on this subject, but from all the information that I have been able to obtain, the number of killed, wounded, captured, and deserters is at least 10,000 men.

Stoeckl's estimate of 10,000 federal casualties proved to be far from accurate. The official figures are: killed, 460; wounded, 1,124; missing, 1,312—a total of 2,896. Similar inaccuracies will be noted in his reports pertaining to some other battles. Remarkably well informed as a rule, the Russian Minister, nevertheless, was reporting contemporaneously, frequently immediately after the event, and had to rely upon unofficial sources and hearsay for his information. Considering the dispatch with which he usually forwarded his quickly acquired information to St. Petersburg, it is surprising how accurate he proved to be in most instances.[12]

Continuing his report of the Battle of Bull Run, Stoeckl depicted the despair and confusion which enveloped the North after the disaster:

The day after the battle, Washington offered a sad spectacle indeed. Groups of soldiers, returned from the battlefield, exhausted and bedraggled, crowded the streets and begged for food from door to door. A deadly fear pervaded the city that momentarily it might be invaded. Fortunately a thousand regular troops performing police functions succeeded in leading the deserters into the camps near the Capital which they had occupied prior to the march on Virginia, and order was restored.

No one was more affected by this disaster than General Scott. He knew from experience the danger of sending untrained volunteers into combat and had resisted as long as he could. But . . . the pressure was too great and he had to yield. When the news of the rout arrived here the President went to the residence of General Scott to ascertain what emergency measures were now necessary. "The first thing that you must do," the veteran answered, "is to accept my resignation because I have committed one of the gravest

offences possible, that of yielding to the clamor of the demagogues." However, General Scott is the only one who has not lost
his head. he has already started to reorganize the army. But he has
declared that he will require ample time before he will again be
in a position to take the offensive.

We do not know what the Confederate army will do following
this victory. It has again advanced toward Washington, the outposts being but five or six miles from here, but it cannot take the
Capital, which is separated from Virginia by the Potomac. The
first attack will probably be directed upon the army of General
Banks. This force cannot venture into Virginia since the main army
has been destroyed. Therefore, General Banks has been ordered to
fall back upon Harpers Ferry where there are entrenchments, and
if necessary to recross the Potomac. But it is a question whether he
can elude General Johnston, who, it is reported, started advancing
immediately after the battle of Manassas Gap to cut off the retreat
of General Banks' forces. The danger to the latter has been aggra-
vated by the fact that his strength has been reduced by reason of
the departure of 17,000 of his men whose terms of service have
expired. On the other hand, Johnston's army has been reinforced
by several regiments added from Beauregard's army. In any event
Johnston will be the master of the upper Potomac and will be able
almost at will to enter the State of Maryland where the secessionists are in the majority and await only the arrival of Southern
troops to issue a declaration of secession from the Union. If that
happens, we will again be surrounded in Washington as we were
three months ago.

However, it is not to be taken for granted that Jefferson Davis,
who directs operations and who up to this moment has demonstrated the greatest of prudence, will decide to extend operations
to the upper Potomac. It is fair to assume that he will continue to
remain on the defensive in Virginia where his greatest resources
are located.

While Washington trembled with fear that Generals Beauregard and
Johnston were planning next to strike at the Capital, President Lincoln
sent out a call to Major General George B. McClellan, in charge of
military operations in Western Virginia, to hasten to Washington to
replace McDowell in command of the Army of the Potomac. He was

a stocky young fellow only thirty-four years of age. Stoeckl included an account of this new military development in a dispatch to the Foreign Office:

> General McClellan is a young man who lacks neither ability nor energy, but who has not yet proven himself as the commander of an army. Before the Civil War, he was a mere Captain. . . . His task now is to reorganize the army shattered by defeat and to replenish the ranks with new regiments of volunteers.
>
> Radicals in Congress, whose clamoring for action is responsible for the disaster at Bull Run, are doing their utmost to oust General Scott, whose moderation and popularity annoy them. In a secret meeting held the day after the battle they decided that Congress should dismiss Scott, order the complete mobilization of the North, and decree emancipation of the slaves. However, because of the consternation the battle has caused throughout the nation, they do not dare to initiate these moves at present. . . . The public fully appreciates the wisdom of eighty-year-old General Scott, who has served the nation for sixty years . . . and it is now generally recognized that the nation would have been spared the disgrace of ignominious defeat if his advice had been followed. The catastrophe at Bull Run has become a personal vindication for General Scott.

As the days passed the impact of the military disaster upon the cause of the Union loomed more and more crushing. As Stoeckl observed:

> The federal defeat is greater than anyone expected. Everyone was sure of a victory. . . . The retreat was disgraceful. . . . Russell, the correspondent of the [London] *Times*, who is here, witnessed the event. He told me that he had never seen such a rout, not even among the Hindus or the Chinese. The Southern troops on the other hand fought extremely well.
>
> It is impossible to describe the confusion which the disaster has caused here. The administration and Congress have completely lost their heads. In the secret meetings being held here day and night no one listens, for confusion is everywhere. No one seems to possess authority to give directions for the future. All that is being done is to request the several States to send additional regiments of volunteers. But they will have difficulty in raising them.

Stoeckl then told of the difficulty the federal army was having in replenishing its depleted ranks. Volunteer enlistees, highly disgruntled, are demanding their releases. "Some eighty thousand men had enlisted for three months. The government is offering a premium of fifty dollars to anyone who will re-enlist for three years, without getting many takers." The Russian Minister related that "on the morning of the Battle of Bull Run, a Pennsylvania regiment whose term of service expired the same day left the army at the moment when the action was to start and returned serenely to Washington."

Prince Gortchakov, reading this paragraph at his office in St. Petersburg, noted on the margin of Stoeckl's dispatch, *"Charmant!"* (How charming!)

> With the passing of time, the situation becomes increasingly more critical. When hostilities end—and they must end sooner or later—new difficulties and more serious ones will appear: How to establish a line of demarcation between the North and the South? What to do with the West linked so intimately to both sections as to make a separation physically and geographically impossible? What to do about disruption of trade and commerce which the dissolution of the Union must inevitably bring about? Such are the questions everyone asks and for which no one has the answers.
>
> During a stay of more than twenty years in America, I have had the opportunity of making a study of the country. But I must admit frankly that I am at a loss to conjecture as to the future. I can only repeat that we can see nothing but the beginning of one of those political convulsions which overturn a nation from top to bottom.[13]

To which Gortchakov added the comment: "I think so too."

Not only had military affairs gone badly on land, but the blockade, too, is more or less of a failure, Stoeckl reported:

> In spite of all its efforts the government has not succeeded in accumulating a naval force of sufficient size to blockade the Southern ports effectively and to halt the privateers which are pursuing federal merchant ships as far north as the Massachusetts coast. More than forty Northern vessels have already been captured,

whereas, up to this time, the United States fleet has seized only one privateer.

But more serious than all other difficulties is the financial situation.... Congress had generously granted the President $500,000,000 instead of the $400,000,000 he had requested. But it was another story when it came to raise this exorbitant amount. An embarrassed Congress is suggesting a direct tax, but representatives of the people are objecting because of the unpopularity of such a tax. . . . The big bankers of New York are in no position to lend the government more than forty to forty-five million dollars. Mr. Chase has sent agents to Europe to float a loan, but its success is doubtful. The recourse will have to be to treasury bonds with the result that paper money will lose its value and public credit will be ruined.[14]

From then on for practically the remainder of the year 1861, Stoeckl's dispatches to St. Petersburg dealt largely with the inactivity of General McClellan's Army of the Potomac.[15] "Since the Battle of Bull Run, military operations on the Potomac are suspended," he wrote on August 13. "It will be some time before General McClellan can take the offensive." In his dispatch of September 9, Stoeckl reported:

No military operations have taken place during the last two or three weeks. The army camped in Washington has been reinforced by several volunteer regiments recruited in the North and it numbers today more than one hundred thousand men. General Mc-Clellan, who commands it, has succeeded in inculcating a certain degree of discipline but in so far as military training is concerned the army is mediocre. It lacks officers, who are more difficult to procure than volunteers. Seventy-five thousand men of this army are encamped on the opposite bank of the Potomac, almost in sight of the enemy pickets, but they have made no forward movement to push back the Confederates, whose flags can be distinctly seen from the top of the Capitol. It appears that the federal troops in other sections have not been any more active than those on the Potomac, for if they had won any success the government would have hastened to publish it.

A state of inactivity is to be expected from the Confederates.

They are acting on the defensive and as long as they can win positions and prevent the enemy from advancing, they have a measure of success. On the other hand, inaction for the army of the North is proof of lack of power and weakness.

Nearly a month passed, and on October 6 Baron de Stoeckl was still writing in the same vein, as indeed was the case on into December:

[October 6:] General McClellan still hesitates to attack the enemy although his strength is 170,000 men. At Washington plans are made and remade daily. Time is being wasted in conferences with bad weather coming on. . . . The newspapers are clamoring for vengeance. The government is endeavoring to comply with public opinion. But matters are becoming increasingly confused and vacillating.

[October 21:] The great Army of the Potomac is still immobile. Two months have passed without delivering a blow. The opposing armies each of 150,000 men content themselves with intercepting communications and destroying bridges and roads.

[November 5:] General McClellan is immobile. He has been in the same position for the last three months. General Johnston is master of the River. For ten days Washington has been under blockade. Supplies are coming in by a single route. . . . The cost of necessities is exorbitant. . . . Washington is cut off from its water route to the outside world by a smaller force than the federals have available.

General Scott has resigned, bringing new gloom to a situation already very dark. In all justice to President Lincoln it must be said that he has always treated General Scott with the highest consideration and regard worthy of his long· and distinguished record of service.

[December 3:] Military operations continue with the same lack of progress. . . . General McClellan is in the same position as four months ago.

However, while McClellan was holding the Army of the Potomac inactive in its camps, the Western armies were up and doing. In his August 13 dispatch Stoeckl reported a battle raging in Missouri. "But the silence of the government, which controls the telegraph wires, indicates a lack of success." As a matter of fact, five days later he was reporting that "the campaign in the West has been to the advantage of the Confederates. . . . General Frémont in command of the Army of the West has set out to retake Lexington. We are awaiting results as they will be decisive to the federal cause."[16]

The Russian Minister also reported that "a strong naval expedition organized by the government several months ago was now prepared to attack New Orleans or Mobile."[17] Less than a month later he was writing of "good news" which "produced a terrific moral effect" upon the nation:

> A naval expedition the government has been preparing for two months, set out and has occupied Beauford off the coast of South Carolina. The administration will be able to announce a victory which should aid the financial situation. It is an important event as it may prove the springboard for expeditions against Charleston and Savannah."[18]

However, on December 3 he apprised Prince Gortchakov that "the naval operations on the South Carolina coast were making no advance." He believed that the cause for the North's military failures lay in the fact that most of the federal commanders were lawyers and merchants by training without any skill for organizing an army.[19]

Nearly nine months without a single major military victory, coupled with the staggering disaster at Bull Run, had their inevitable effect upon the nation. The same people who in midsummer were clamoring, "On to Richmond," were by the end of the year crying, "Down with Lincoln." "The situation of the country is deplorable," Stoeckl had informed his government on September 9, 1861.

> It is sad to see a nation which was so prosperous hardly a year ago dragged toward its complete ruin by demagogues who have risen from the scum of the population, whose personal interest is their only guide—who risk everything, for they have nothing to lose. During the several days I spent recently in the North, I personally became aware of the change which has come about everywhere. One doesn't see either the industrial activity or the prosperity which used to exist in the cities and even in the villages. These have been replaced by gloom and depression and for the first time in America I saw beggars seeking alms in the streets. One of the tricks employed by the radicals is to spread rumors that the

South is in a deplorable condition and that all will be ended in one or two. months. Thus the first question I was asked everywhere was: "Will the South surrender? Is the war going to end?"

The President, honest man that he is, sees this evil but is helpless to stop it. As for Mr. Seward, he continues to lean first toward one faction, then toward the other. Evidently he is looking for a road of conciliation but he is afraid and doesn't dare to act. The radicals who suspect him of moderation work to overthrow him and it is very possible that they will succeed.

If the reign of the demagogues continues for a long time, General Frémont is destined to play an important role. He is already the standard-bearer of the radical party, and he will become the head of the party because of his superiority over the other leaders, among whom are only mediocre men and not a single leader of talent and energy.

A contributing factor to the disorder which prevails everywhere in the administration, as in the army, is that everyone here believes that he has the right to meddle in the affairs of state, or at least to give advice. There is not a newspaper which does not recommend its own military strategy and plans, and which does not have its favorite general whom it extols to the skies. Spinster ladies visit the hospitals and create embarrassment or annoyances, but every one of them wants to play the role of Miss Nightingale. Some committees named by charitable organizations go through the camps followed by doctors and French cooks to teach the soldiers to take care of their health and to cook. Finally, religious sects, of which there is a considerable number here, send deputation after deputation to enjoin the President to observe the Sabbath strictly in the army.

The President is forced to meet all of these people, to listen to them, to talk with them, and often to yield to their demands, absurd as they may be. In order to please the Puritan clergy, the commanding general, by order of the President, has just ordered the heads of the different corps to observe the Sabbath religiously, and not to engage in any military operations on Sunday other than to defend themselves in case of attack. All of this will give an idea of the chaos which exists.

Americans who refuse to take cognizance of the true condition of the country look upon the diplomatic corps with distrust. They see in us troublesome witnesses of their misfortunes, and our reports, which are as often as official as they are social, are on occasion rather annoying to them. Our personal position is hardly better. We have for a garrison a large undisciplined army of volunteers recruited for the most part from the dregs of the large cities and who from what some of my colleagues who recently returned from Turkey say, are no better than the *bashi bozouks* (Turkish irregulars). More than once, I and my colleagues have been exposed to the excesses of these volunteers, but we have not complained formally in order not to embarrass the government which already has troubles enough.

Luckily the Potomac shelters us from sudden attack by the enemy whose advance posts are only 4 or 5 versts [a verst is about two-thirds of an English mile] from here. But they can cross the river easily twenty-five miles from here and surprise the city from the rear. In such case I do not know from where we would be threatened most—from the soldiers who are here to protect us, or from the Confederates who may attack us. Probably we would be plundered by both. My wife along with the families of all the diplomats have gone North, and as for us we are so accustomed to these conditions that we don't think anything about them.[20]

Continuing his analysis of the "deplorable situation," Stoeckl discussed in some detail the efforts of the radicals to gain control of affairs:

The danger to the country lies not so much in the lack of success in military operations as in the intrigues and secret dealings of the radical parties and the weakness of the administration which, without sharing the views of the demagogues, succumbs to their evil influence and permits itself be dragged blindly along to certain ruin.

In one of my preceding reports, I had the honor to tell Your Excellency that the radicals were seeking a man devoted to their interests to place him at the head of the army. They had eyes on Mr. Frémont, a veteran officer of that type, but who had left the army to devote himself to political activities. In 1856 he was the candidate of the Republican Party. He is an ambitious man of great daring and perhaps destined to play an important role in this revolution. His followers desired him for the supreme command of the army, but the President would not consent to replace General Scott. Instead he placed Frémont in command of the federal troops in the West. Scarcely had Frémont arrived at his headquarters in St. Louis than he issued a proclamation establishing martial law in the whole State of Missouri, and announced that all insurgents would be shot. Moreover, he declared free the slaves of all persons who directly or indirectly had taken part in the secessionist movement.

General Frémont acted without authorization of the President and even contrary to his instructions, which forbade him to act in regard to the slave States of the West where Unionists are still fairly numerous. So the President was greatly astonished to learn about the proclamation of General Frémont. He regarded it as an act of insubordination. For a while there was consideration of dismissal, but after all he did nothing and did not even dare to reprimand him. The radicals, emboldened by this triumph, demand today that the edicts laid down by General Frémont in Missouri shall be applied everywhere. In other words, they demand that the government should convert the present struggle into a war of extermination.

What the radical party fears most is a reaction which would bring its ruin. So it takes advantage of the hold it has on the administration in order to drive it to extreme measures. The government has forbidden postmasters to carry newspapers in the mails which advocate conciliation and compromise. The result has been that the majority of newspapers which were opposed to war have had to suspend publication. In several towns the extremists have gone even further. They have stirred up the populace, which has smashed the plants of the moderate newspapers. Conditions are such that mere denunciation by a general is sufficient for a person to be arrested and imprisoned. The act of habeas corpus and all the personal guarantees which the Americans have appeared to prize so much, have vanished and have given way to martial law, which . . . is being enforced throughout the North. . . .

We are not far from a reign of terror such as existed during the great French Revolution, and what makes the resemblance more striking is that all these acts of oppression are made in the name of liberty.

Stoeckl wrote that the people of the North were being misled into
believing that these drastic measures would hasten the peaceful restoration of the Union. But he did not believe the deception could persist:

> People will not be duped long by their political leaders. The re-
> action will necessarily take place. But unfortunately it will come
> too late to repair the harm that the demagogues have done to the
> country.
> The Civil War will be prolonged until the end of the year, per-
> haps even until spring but without result, and as I have already had
> the honor of telling Your Excellency, the separation can be con-
> sidered as a *fait accompli*.
> But when the separation is completed the North, exhausted of
> men and money, will submit as a sad necessity, and the two con-
> federations will find themselves facing new and grave difficulties.
> It will be necessary again to reconcile the rivalries of the different
> States, to combine the needs of the manufacturing States of New
> England with the interests of the great State of New York and
> those of the West, where agriculture is the principal source of
> wealth. It will be the same in the States of the South which are
> united at this moment but where discord will break loose the day
> when they have acquired their independence. It will be necessary
> finally to revolutionize the political and administrative institutions
> which function well enough in peaceful times but which have
> weakened upon the first rock against which the nation has been
> hurled. In the North and in the South they will have to reconstruct
> the edifice which the founders of the Republic have had so much
> trouble in building. . . . The present war is only the prelude of the
> political convulsions which this country will have to pass through.[21]

5

Domestic Trouble Invites
Foreign Intervention

THE Old World powers were not displeased at the trials which democracy was encountering in the United States. Their ruling aristocracies rejoiced at the news that democracy across the Atlantic was riding to a fall. The breakup of the American democratic republic would be a blessing to Europe's monarchies. The example of successful republican government in the United States was a constant source of inspiration to European agitators and of apprehension and exasperation to the ruling authorities of the monarchial states. Its failure here would be a setback to democracy everywhere. If the North should win, her leveling idea in government would become almost irresistible in lands where the masses were still disenfranchised. But this was not likely now, as European observers regarded the dissolution of the Union inevitable.

In England, few if any tears were shed over the impending breakdown of her formidable maritime rival. British aristocracy had much in common with plantation aristocracy and little with the "vulgar, boastful Yankees." Let the Union split in two. Independence of the Confederate States would weaken a dangerous commercial competitor, remove a barrier for the advancement of England's interests in the Western Hemisphere, and free a source of cotton supply on which hundreds of thousands of her textile workers depended for a livelihood.

Even European liberals and antislavery humanitarians withheld their sympathy for the federal government, because Lincoln, striving desperately to keep the border States in line, announced emphatically that the Civil War would be fought to save the Union and not to destroy slavery.

Fully fifteen months before the bombardment of Fort Sumter, Stoeckl had already prophesied "the approaching dissolution of the American Union." But what concerned him most, he wrote on that occasion in his reports to the Foreign Office of imperial Russia, was that Great Britain—Russia's bitterest enemy—was to become the sole gainer from the impending American tragedy. Sadly he predicted in his dispatch of January 4, 1860 to Prince Gortchakov: Great Britain is about to experience one of those "strokes of fortune" which occur but rarely in the history of nations, in the approaching dissolution of the American Union. She alone of all the nations of the world, would benefit by it through the expansion of her power, hitherto blocked by the might of the United States. Broken into two or more hostile pieces America would be at the mercy of England, to become her plaything. "The Cabinet of London is watching attentively the internal dissensions of the Union and awaits the result with an impatience which it has difficulty in disguising." Great Britain would soon, in return for cotton, give recognition to the South and, if required, armed support. For this same cotton she would oppose emancipation of the slaves. The breakup of the Union will be no less than a disaster for all nations save England, since hitherto the "struggle" between England and the United States "has been the best guarantee against the ambitious projects and political egotism of the Anglo-Saxon race."[1]

On April 14, 1861 Stoeckl advised his government that "England will take advantage of the first opportunity to recognize the seceded States and that France will follow her." On the same day in a separate dispatch he also reported a new worry for Lincoln's sorely troubled government—Spain's occupation of Santo Domingo. Later he added:

> Mr. Lincoln has placed himself in the position where he must either discontinue these protests or wage war against Spain. Tassarra assured me that . . . if Lincoln dared to threaten Spain, his government would immediately recognize the independence of the Southern Confederacy. Spain has a rather large squadron of ships in the port of Havana and in the Gulf of Mexico, and the garrison in Cuba has been augmented to 25,000 men, all excellent troops. Thus prepared, Spain does not fear a war. Tassarra would relish

such a conflict to avenge her many grievances against the United States."[2]

But of all European enemies of the Union none was as dangerous and persistent as Napoleon III. He became the head and front of the foreign conspiracy against the North. Greedy for glory and prestige and eager to distract the public mind from the popular discontent kept alive by the friends of the betrayed republic, the French Emperor launched an adventurous foreign policy in which the American continent figured most prominently. He was most pleased at the prospect of the United States breaking into two hostile parts too weak to enforce the Monroe Doctrine, which stood in the way of his plans.

The political chaos in Mexico offered him the springboard he sought for devitalizing the Monroe Doctrine and for reviving his plans for a French colonial empire. So he laid plans to establish Maximilian in Mexico. This would again make France a world power, give a new outlet to French trade and create a bulwark against American aggression southward.

Already in April 1861, only a few days after the outbreak of hostilities in the United States, at the order of his government, French Minister Henri Mercier was making overtures to Lord Lyons and Stoeckl to secure authority from their governments to recognize the Confederacy whenever they thought "the right time" had come. But the British representative advised Mercier that he was loath to assume this responsibility as such a step might embarrass him in his relations with the North. Stoeckl also opposed the plan. He explained that Russia preferred to wait until Great Britain and France had acted. Then she could recognize the Confederacy without offending Lincoln's government.[3] Stoeckl then advised St. Petersburg that the French Minister

has written to M. Thouvenel that as long as there had been any hope of settling the dissensions which had arisen between the North and South and there remained a possibility of reconciliation, it was improper to conduct diplomatic relations with the seceded States. But now the situation was entirely changed. The States of the South had a regularly organized government; secession had become a *fait accompli*, and France must think above all else of safeguarding her commercial interests which the hostilities between the North and South would seriously damage. In recognizing the Confederation of the South, the French government would give to the conflict the characteristic of a war, nation against nation, and would thereby give her commerce the benefit of neutrality rights.

The Minister of France points out that the United States has at all times recognized governments without concerning herself too much whether they had obtained their independence by revolution or otherwise; consequently, she had no right to be offended if the European powers followed the same policy towards her. Finally, M. Mercier commends to his government the necessity of being in agreement with England and the other great powers and of leaving to the discretion of their representatives in Washington the task of recognizing the Confederacy of the South at such time as they deem proper.

Lord Lyons, with whom M. Mercier discussed this question before referring it to his government, said that he agreed entirely with the views of the Minister of France, and that he had written to this effect to Lord John Russell. But he adds . . . that he does not wish to assume the responsibility of deciding the time when it would be opportune to recognize the Confederacy and that, besides, such a step on his part would compromise his position with the government of Mr. Lincoln. It is more than probable that France and England will make overtures to us on this matter. . . .

Today the rupture between the North and the South unfortunately appears to be irrevocable, and it is no longer to our interest to observe strict impartiality between the two sections. The recognition of the Southern Confederacy by France and England will offer us a very natural excuse to follow their example in recognizing a *fait accompli* without, however, giving us the appearance of a previous agreement with these two powers.[4]

From the outset it was apparent to President Lincoln that the first task of his government in its conduct of foreign affairs was to prevent the great powers of the world from recognizing the rebellious States as a sovereign nation. But his administration got off to a bad start in its wartime relations, not only with Spain but, what was far worse, with England and France.

Lincoln's call for volunteers for the purpose of "repossessing" federal forts seized by the South, was followed on April 17 by a proclamation of Jefferson Davis offering letters of marque and reprisal for commissioning privateers to prey upon the commerce of the North. The bait was most tempting as the American merchant marine was then the largest on the seas. Two days later President Lincoln set on foot a blockade of the entire coastline of the seceded States. Foreign trade was the lifeblood of the South. If this traffic could be cut off, the new Confederacy would perish. The insurrection would be snuffed out without firing a shot.

But even before official news of the blockade had been received by Queen Victoria's government—on May 13, 1861, the very day that Charles Francis Adams, America's new Minister to the Court of St. James, reached London to present his credentials—England issued a formal proclamation enjoining strict neutrality upon her subjects. As England was most intimately related with the contestants, France, Spain, The Netherlands, Brazil and other maritime powers followed Britain's lead and subsequently issued similar proclamations of neutrality.

The North rose in anger against England for her shocking discourtesy and hasty action in giving recognition to the South as a belligerent without even giving Lincoln's spokesman an opportunity to be heard. Although England's declaration of neutrality did not amount to a recognition of the independence of the Confederate States of America, it did mean a recognition of her flag on the high seas and the granting of her ships of war and commerce the same privileges in neutral ports as were accorded to the ships of the federal government. The British recognition of the belligerency of the Confederate States while the President was branding the conflict as a local insurrection in which no foreign power had a right to meddle, was deeply resented by Lincoln as an unfriendly act and the first step toward ultimate recognition of the Confederacy.

The Russian Minister, closely watching this British-American rift, reported to his own government that the Lincoln administration in its foreign affairs was displaying the same ineptness and the same lack of foresight as in military affairs:

> The North, and especially Mr. Seward, led themselves to believe that England would sympathize with them for humanitarian reasons arising out of the question of slavery. For the first time the American press expressed kind words for Great Britain. England, said these journals, would never place her commercial interests

above her regard for human rights in a struggle between liberty and slavery. But the British press is not impressed by such flattery. It barely mentions slavery but gives much space to the question of cotton.

The London Cabinet does not appear any more disposed to sympathize with the Northern States than does the English press. . . . Lord John Russell refused to promise Mr. Dallas that England will not recognize the Southern Confederacy. The negotiations of Mr. Adams, the new United States Minister to London, are being awaited impatiently. But the Secretary of State told me that he is no longer deluded regarding England's unfavorable attitude since Lord Russell's declaration in Parliament that the Southern Confederacy in its capacity as a belligerent has the right of issuing letters of marque and reprisal.[5]

The South relied upon "King Cotton" to smash Lincoln's blockade. Her statesmen pointed to the dependence of the French and English textile industries on the South's plantations for fully eighty percent of their requirements of raw cotton. This fact, they believed, was bound to force these powerful nations to intervene and recognize the Confederacy as an independent republic. It was also Stoeckl's prediction that "cotton will decide England's attitude":

A blockade of the Southern ports would harm every country including Russia. However, the cotton exported to Russia is not shipped until the end of January or the beginning of February, and the blockade can under no circumstances last until then. If the Civil War lasts until winter, and if the British lift the blockade, all their cotton will be shipped to Europe on neutral vessels. Our maritime fleet in the Baltic should not overlook this opportunity to realize considerable profits.[6]

At first, hope of an early peace was entertained widely. Stoeckl felt confident the war would be over by winter. But the Union disaster at the Battle of Bull Run changed his forecasts completely. Writing to his Foreign Office on June 3, he described the mounting resentment throughout the North against Great Britain on account of the Queen's declaration of neutrality. The North sees in Great Britain "a declared enemy," while at the same time, England views with satisfaction the political convulsion in America.[7] But he advised that the United States should be cautioned against breaking relations with England as "they are entirely at the mercy of their rivals." The American naval force is woefully outclassed by that of Great Britain.

> Among the American fighting craft are six to eight frigates and corvettes with propellers, which although not of the most modern construction could render effective service, for they are well equipped and ably commanded. But the remainder of her naval forces consist of old sailing vessels most of which are hardly seaworthy. The blockade of the Southern ports is accomplished in a large measure by merchant vessels armed with one or two cannon and commanded by navy officers. England already has several warships off the coasts of Canada and the West Indies. She need only reinforce this squadron with a dozen frigates to sweep away all the American ships engaged in the blockade of the ports of the seceded States. . . .
>
> But whatever may be her superiority, and however propitious may be the time for humiliating the United States, England may be expected to act with great circumspection and abstain from any aggressive measure unless forced either by the necessity of procuring cotton or by the instigation of the Americans. The latter are extremely sensitive on this subject. Other international quarrels have not lessened their vanity. They are threatening England in the same manner as in the past. If, therefore, a conflict between these two powers takes place, and I doubt that it can be avoided between now and the end of the year, it will be brought about by the imprudence and provocative acts of the Americans.[8]

Although the people of the North appeared angrier with the British than with the French, Louis Napoleon was far more eager and insistent to recognize the Confederate States as an independent republic, and therefore was more dangerous. The French Emperor, harboring far-reaching colonial designs, early decided not only to recognize the Southern Confederacy but to assist her at the proper time by an armed intervention.

Stoeckl reported that he had been advised by Mercier that although the French Foreign Minister would not officially receive the commissioners of the Southern Confederacy,

> he could not avoid seeing them and conversing with them. Secondly, that French ports are open to all merchant ships . . . and

that France could not deviate from this principle without creating serious hindrances to her commerce. Finally, concerning the recognition of the seceded States . . . no early action was contemplated . . . but that if the conflict were protracted and the separation became a *fait accompli*, the French government naturally would follow the course which would serve her own best interests.

What places the United States in an extremely awkward position as far as Europe is concerned is that her action is a contradiction of her own traditional policy. Every revolutionary movement in Europe has been applauded here. The Americans are not content merely with giving ovations to Kossuth, Kinkel and other demagogues; they supply them with money for the express purpose of inspiring new disorders. The Secretary of State requests European powers not to recognize the representative of the seceded States, but he seems to forget that hardly five years ago the President of the United States officially recognized the Minister of the Nicaraguan Republic, accredited by the government after the famous Walker filibuster. Finally, at the very moment when they clamor for the extermination of the Southern rebels, the New York newspapers call the disorders which have recently broken out at Narsorie patriotic uprisings, and accuse us of cruelty for having suppressed them.[9]

On June 10, Stoeckl reported to St. Petersburg that Louis Napoleon's government in emulation of England's recent proclamation of neutrality, is of the opinion that

the Confederate States of the South have today an organized government and forces effective enough to make the result of the struggle doubtful. The French government found it necessary to recognize them as belligerents, and has expressed approval of the right of the Confederate States to issue letters of marque and reprisal. . . .

Mr. Seward became greatly irritated about this. He replied to M. Mercier that he had hoped that Emperor Louis Napoleon, after the friendly statements that he addressed to the representative of the United States in Paris, would be on the side of the government, but that he realized with regret that the French shared the views and the intentions of Great Britain. "We have not yet," he said, "been officially informed of the recognition of the seceded States as a belligerent. As soon as we are formally notified about it, we will vigorously protest the attitude of the foreign powers. We are ready to face eventualities." As a result of these developments a rupture between the United States and England and perhaps with France seems to be inevitable.

A new conflict would thus be added to all those which are at present agitating the entire world. With this possibility it is of major concern to us to watch events carefully.[10]

With the threat of foreign intervention hanging heavily over the nation, a new international crisis arose which brought the United States to the very brink of a war with Great Britain. Captain Charles Wilkes of the USS *San Jacinto*, learning that John Slidell and James Mason, Confederate emissaries to Paris and London, respectively, were on board the British steamer *Trent* bound for England, stopped the vessel twenty-five miles out from Havana by firing a shot across her bow, and removed the Confederates by force.

The United States went wild with joy over the exploit of Captain Wilkes. The capture of two Confederate hostages seemed to atone, in a measure, for the military disasters at Bull Run and Ball's Bluff. So the whole North broke out in enthusiastic approval of the deed. Wilkes became the hero of the hour. Secretary Welles sent the "hero of the *Trent*" the official approval of the Navy Department, and Congress voted him a gold medal.

The diplomatic corps buzzed with disapproval of Wilkes' exploit. Stoeckl, Mercier, and the Ministers from Prussia, Italy, Denmark and other lands called on Lord Lyons to assure him of their belief that the United States was wrong in the matter. In his report to St. Petersburg about this "event which may entail serious consequences," Stoeckl wrote, "Lord Lyons told me that he considered the action of Captain Wilkes as the gravest insult ever perpetrated against the British flag."[11] He added:

Upon receipt of this news, the President was disposed to disavow Captain Wilkes' act, restore the prisoners, and apologize to England. But he ran into strong opposition from his Cabinet and from the demagogues among his advisors who believed . . . they [the federals] were stronger than ever and could defy England.

I have learned from a reliable source that the captain of the *San Jacinto* had acted under the specific instructions of the Secretary of State, who having learned of the arrival of Mason and Slidell in Havana, and believing they would go to Europe on the English vessel, ordered the *San Jacinto* to the Cuban coast with instructions to seize the two commissioners in disregard of the British flag. I have learned also that this order was issued without the knowledge of the President.[12]

This information caused Prince Gortchakov to write on the margin of Stoeckl's note: *"Charmant!"*

When at the end of November 1861 the full report of the *Trent* affair was made public by the British government, all England went wild with rage. Excitement swept across the country like a hurricane. The newspapers filled their columns with abuse of the United States. No time must be lost in teaching those damn Yankees "how to respect the flag of a mightier supremacy beyond the Atlantic." The Cabinet met in extraordinary session. Orders went out to the navy yards to dispatch 10,000 picked troops to Canada, and to prepare for war. An ultimatum was prepared: within seven days Lincoln was to release the prisoners and apologize to the British government for the "gross outrage and violation of international law."

Lincoln kept his head when all around him were losing theirs. "One war at a time," he said. The United States had a bad case in international law, and he said so to Attorney General Bates.[13] Lincoln drew up a proposal for submission of the controversy to arbitration. But Lord Lyons replied that his instructions were to demand immediate yielding, and allowed no time and no discretion. This left Lincoln no alternative.

Over the Christmas holiday Lincoln and his Cabinet struggled with the problem. On Christmas Day Seward finally completed the American answer: Lincoln's conclusion—"We must stick to American principles concerning the rights of neutrals"—determined its terms. The British demand for the surrender of the hated Southerners was acceded to. But no apology was made on the ground that Wilkes had acted without orders. To the country it was, as Secretary Chase called it, "gall and wormwood." But it was the common sense thing to do. "One war at a time" was all the United States could afford.

On New Year's Day 1862, the Confederate emissaries were handed over to the commander of an English gunboat at Provincetown. Thus ended the immediate threat of a war with Great Britain. But the danger of recognition of the Confederacy by England and France continued unabated.

The French people generally, hating slavery, favored an undivided America. But their Emperor remained outspoken in his desire for a weakened Union through the establishment of an independent Southern nation. On January 14, 1862 Louis Napoleon's representative in Washington wrote Thouvenel that "there is no other outcome of the crisis except a pacific arrangement based upon separation."[14] Under instructions from the French Foreign Office, Mercier undertook to mobilize the foreign diplomatic corps in Washington to undertake the mediation of the American dispute. He induced President Lincoln to grant him a pass to visit Jefferson Davis in Richmond.

On April 10, 1862 the French Minister came to Lord Lyons, and told him he was about to set out for Richmond, to discuss possibilities of mediation with leaders of the Confederacy. He expressed the opinion that the three great powers—Great Britain, France and Russia—ought to act in concert. But he was loath to ask Lyons to accompany him because of American "extreme susceptibility" to any interference by Great Britain. However, he believed it would be proper for Stoeckl to go along, and he stated that the Russian Minister was "pleased with the idea." Lord Lyons was frank in saying that he was glad to be relieved of the necessity of declining to go. However, he expressed regret that Mercier was determined to proceed without Britain and objected strenuously to Stoeckl participating, as this meant a break in "joint policy."[15]

Stoeckl's report to St. Petersburg was at variance with Mercier's statement:

> M. Mercier invited me to accompany him on the trip in the hope of establishing negotiations or at least of exploring the possibilities for conciliation. I replied that in the present state of affairs I would have to refuse because I did not see any chance for the success of his plan. . . . In the interview which M. Mercier had the next day with the Secretary of State, Mr. Seward acted coldly to the offer of the Minister of France and refused to permit him to make any overtures to the Confederates.

> Two days later, I had the occasion of seeing the Secretary of State, who spoke to me of this affair. "I do not know," he said to me, "if M. Mercier has acted with or without the authorization of

his government. But the fact is that Louis Napoleon has more than once attempted to force us to accept mediation. However, the conduct of the French government during the present crisis is not such as to inspire great confidence. If any power should be called upon to mediate, it certainly should be Russia who has given us so many indications of friendship. But mediation," he said, "from whatever source will not be popular with our nation. This is a domestic quarrel which must be settled among ourselves. In any event, there is nothing to do at present except to follow events and await the result of military operations."

So the trip of M. Mercier which occasioned so many interpretations in the press of the United States, and which will also become the subject of comment in the European press, did not bring about any results.[16]

Napoleon, despite his "sympathy for the South," was afraid to act alone in the American conflict. He pressed for a European coalition to bring about straight-out recognition of the Confederate States. Mercier declared that if France took the initiative, supported by the other powers, especially by Russia, America would be forced to yield.

Stoeckl reported on September 28 that Mercier was of the belief that the United States was in no position longer to refuse a joint request of the world powers to stop hostilities for the sake of the world's economy. But Lord Lyons was still fearful of pressing unwanted mediation. He told Stoeckl, "We ought not to venture on mediation unless we are ready to go to war."

The Russian Minister agreed with Lyons that efforts at mediation would fail at the present time unless backed by the force required to open up the Southern ports. But he believed "that eventually, America, suffering from the ravages of war, would beg the world to mediate the conflict."[17]

After news of General McClellan's defeat in the Peninsular campaign reached Napoleon in Paris, he concluded that the stage was cleared for European intervention. The French Emperor took the British Minister aside at a dinner, and told him in so many words that France was ready to recognize the Confederacy as an independent nation if England would go along.

Prime Minister Palmerston and the Foreign Minister, Lord Russell, gradually yielded to Napoleon's views. Gladstone, declaring the moral duty of intervention, made a celebrated speech at Newcastle on October 7 in which he said: "Jefferson Davis and the other leaders have made an army; they are making, it appears, a navy; and they have made what is more than either, they have made a nation." With such a pronouncement coming from a prominent member of the Cabinet, the natural construction put upon this speech was that the British had decided to recognize the Confederacy. A Cabinet meeting of Queen Victoria's Ministers was called for October 23, 1862, to consider formally France's proposal to intervene in the American situation.

To thwart any American attempt to interfere with his scheme to set up an empire in Mexico, the French ruler had launched anew his campaign for joint direct interference on the part of the European powers to settle our Civil War on a basis that would insure the permanent split of the Union.

On October 30, Drouyn de Lhuys, an imperial henchman who had replaced Thouvenel as Napoleon's Minister for Foreign Affairs, wrote in the Emperor's name to invite England and Russia to join France in a tripartite scheme to take action in the American affair. The Emperor, according to Lhuys, was very anxious to "put an end to the war." A few days later, Stoeckl reported that Mercier had informed him confidentially that Drouyn de Lhuys was insisting

> that France can no longer remain neutral in the conflict which was affecting her interests so vitally. Neither Mercier nor Lyons have any illusions about the chances of their offer of mediation being accepted. . . . The next step will be recognition of the South. . . . A high administration official told me that if France and England recognize the South, the federal government will not hesitate to sever diplomatic relations. . . . What good will this recognition do France and England? It will not end the war and what is more, it will not procure cotton for them, and the distress of the manufacturing districts will not be lessened. It can be accomplished only by forcing open the Southern ports, thus leading to a clear rupture with the North.
>
> Drouyn de Lhuys in his telegram to M. Mercier speaks of the intention of the French government to seek the cooperation of Russia in case of intervention. Lord Lyons . . . added that the Cabinet of London desires to associate itself not only with Russia, but with the other great powers so that the attempt to stop the

fearful bloodshed will come not only from France and England but from the entire civilized world.[18]

Horace Greeley, chameleonic editor of the influential *New York Tribune*, like a prophet of doom, became more and more convinced as the Union government staggered under a series of sickening military reverses that the South could never be subjugated. He began to clamor for a compromise that would restore the Union. Beguiled by the profuse professions of good will of the wily French Emperor, Greeley readily accepted his plan of mediation by the European powers. Personally and by letter Greeley urged Mercier to secure the intercession of the French government to put an end to the war. Mercier naïvely believed that Greeley was a representative spokesman, if not for Lincoln's administration, then at least for the Republican Party. Relying on Greeley's representations, Mercier suggested that the English and Russian Ministers in Washington advise their governments that the time was opportune to act in the American conflict.

On January 26, 1863, the day after Lincoln had replaced General Burnside with General Hooker as commander of the Army of the Potomac, Stoeckl called his government's attention to Greeley's activities.

The *New York Tribune*, the chief organ of the radical party, recently published an article in which it suggested submitting the conflict between the North and the South to the arbitration of the Swiss Confederation. Some days after the appearance of this article, Mr. Greeley, editor of the *Tribune*, came to Washington to confer with the Minister of France. He asked him if the French government was ready to undertake mediation and assured him that the good offices of Emperor Louis Napoleon would be accepted. He added that the article suggesting arbitration by the Swiss Confederation was intended only to prepare public opinion for the idea of mediation, but that after all, it was France who could more ably act in this situation.

When Mercier spoke to me about this interview, I replied that it was true that Mr. Greeley wielded great influence through his newspaper, but that it was highly essential to find out if the request which he had made was supported either by the government or by members of Congress. The Minister of France replied that he didn't know and added, "Since your relations with the Secretary of State are older and more intimate than mine, you will perhaps be better able to discuss this subject with him." I saw the Secretary of State the same day and told him confidentially what M. Mercier had said. Mr. Seward replied that he had not seen Mr. Greeley at all and that the administration was completely opposed to his plan.

"As for the leaders of Congress," Mr. Seward said to me, "you know them too well to think that they would favor foreign mediation at a time like this." Mr. Seward asked me to tell M. Mercier not to put too much faith in Mr. Greeley's words. Accordingly, I told my French colleague that I shared the opinion of Mr. Seward, and that I knew Mr. Greeley by reputation as a man not to be trusted. However, I could only half convince M. Mercier. He wrote to his government and asked for instructions and full powers to act as mediator if the occasion arose.[19]

Stoeckl then explained that although some individuals like Greeley favored mediation as the only way to end hostilities, actually the government, or rather the radicals who have control of it, are strongly opposed to the idea.

It is my opinion that if the powers friendly to the United States wish to stop this dreadful bloodshed by mediation, it is essential to await the propitious time. Any precipitate action would only serve to make more difficult the later accomplishment of this humanitarian objective.

In the course of conversation the French Minister asked me if he would be able to count on my cooperation in the event of mediation. I replied to M. Mercier that I felt myself authorized to offer my aid only in case that our good offices would be sought by the federal government or at least upon the assurance that our offices would be favorably received. As for the means of mediation, I told M. Mercier that in my opinion the action of the several powers which might be called on to intercede should be strictly limited to effecting the cessation of hostilities and the opening of negotiations.[20]

In a dispatch dated two weeks later, Stoeckl stated that "the Minister of France . . . is moving heaven and earth to bring about mediation."

For my part, I am holding myself in reserve. To people who have spoken of mediation, I have replied that the intentions of good will on the part of the imperial government are too well known to leave any doubt about the dispatch with which we will act should the proper occasion present itself, but that I could not deal with this matter except directly with the federal government. ... It might be that the federal government may ask or consent to accept the good offices either of France alone or of France and Russia, excluding England. In this case, am I authorized to act jointly with the Minister of France?

Louis Napoleon's persistence in meddling with the American crisis served only to strengthen the Russian Minister's oft-repeated belief that the Union was permanently destroyed. As much as Stoeckl regretted it, he hoped that Lincoln would make a virtue of necessity and accept the inevitable by seeking cooperation with the South in a commercial union and in foreign relations. In time perhaps the split sections would knit together again.

On February 10, 1863, Stoeckl hastened to advise his superiors in St. Petersburg of Napoleon's "latest plan of mediation" as contained in a message from Drouyn de Lhuys which Mercier showed him.

It was an offer of mediation directly to the American government. The note stated:

"The French government regrets that its views were not supported by Russia and England, and that, full of solicitude for the well-being of the United States, Emperor Louis Napoleon will continue, with the other powers if they wish to be associated with him, or alone if necessary, to make efforts to put an end to this disastrous war. M. Drouyn de Lhuys proposes a means which, without wounding the feelings of the nation and without stopping the military operations which the federal government hopes to see turn in its favor, will perhaps bring about a peaceful solution. This means would consist in appointing commissioners from each side, who would meet at a neutral point and who would discuss the basis of an agreement while the war continued its course."

The Minister of France, on order of his government, has sent a copy of this message to the Secretary of State who has promised to give him a reply after consulting with the President.

I saw Mr. Seward the day before yesterday and he asked me how the imperial government would regard this new stand on the part of France. I replied to Mr. Seward that I could not answer directly but that the message of M. Drouyn de Lhuys carefully avoided any suggestion of pressure, and that the proposition of France was nothing more than friendly advice which coincided perfectly with the thoughts on peace and conciliation which we ourselves have addressed more than once to the federal government.

Mr. Seward did not wish to commit himself on the reply of his government, but told me that Europe was mistaken as to the situation of the federal government and that it had a false impression of the exhaustion of the resources of the country. He expounded at length on this subject and sought again to make me share the illusions to which he is a prey. . . . He told me that the proposition of France had no chance for success. . . .

The fact is that the men who are in power . . . know that their downfall is certain the day that they stop. So they have decided to go forward and brave the consequences of their acts so as to keep the power which is slipping from them and prolong their political existence.[21]

The cabinets of the Old World were acting on the conviction that the restoration of the national authority was impossible. It was a hypothesis that was completely repugnant to Lincoln's feelings. He, therefore, instructed Seward to prepare a note to William L. Dayton, our Minister in Paris, for the attention of Drouyn de Lhuys. It was to serve as an unequivocal answer to Emperor Louis Napoleon's new proposal of mediation.

The note reiterated President Lincoln's view that "the protraction of the struggle has not shaken the confidence [of the federal government] in the definite success of its efforts . . . to preserve the integrity of the country." It rejected with absolute finality the French Minister's fantastic suggestion that the federal government shall appoint commissioners to meet with the commissioners of the insurgents and enter into diplomatic discussions upon the questions of "whether or not the country shall not be delivered over to disunion."[22]

Lincoln's firm rejection of "the latest proposal of France" was according to expectations, Stoeckl observed in his next dispatch to St. Petersburg. However, he hastened to take issue with Seward on "the bright picture of the condition of the country" which the Secretary of State painted in his note to Dayton. "Unfortunately," Stoeckl wrote, "it is not a true picture."

He maintains that in no part of the world in ancient or modern times has any nation put forth such energy and achieved such victories as those which have marked the progress of this contest on the part of the Union.

Mr. Seward claims that the French government has a mistaken notion about the existence of dissension in the North and maintains that the American people are united on the question of war; that they have decided to fight on until they have subjected the whole South.

No one will question the enormousness of the resources displayed by the American nation in this war. But to speak of the success of the Union army and to extend them beyond any comparison in history, is to stretch exaggeration too far. It denies the cold facts which are before our very eyes. The outposts of the enemy are a few versts from the Capital. And only the day before yesterday we could still hear the cannon of the Confederates.

The Secretary of State is no more accurate when he says that the Americans are united in their desire to continue the struggle. On the contrary, the people are exhausted and clamoring for peace. This feeling is particularly manifest in the West where they are staging open demonstrations for peace at any price.

As to the proposal of Mr. Seward to call the representatives of the South to Congress, it would be strange and very embarrassing if the French government were to ask him by what right the deputies of the seceded States could be requested to sit in the Congress at Washington.

The Secretary of State has evidently issued his message with the view of producing a favorable impression on his countrymen who more than any other people are subject to flattery. It must be admitted the impression produced on the public by this publication was rather favorable to Mr. Seward.

It remains to be seen what the reaction of the Cabinet at Paris will be. Here we are concerned about this as it is feared that this may be the preliminary for the recognition of the South by France.

A few days later Stoeckl informed St. Petersburg that Louis Napoleon's proposal of collective mediation had stirred up bitter resentment throughout the United States. Northerners regard it as a decisive step toward recognition of the independence of the Confederate States by France in the near future. The radicals in Congress are taking advantage of the rumors of impending foreign intervention by pressing for their extreme measures, especially the conscription bill which is very unpopular. "Senator Wilson, the author of the bill, told Congress that the government regretted the necessity of imposing conscription, but in view of the hostile attitude of the European powers, it was essential to take all precautions for the safety of the country."[23]

On March 2, Senator Charles Sumner, Chairman of the Senate Committee on Foreign Affairs, told the Russian Minister that he would present a resolution to Congress that day declaring that any offer of mediation or of intervention on the part of foreign powers will be considered an unfriendly act, and offensive to the American nation. It would express his feeling that Napoleon's offer to procure a joint mediation in our affairs, whatever its motive, is "an encouragement to rebellion." "Trampler upon the republic in France, trampler upon the republic in Mexico," Sumner stated, "it remains to be seen if the French Emperor can prevail as trampler upon this republic."[24]

Stoeckl thought that Sumner had a purpose other than just that of warning foreign powers to stop meddling in American affairs:

> Congress will complete its sessions in three days and the radicals fear that the President and Mr. Seward may let themselves be carried away by manifestations in favor of peace which are beginning to appear in the country and that they may accept proposals for a compromise. This resolution aims to constrain the administration not to retreat from the policy of all-out war.
>
> It is to be feared that this move, prompted by the latest proposal of France, may produce a bad effect in Paris. It may stir up Emperor Louis Napoleon who already, as is commonly known, is not too well disposed towards the federal government.[25]

Stoeckl wrote that "these resolutions were adopted without debate in the waning moments of the last session. They have produced little interest in the country at large and the press has scarcely taken notice of them. Lord Lyons told me that the London Cabinet will not pay any attention to this act of Congress. But M. Mercier is of the opinion that Emperor Louis Napoleon will regard it as a gesture hostile to France."[26]

Moreover, Lyons informed the Russian Minister that "England would have already intervened were it not for the fact that she is convinced that the subjugation of the South is impossible. . . . The English want cotton and want it as cheaply as possible, and it is only by the toil of slaves that they can obtain it thus. They would, therefore, be loath to see emancipation come about, no matter what the orators of Exeter Hall may say."[27]

Cassius Clay's Mission to Russia

LINCOLN, aware of Russia's intense anti-British feeling and her desire to maintain the balance of power—the "universal equilibrium" of which the United States was so important an element—looked around for an envoy to St. Petersburg possessed of the skill to reap the full benefits of this fortuitous circumstance. For it was evident both to Lincoln and Secretary Seward that the ability of the North to counter the hostility of England and France would depend to a large degree on the measure of Russian support.

For the vitally important mission to St. Petersburg, Lincoln finally decided on Cassius Marcellus Clay, eminent and picturesque Kentuckian and kinsman of the famous Henry Clay. He was one of those rare specimens, a rabid antislavery Union man in a border State. A Yale graduate and a veteran of the Mexican War, he published *The True American*, a weekly newspaper devoted to the overthrow of slavery. It aroused such indignant opposition that his press was seized by a mob and he was threatened by public resolution with assassination. By keeping a bowie knife and two pistols constantly on hand he managed to continue his abolitionist agitations and stay alive.

Clay was a firebrand, a spell-binding orator who took his politics very seriously. Once at a rally his persistent heckling provoked a pro-slavery political opponent into felling him with a club and then firing his pistol straight at Clay's heart. The bullet struck the scabbard of the bowie knife which hung around his neck; the Kentuckian drew the knife, began to slash and cut with it, and ended up by burying it to the hilt in his assailant's body.

He came to the Republican convention in Chicago with a number of Kentucky emancipationist delegates pledged to him for the presidency, but at the right moment he followed Cameron, Bates and Dayton in releasing his delegates to insure the nomination of Lincoln over Seward. Then he received a substantial vote for the vice-presidential nomination, but lost out to Hannibal Hamlin.

Clay then stumped Kentucky for Lincoln's election. With victory achieved, he expected his reward by an appointment to the Cabinet, and did not hesitate to let Lincoln know about it. He had hoped for the post of Secretary of War and had considerable support for this office. But political considerations dictated that the appointment should go to Simon Cameron, who had swung Pennsylvania's bloc to Lincoln at the Republican convention.

Bitterly disappointed, Clay then informed the President that, "Since the Cabinet was full, I will go to England or France as Minister." Lincoln replied that Seward had promised these two most important ministries to Charles Francis Adams and William L. Dayton. Undaunted, Clay expressed his next preference to be the post of Minister Plenipotentiary to Madrid, although he did not particularly care for "an old effete government like Spain." But here again political considerations thwarted the Kentuckian's wishes. A place had to be found for Carl Schurz. A political refugee, Schurz would not be acceptable in the Russian court. The Spanish post seemed to be the only spot into which he could be fitted.

Clay was angry, but Lincoln promised he would not forget him. Senator Baker of Oregon, with whom Clay had served in the Mexican War, interceded with the President on behalf of the Kentucky politician. What about appointing Clay envoy to Russia? Within a few days, a telegram reached Clay at his home in Lexington, Kentucky. It was from Montgomery Blair, Lincoln's Postmaster General. The President was prepared to offer him the post of Minister to St. Petersburg, Blair wrote. Would he accept? Quickly, on March 27, 1861, Clay telegraphed Blair his reply: "For the sake of the cause I accept the Russian mission."[1] The next day he wrote to the President:

> I yesterday received a telegram, by the Honorable M. Blair,
> intimating that it would be agreeable to you that I should accept

the mission to Russia instead of Spain, in order to allow you to send (as I conjecture) Carl Schurz, Esq., to Spain; as his mission to Central and Northern Europe might be offensive to those powers. My family preferred Spain, as well as myself, because of the climate and possible negotiations; but as I had urged the appointment of these German leaders to satisfactory missions for Party reasons, I desire to give you assurance of my fidelity to my suggestions and my personal regard for yourself, by yielding to your wishes and freeing you from your embarrassment. But the Court of St. Petersburg is an *expensive* one—even necessaries being very high: So that my family are in doubt whether it will not be necessary (seven of us!) to split and a part remain in the U. S., for economy's sake—and this was the chief source of my disappointment in not having a place in the Cabinet. Many senators promised to raise my salary in Spain to 15,000$, if I would accept that: I beg that you will use your influence to have the Russian Mission put upon an equality with the English and French 17,500$: As it is an equal power, becoming cosmopolitan, full of Americans and other travelers—and the most expensive Court in Europe. Another thing, I must employ a private secretary who speaks French, which will greatly add to my expenses.

Now, Mr. Lincoln, in consideration of my lifelong sacrifices, and my being again and again put back for the Party's sake, (all of which I have done with good grace) would it be too much for me to ask you to gratify me at last to some extent by appointing me (in case of a vacancy) Minister to France or England?[2]

Clay hurried to Washington and met with Senator Baker, who assured the Kentuckian that the President was anxious to satisfy his aspirations. In an account of this meeting, Clay wrote:

Baker said, "the country was divided into personal and political factions and it was hard to solidify the party—" would I not accept the mission to Russia? . . . I then said, "Well, Russia is a young and powerful nation and must figure greatly in our affairs. I will accept." Without ceremony, Baker said: "Get your hat, and we will go to the White House at once." We went; and without sending up a card we entered Lincoln's reception room. He was alone and evidently awaiting us. He was quite sad and thoughtful. With his head bent down in silence he awaited Baker's report, who, without sitting down, said: "Mr. Lincoln, our friend Clay will accept the Russian Mission." Lincoln then rose up, and advanced rapidly toward me, firmly took my hand and said: "Clay, you have relieved me from great embarrassment."[3]

The Cunard Line steamer *Niagara* which sailed out of Boston Harbor May 1, 1861 for Liverpool, carried among its passengers somber, dignified Charles Francis Adams, appointed to the arduous and important post of Minister to the Court of St. James in London, and also "the Kentucky ambassador," Cassius M. Clay—spectacularly dressed, garrulous and belligerent as ever—bound for Russia. He was accompanied by his wife and five children and their nurse. Henry Adams, attending his father as secretary, met the frank and blunt Kentucky politician and promptly labeled him a "noisy jackass."[4] Lincoln's new envoys to England and Russia hardly spoke to each other during the long voyage across the Atlantic. On shipboard somewhere "off Ireland" Clay penned a note to the President: "I think my talent is military. . . . Make me a general in the regular service . . . and I'll return home at once upon notice."[5]

But, landing on British soil, Clay was "persuaded by Americans to have a frank talk with members of the House of Commons and House of Lords, and also with Lord Palmerston . . . because our affairs were not at all understood in London and on the Continent." From Paris, he wrote to Secretary of State Seward: "Lord Palmerston received my remarks in a very kindly spirit: so did Lord Brougham and others. I was also persuaded to write a popular article for the *Times* on the American question [which] was . . . translated and put in the French papers also."[6]

In his effort "to make public sentiment for our cause," Clay declared that the United States was fighting for nationality and liberty. This caused the *London Times* to comment sarcastically that it was difficult to understand how "a people fighting . . . to force their fellow citizens to remain in a confederacy which they repudiate, can be called the champions of liberty or nationalism."[7]

Minister Adams was highly offended by the "Kentucky ambassador's" activities in England and protested that they were a trespass on his own diplomatic mission. Unperturbed, Clay wrote to Secretary Seward, "I have it from private and confidential sources, England—the government—*not* the people, probably would rejoice in our calamities."

But more bothersome to Clay, as he was traveling to his post of duty in St. Petersburg in slow and easy stages, were his private financial troubles and the high cost of serving one's country in a diplomatic mission. He complained to Secretary Seward:

> You have drawn my letter of credit so that I cannot get my salary till I get to "my post of official duty." Here I am in the midst of my journey *without means*—the very railroad and boat fares having exhausted my advanced $1000—I left home on the 11 day of April on my mission, and have not spent a day which was not absolutely necessary since on the way—as I was detained partly in Washington by you, and then by the blockade of the city.
>
> I trust, therefore, you will send me and the Baring Brothers & Company a new letter of credit giving me pay from the 10th of Apr. until now: until I get to St. Petersburg. I shall go on then in a few days: borrowing money of friends till I hear from you there. I have a wife, five children, a nurse (8 of us) and I am compelled to hire a private secretary who can speak French, at a high rate: and the Russian Court is the most expensive in Europe. Under all the circumstances I earnestly ask you and the President to urge upon Congress at its next session on the 4th of July to raise my salary to 17-½ thousand dollars: as is the case in England and France. As I do not believe the government desires me to live in a worse style than the poorest Ministers here: and then not have a dollar after four years service in the cause of the country, in my still more advanced years. I am sorry to trouble you with these private matters during the Public Crisis but the necessity with me is urgent and what the department and the President intended to be to me an honour will prove a humiliation.

Clay concluded by urging Seward "to call the attention of the President to this matter and show him this letter."[8]

Clay finally arrived in St. Petersburg in June 1861, and was disappointed to learn that Czar Alexander II was gone on a visit to Poland where a peasants' insurrection had broken out. John Appleton, our retiring Minister, presented the Kentuckian to General Tolstoi, the Deputy Minister for Foreign Affairs. But not until a month later, when the Emperor returned to St. Petersburg, did Clay formally present his credentials. He went to Peterhof Palace and there met His Imperial Majesty and extended to him the greetings of President Lincoln. In his official report to Washington, Clay gave his first impressions of the Russian monarch who had succeeded to the throne March 2 1855, on the death of his father, the late Emperor Nicholas I. "The Emperor," he wrote, "is about my size and weight, grey eyes, auburn hair." A member of the American legation present on the occasion described the Czar as tall and soldierly in personal appearance. "He is about forty-five years of age, stoutly built and of an exquisite figure. Very handsome, rather a round face, eyes a beautiful light blue, mustache, hair shingled, and of a dark auburn color. Speaks 'American,' voice pleasant and looks and walks and is every inch a King."[9]

As a lifelong militant abolitionist, Clay was greatly stirred by Alexander II's recent edict liberating Russia's millions of serfs. He was sure that Lincoln was highly elated over this epoch-making humanitarian act which had freed these slaves from the "disposition" of the landed nobility. So he hastened to report to the President how he had favored the Ruler of All the Russias with a stump speech, congratulating him for his historic deed. "The Emperor seemed much gratified and really moved," Clay wrote, and the Czar replied that Russia and America "were bound together by a common sympathy in the common cause of emancipation." With unrestrained self-praise the Kentuckian was eventually to boast: "I did more than any man to overthrow slavery. I carried Russia with us and thus prevented what would have been a strong alliance of France, England and Spain against us, and thus saved the nation."

Clay also wrote to Lincoln that the Czar inquired during his visit to Peterhof Palace about the reports of England's intention to interfere in the American conflict. Clay advised the President that he told the Emperor, "We did not care what she did, that her interference would tend to unite us the more—we fought the South with reluctance."[10]

In his reports to Washington, Clay told Lincoln and Seward about Prince Alexander Mikhailovich Gortchakov, the Czar's Minister for Foreign Affairs, whose policies were to affect American affairs so vitally. In the last analysis the Prince would be the one who would make the vital decision whether or not Russia would join England and France in an intervention in the internal affairs of the United States. Prince Gortchakov was a man of medium size, about sixty years old, with short hair, a little gray—shrewd and agreeable. In 1854, during the Crimean War, he served the Czar as Ambassador at the Court of Vienna. It was due chiefly to his influence that Austria maintained her neutrality. Two years later he replaced Count von Nesselrode as Minister for Foreign Affairs. In time he was to become Vice Chancellor of the empire and ultimately Chancellor. He was generally regarded as one of the most able and experienced statesmen in Europe. He was a scholar with an expansive intellect, and also a brilliant linguist. But, born an aristocrat and essentially an autocrat, he was never popular with the people.

Shortly after Clay assumed his duties in St. Petersburg, he received a letter of instruction from the Secretary of State. "Nations, like individuals," said Seward's note, "have three prominent wants, first freedom, secondly prosperity, and thirdly, friends. The first two were early secured by courage and enterprise, but in spite of singularly moderate practices, the United States has been slow in winning friends."

An "exceptional case" is Russia, Seward pointed out. The surprising friendship between two such remote and unlike nations may be explained by the fact that Russia and the United States are "both improving and expanding empires," one toward the East and the other toward the West, each conveying civilization to new regions, and each resisted, at times, by nations "jealous of its prosperity or alarmed by its aggrandizement." "It will be your pleasing duty to confirm and strengthen these traditional relations of amity and friendship."

To Russians who would ask about the causes of the American Civil War, Clay was instructed to explain that the object of the revolution was the South's attempt to build a nation on the "principle that African slavery is necessary, just and beneficent, and that it may and must be expanded over the central portion of the American continent and islands, without check or resistance, at whatever cost and sacrifice to the welfare and happiness of the human race."

Should this revolution prove successful it would result in a "division of this great and hitherto peaceful and happy country into two hostile and belligerent republics," which might later break into a number of petty, hostile and belligerent states. Failure of the revolution, on the other hand, would have as its consequence "the continuance of the country in the happy career that it has pursued so auspiciously to the repose of nations and the improvement of the conditions of mankind."

Finally, Seward's letter added, the President wished but one thing of Russia's Emperor: "that the Sovereign is expected to do just what this government does in regard to Russia and all other nations, it refrains from all intervention whatever in their political affairs and it expects the same just and generous forbearance in return. It has too much self-respect to ask more and too high a sense of its rights to expect less."

But Clay did not confine himself to Russian-American relations. The outspoken Kentuckian believed it his duty to advise Lincoln, Seward and the United States government in general concerning nearly every current national and international issue. Despite instructions he would not restrict his dispatches to subjects concerning his ministry or those of a diplomatic agent. He irritated Seward by requesting that his letters be called to the attention of the President. Again and again the Secretary of State was to caution him to confine himself to the immediate purposes of his mission to Russia. But impulsively the Kentuckian would write his opinions on the attitudes of the various countries of Europe which regarded our Republic with "jealousy and distrust." "In case of war with England," he advised the President and the Secretary of State, "Canada should be seized, money sent into Ireland and India to stir up revolt; slaves as property should be summarily confiscated; while extending the olive branch in case the rebels lay down their arms and return to duty and the Union."

He even presumed to advise Lincoln concerning his attitude toward General Frémont who, contrary to the announced policy of the administration and to the consternation of the President, had issued a proclamation emancipating the slaves within his military district. Clay wrote from St. Petersburg to Lincoln, "I hope you will stand by Genl. Frémont's proclamation—the hour has come for that vital blow to secession—and the cause of all our woes."[11]

Soon irritations and frictions arose between Seward and Clay, and the blunt Kentuckian did not hesitate to manifest in his official correspondence his dislike for the Secretary of State, Senator Sumner—Chairman of the Senate Committee on Foreign Affairs, and all others whom he suspected of obstructing his activities.

On July 25, 1861 Clay wrote a private note to President Lincoln to compliment him on his July 5 message to Congress, which, according to the Minister to Russia, "is published in all the European journals":

> I hope you will believe me when I say it is a very able paper, and one which will add to your reputation very much. It comes forcibly to the point, in that simplicity of words and structures of sentences which is the true style of all great effort. I rejoice that you have pursued steadily your way to this one end—the reunion

of the Union. The *St. Petersburg Journal* in summing up its judgment of the message says, "The message of the President of the United States is moderate in its tone (*dans la forme*), clear in its style, firm in the maintenance of principles, trustful of the future of the republic." It has produced a good effect upon the European press.

Clay was sure that President Lincoln would be interested in his own observations concerning the attitude of the great European powers toward the United States. So he cautioned the President to be on his guard against England:

I saw at a glance where the feeling of England was. They hoped for our ruin! They are jealous of our power. They care neither for the South nor the North. They hate both. Even the *London Times* at this late date in concluding its comments upon your message says, "And when we prefer a frank recognition of Southern independence by the North to the policy avowed in the President's message, it is solely because we foresee as bystanders that this is the issue in which after infinite loss and humiliation the contest must result." And that is the tone of England everywhere. Of course, the hope is the father of the conclusion. Seeing that was the spirit of the English, I thought the true policy was to set them at defiance. . . .

Our only hope was to conciliate France, and to this end all our efforts have been directed. The consequence was that while England was on the way to allow privateers to bring their prizes into English ports—which would have brought us at once to war, the French Emperor refused: and only then, as he admitted to the House of Commons, did Lord Palmerston following in the wake of the French, come to the conclusion! If England would not favor us, whilst following the lead of the antislavery policy—she will never be our friend. She will now if disaster comes upon our arms, join our enemies! Be on your guard. . . . I think our policy is for the future to keep upon the best terms with France: Her people love and admire us—the Emperor though not a man to give way to sentimentality, is friendly: After all the billing and cooing between England and France, England *fears* and France *hates*! They can never be long friends. . . .

All the Russian journals are for us. . . . In Russia also we have a friend. The time is coming when she will be a powerful one for us. The emancipation move is the beginning of a new era and new strength. She has immense lands, fertile and undeveloped in the Amoor country, with iron and other minerals. Here is where she must make the centre of her power as against England. Joined with our navy on the Pacific Coast we will one day drive her from the Indies: The source of her power: and losing which she will fall.

Then Clay proceeded to tell the President how to conduct the war. "You are now pressing war rightly. Go into the slave States and their power is gone. The sooner you send troops into them—Tennessea— [*sic*] the better for them and us. You thus save the Union men and destroy the resources of the cotton States." Clay went on to recommend the sending of troops down the Mississippi, and to extend the blockade to every possible place of entry—"so that if England does break in—she will be the aggressor before all the world. Don't trust her in anything."

Clay took advantage of this note to the President again to urge an increase in his salary. "I find this court more expensive than I was told even. It is not possible for us to live here on 12,000$, without having all my family excluded from court and entertainments, which we cannot reciprocate. I could live on 15,000$. If my salary is not raised, I shall be forced to return home: for Russian etiquette requires certain forms and style which cannot be evaded without disgrace—which would make my presence worse than useless. As the government allows me no private secretary, I have been compelled to employ a French one at my own cost."[12]

But President Lincoln, burdened with the colossal task of crushing a widespread rebellion, had other things to worry about.

Cameron's "Exile to Siberia"

By the light of the midnight sun Cassius Clay continued to pen long notes to Seward on sundry subjects and appeals to President Lincoln to get his $12,000 salary raised. He was sinking deeper and deeper into debt, he wrote. He might have saved a few dollars had he been appointed Minister to Madrid, as he had requested; now he longed for a return to the United States. If a vacancy would occur in the Cabinet, he wanted to be given first consideration. He would prefer the navy post. Otherwise he would be better off with a commission in the regular army. Nothing would please him more than to don the uniform of a general and fight for the antislavery cause.[1]

It was a fortunate circumstance for President Lincoln, who had become highly displeased with Simon Cameron as Secretary of War. The Pennsylvania politician's slovenly administration of the War Department and his sudden advocacy of freeing and arming the slaves made his dismissal imperative. But Lincoln was in a dilemma as to the means of easing him out without inflicting loss of face and without creating too great a public furore.

Then suddenly on January 11, 1862 the harrassed President dashed off a couple of notes for delivery to his incompetent war minister. The one that was made public was curt. It read:

Hon. Simon Cameron, Secretary of War
My dear Sir:
*   As you have more than once expressed a desire for a change of position, I can now gratify you consistently with my view of the*

*public interest. I therefore propose nominating you to the Senate
next Monday as Minister to Russia.*

*Very sincerely, your friend
A. Lincoln.*[2]

But on the same day in a private communication to Cameron, Lincoln
discussed the situation in a less formal manner. He had not been un-
mindful of Cameron's long-expressed wish to resign, he wrote. "I have
been only unwilling to consent to a change at a time and under circumstances which might give occasion to misconstruction, and unable
till now to see how misconstruction could be avoided." Now he had a
solution. Cassius Clay's mission to St. Petersburg was about to end. He
was going to be appointed a major general of the army. This turn of
events enabled Lincoln to gratify Cameron's wish to resign,

> and at the same time evince my personal regard for you, and my
> confidence in your ability, patriotism, and fidelity to public trust.
> I therefore tender to your acceptance, if you still desire to resign
> your present position, the post of Minister to Russia. Should you
> accept it, you will bear with you the assurance of my undiminished
> confidence, of my affectionate esteem, and of my sure expectation
> that, near the great sovereign whose personal and hereditary
> friendship for the United States so much endear him to Americans,
> you will be able to render services to your country no less impor-
> tant than those you could render at home."[3]

Thus by banishing Cameron to the faraway, cold, damp, foggy
Russian capital did Lincoln get him out of the vital war secretaryship
where he had proved himself a misfit. As a diplomatic exile on the banks
of the late-thawing Neva River, this political troublemaker could do
little mischief at home. This prompted *Vanity Fair* to publish a derisive
cartoon depicting the President as saying to Cameron: "I am resolved
what to do, Simon. I will send you to St. Petersburg where you may
serve nobly the cause of your country at the Court of the Kezzar."

In a reply to the President, predated January 11, the Cabinet
officer, though deeply hurt by his "exile to Siberia," nevertheless expressed gratitude for Lincoln's confidence in his "ability, patriotism and
fidelity to public trust." "I have done my best. It was impossible, in the
direction of operations so extensive, but that some mistakes should have
happened and some complications and complaints should have arisen."

The "proffer for my acceptance [of] one of the highest diplomatic positions at your bestowal" is "an additional mark of your confidence and esteem. . . . I, therefore, frankly accept the new distinction you have tendered me. . . ."⁴ Although no Cabinet officer had ever received a more complimentary endorsement from a President than did Cameron, the new envoy regarded the shift to the post of Minister Plenipotentiary to Peterhof Palace as political degradation. He "was affected even to tears, and wept bitterly over . . . [the] personal affront from Lincoln."⁵

Members of the United States Senate wrestled long behind closed doors with the question of Cameron's confirmation. Some attacked the appointment as the whitewash of an incompetent and unfaithful public servant. Others branded it as an immoral act. But after four days of protracted debate and wrangling the ousted Secretary of War was confirmed as Minister to Russia by a vote of 28 to 14. Said the *New York Herald*: "The array against the nomination . . . deprive the confirmation of any complimentary complexion, and amount to a censure of the conduct of the War Department."⁶

Edwin M. Stanton, a Pennsylvania lawyer and an 1860 Democrat who had served in Buchanan's Cabinet, was named by President Lincoln to the war secretaryship. This despite the fact that only a few months before his appointment he had voiced open and bitter opposition to the administration.

Lincoln's nomination of Cameron as our Russian envoy and the Senate's reluctant confirmation were met with derision by a hostile press. *Leslie's Weekly* captioned its comment, "The Exiles of Siberia." It declared:

> Mr. Lincoln has a wide reputation as a humorist. The nomination of Mr. Cameron to St. Petersburg, which is a long way on the road to Siberia, looks as if he were addicted to practical joking. It would be no joke for the ex-Secretary of War, however, if the Czar were to take his appointment as a hint to "pass him on" to that land of penance, and the companionship of that goodly company of army contractors and speculators whose exploits in the Crimean War failed to receive the imperial approval!

Harper's Weekly lampooned the affair by picturing Cameron with a packed carpetbag in his hand, standing at the desk of the Secretary of the Navy, and saying: "Good-by Welles. I'm off for Russia. There's too much talk of hanging here to suit me!"

Thus did Simon Cameron, the political czar of Pennsylvania, undertake the mission to meet the Czar of all the Russias and to represent the United States in that cold capital city beyond the Baltic Sea where a predecessor, James Buchanan, had once complained that "the tall wood stoves failed to heat decently the big rooms."

Cassius Clay, sitting in his cold chambers in St. Petersburg awaiting news from Washington of his replacement by a successor, took his quill in hand and wrote to Secretary Seward concerning numerous subjects. Among the leading topics of diplomatic conversations in the chancelleries of the continent was the subject of European intervention in the American conflict. So, on April 13, 1862, from far-away St. Petersburg, the Kentuckian felt it incumbent upon himself to impart this advice to Lincoln and Seward:

> Since steam can throw, in twelve days or less, the entire navies of Europe upon our country, it is useless to deceive ourselves with the idea that we can isolate ourselves from European interventions. We became in spite of ourselves—the Monroe Doctrine—Washington's Farewell—and all that—a part of the "balance of power," and constitute a portion of that "universal equilibrium" of which Prince Gortchakov so aptly spoke. We must then strengthen ourselves like other nations. . . . We must make and keep a navy equal to any other nation. This we can well do without jeopardizing our liberties. . . . Here has been the secret of English liberty—a small army, and a large navy. Let us go, and do likewise.[7]

Not until a package of weeks-old newspapers arrived by steamer from the United States was Clay to learn about Cameron's appointment. Reading the general condemnation of the Pennsylvanian's unsatisfactory record as Secretary of War, the outspoken, retiring Minister characterized Cameron's appointment to the court of St. Petersburg as "a parachute to let him down gently."

By the time Cameron and Bayard Taylor, his Chargé d'Affaires, arrived in St. Petersburg in June 1862, Clay had undergone a change of heart about quitting the Russian ministry. In a "private" letter to President Lincoln, the unpredictable Kentuckian complained:

My appointment as General came so late and so unexpectedly, that I had made up my mind to worry it out here, and by sending my family home, I had made arrangements for a stay here and made the necessary expenditures accordingly. I have several thousand of roubles of property here, which is usually turned over to successors—but Mr. Cameron cannot buy: he says he will positively ask leave to retire from this post at the end of the next quarter, the 1st of Sept. next. He proposes to come home on your leave of absence, and then remain. So not knowing what you propose to do for me after the war into which I have long since lost all hopes of taking any efficient part, as you now have already too many generals in the field, I ask that you will return me to this court on Mr. Cameron's leaving. For at this season it is impossible to sell second-hand property for anything like its value, and I have concluded to let Mr. Cameron use some of it and store the balance till I see you and know your intentions in respect to me. As I said before, I am now in a much worse pecuniary condition than when I entered the public service, but have hopes of being again sent here to save in part my outlay, and some of my salary in the future.

I am mortified to have to trouble you so much with my "private griefs" but circumstances compel me to smother all ill-timed sensibility upon this subject.[8]

Clay's request to remain in St. Petersburg was not granted. Although Cameron kept delaying his departure for his post of duty in the domain of the Czars, he eventually began his "exile in Siberia." He presented his credentials to the Emperor, and within a few days he dispatched a request to Secretary Seward in Washington for leave to return to the United States.

Before Cameron's reluctant departure on his mission to Russia, Lincoln advised him that, after settling down to his new duties in St. Petersburg, he should endeavor to secure a personal and confidential interview with the Czar to learn the Russian monarch's attitude in the event England and France forced their unwelcome intervention. Shortly afterwards, Cameron reported that the Czar's spokesmen assured him that in case of trouble with the other European powers, the friendship of Russia for the United States would be shown in a "decisive manner, which no other nation will be able to mistake."[9]

The Russians were evincing the most candid friendship for the

North, our new Minister wrote to Secretary Seward. The government, he stated, was showing a "constant desire to interpret everything to our advantage. There is no capital in Europe where the loyal American meets with such universal sympathy as at St. Petersburg, none where the suppression of our unnatural rebellion will be hailed with more genuine satisfaction." Heartened by such dispatches from Cameron, Secretary of State Seward wrote to John Bigelow, United States Consul at Paris, on June 25, 1862:

> Between you and myself alone, I have a belief that the European state, whichever one it may be, that commits itself to intervention anywhere in North America, will sooner or later fetch up in the arms of a native of an oriental country not especially distinguished for amiability of manners or temper. . . . It might be well if it were known in Europe that we are no longer alarmed by demonstrations of interference.[10]

During his brief sojourn in the Russian Capital, Cameron had a very capable and dependable assistant in Bayard Taylor, serving as Secretary of the United States legation. He had succeeded Green Clay, nephew of Minister Cassius Clay, who had returned to the United States with his uncle. Taylor, a poet and author of travel volumes, novels and magazine articles, accepted the minor diplomatic post confident that it would be a stepping stone to something more important—perhaps the St. Petersburg ministry itself, since he knew with what reluctance Cameron had accepted the appointment.

Only ten days after being presented to Czar Alexander II at Peterhof Palace, Cameron was already writing to Secretary Seward expressing his desire for a furlough. He chafed under the restraints of his "Siberian exile." He had no desire for St. Petersburg's notorious excessively cold, long and gloomy winter nights and debilitating social functions. He was anxious to resume active political life by standing again for the United States Senate from Pennsylvania.[11]

Bayard Taylor, now as Chargé d'Affaires, nursed even brighter hopes of becoming Cameron's successor. He was sure Secretary Seward "can testify from my dispatches, that I am fully capable of conducting the legation." Taylor was encouraged by the Secretary of State's note advising that President Lincoln had expressed gratification regarding his services. But the unpredictable Cassius Clay, strutting around in Washington with his shoulder straps of a major general, was writing the

President: "I . . . await your pleasure about again entering upon [diplomatic] service as you promised me. . . . I trust you will allow him [General Cameron] to come home at once on leave of absence and he will resign so you will not lose public money by such leave."[12]

Even if his duties as Major General took him into the field, Clay wanted Lincoln to know "I don't mean to waive my right to avail myself of your kind promise to allow me—should Mr. Cameron resign—or be recalled—to return to St. Petersburg as your Minister."[13]

In the meantime Clay was causing the administration considerable embarrassment by his intemperate speeches on behalf of emancipation. He had reported to Lincoln on his return from Russia that all over Europe he had found governments ready to intervene in America's affairs and recognize the independence of the Confederate States. He insisted that only a forthright proclamation of emancipation would block these European autocracies. Russia had emancipated her serfs. Why does not democratic America liberate her slaves? In a speech at Odd Fellows' Hall in Washington, Clay declared:

> I think that I can say without implications of profanity or want of deference, that since the days of Christ himself such a happy and glorious privilege has not been reserved to any other man to do that amount of good; and no man has ever more gallantly or nobly done it than Alexander II, the Czar of Russia. I refer to the emancipation of the 23,000,000 serfs. Here, then, fellow citizens, was the place to look for an ally. Trust him; for your trust will not be misplaced. Stand by him and he will, as he has often declared to me he will, stand by you. Not only Alexander but his whole family are with you, men, women, and children.[14]

Thus imbued with the ideal of emancipation, Clay declared openly for liberation of the slaves captured in war, and of those of all the States in rebellion. Meeting with opposition from Lincoln's administration, Clay was eager to return to Europe, if he could. For, as he said, "What was the use of fighting for the old Union with the cancer of slavery left?"[15]

Lincoln commissioned Clay to sound out public opinion on emancipation in his own State of Kentucky. He also invited the Kentuckian's opinion on the practicability of a plan to restore Florida to the Union by armed colonization. The first chore enabled Clay to deliver more speeches on emancipation. In Frankfort he declared, "If fall we must, let us fall with the flag of universal liberty and justice nailed to the mast head. . . . The autocracies of Europe would not hesitate to destroy a republic but they would not dare to interfere in behalf of slavery." Regarding the President's Florida plan of armed colonization, Clay stated it was "highly practical. . . . What can be done in Florida can be done in Texas and other slave States."[16]

There was a danger, Lincoln was advised, that Clay's unrestrained agitation for emancipation would yet drive Kentucky into joining the secessionist States of the South. So upon learning of Cameron's determination to resign his Russian ministry, Lincoln decided to send Clay back to St. Petersburg, upon receipt of Cameron's formal resignation, and notified the Kentuckian accordingly.

Clay promptly tendered his own resignation as Major General of volunteers in the United States army—"to take effect on the resignation of Simon Cameron, Esq. as Minister Plenipotentiary to Russia. I do this to avail myself of your kind promise to send me back to my former mission to the Court of St. Petersburg and where I flatter myself that I can better serve my country than in the field under General Halleck who cannot repress his hatred of liberal men into the ordinary courtesies of life [sic]."[17]

Clay then reminded the President that the 1,000th anniversary of Russia's national existence was being celebrated there with great pomp and ceremony. In view of the Emperor's known expressions of sympathy for the cause of the Union, "would it not be well to write him an autograph letter of congratulation?"[18]

Within less than a year after his appointment as envoy to Russia, Cameron resigned, and President Lincoln nominated Clay for reappointment to his former diplomatic post. But much opposition arose in the Senate against confirmation. Greatly alarmed, Clay wrote to the President:

> I am informed that the Committee of Foreign Relations will report against me on the ground that I am unacceptable to the Russian government. It is a false allegation. I can show more evidences of the good feeling of the Russian Court than any Minister there. . . . I have letters at home of the most flattering kind from Prince Gortchakov before and since my arrival here. Baron de Stoeckl called on me today and says if you will send for him he would make a most favorable report of me. Please send for him

and write to the Committee who takes the vote in the morning. Don't allow me to be slaughtered by a calumny. I have stood by you in good and evil report, and hope now you will see justice done me.[19]

After a long delay, the Senate finally approved the reappointment of the controversial Kentuckian to the Court of St. Petersburg. Then immediately a new vexation arose to annoy the President. This time it was a strange controversy between Clay and Secretary Seward over the naming of a Secretary of legation.

Bayard Taylor was bitterly disappointed over his failure to be selected as Cameron's successor. He had superior qualifications for the post, he wrote to a friend in Philadelphia.

> On the other hand, a man (*entre nous*) who made the legation a laughing stock, whose incredible vanity and astonishing blunders are still the talk of St. Petersburg, and whose dispatches disgrace the State Department that allows them to be printed, will probably be allowed to come back to his ballet girls (his reason for coming) by our softhearted Abraham Lincoln. Let the government send a man who will not be laughed at—who has a grain of prudence and one drachm of common sense, with a few moral scruples—and I shall gladly give up all my pretensions and go home. From my private correspondence I know that Lincoln says Clay is not fit for my place, but he is an elephant on my hands, and I guess I will give it to him!

Secretary Seward had high regard for Taylor's ability and services. He desired that he should at least be retained in his position as Secretary of legation. But Clay wished to appoint Henry Bergh, the eccentric son of a wealthy shipowner whom General Hooker and General Butterfield had recommended highly. Going over the head of the Secretary of State, Clay wrote directly to the President, "I trust you will allow me to choose my Secretary as I was allowed no patronage in Ky. but the appointment of my nephew Green Clay."[20] Two weeks later from New York, he wrote another letter of bitter complaint to the President because the Secretary of State had ordered him "to set off to St. Petersburg and leave the subject of Secretary of legation—there was already one at that place." Clay declared he had asked Bayard Taylor if he were

interested in remaining as Secretary of legation, and he had "peremp-
torily declined."

> Yet Mr. Seward accuses me of treating B. Taylor badly, by
> asking my legal rights of a Secretary. You see all this is merely a
> pretext to insult me by insulting my friends. Mr. Henry Bergh is
> a descendant of American ancestors of revolutionary fame: is a
> man who speaks most of the modern languages—is an author—and
> in every way my or Mr. Seward's equal. Yet he is insulted because
> I ask his appointment. The custom in all Europe is for the minister
> to appoint his secretary—for the most obvious reasons. It has
> always been the custom in this country. I feel that I have this
> right.

It wouldn't be just to him, Clay protested, to have "a Seward spy in
my house. I name Wm. H. Bergh as my Secretary and no other can
render me any service. If a Sewardite is thrust upon me I shall regard
it as an unfriendly act on your part."

Clay had more complaints for the harassed President. "The rebels
have ruined my already poor means of living by their continuous raids."
Now Seward was delaying his letter of credit, and he was unable to
get a civil answer from the Department of State. "Mr Lincoln, I am
poor but honest. You have given me an office. I have discharged it faith-
fully and to the interest of my country—treat me justly. . . . I grieve to
trouble you with this matter, or any matter. But I am not master of my
own movements. I am in the hands of men who seek my ruin. I ask
your protection."[21]

In the meantime, Bayard Taylor, piqued by his failure to win promo-
tion and unwilling to remain as a subordinate to a man for whose ability
he had little regard, resigned as Secretary of legation. When Clay arrived in St. Petersburg in the spring of 1863, he was accompanied by
his new Secretary—Henry Bergh. A dandy who wore clothes adorned
with gold lace, America's new Secretary of legation was soon to become a notorious character in that far-off capital of the Czars.

Clay was to remain as Minister until 1869; he was resolved to outlast
Secretary Seward, whom he despised.

United States and Russia:
Strange Bedfellows

THE "traditional relations of amity and friendship" between the United States and Russia which Ministers Clay and Cameron were instructed "to confirm and strengthen" during their respective missions to St. Petersburg, were the incongruous relations between two of the most mismated international bedfellows in all recorded history.

No two civilized nations were more unlike than the United States, where the people had elected Abraham Lincoln President, and imperial Russia, where Czar Alexander II ruled by the divine right of kings. Their peoples had different backgrounds, different cultures, different outlooks on life. Russia of the Czars was an absolute monarchy—the most repressive despotism on earth, where the Emperor reigned without any constitutional limitations whatsoever. The Republic of the United States—with its government of the people, by the people, for the people—was the most liberal democracy in the world, hated and feared by the autocrats of Europe. James Buchanan, U. S. Minister at St. Petersburg (1832-33), had observed that the Czar's regime was morbidly "afraid of the contamination of liberty." Russian imperialists would have been pleased to see American democracy destroyed. The expected end of the Union was regarded in St. Petersburg as a "turn for the better." Even a friend like Stoeckl predicted that the downfall of the democratic system "will serve as an instructive lesson to European anarchists . . . revolutionaries and demagogues . . . who have always found moral support and often also material help in American democracy."

But Russia's great enemy—England—was also our rival. Out of a common hatred and fear of England emerged an "historic friendship" between two mismated great nations. In practical world politics, the enemies of our enemies are our friends. George Mifflin Dallas, an earlier Minister at the Court of St. Petersburg than Clay and Cameron (1837-39), had duly recorded these significant words of Czar Nicholas I in his diary: "Not only are our interests alike, but," with emphasis, "our enemies are the same."[1]

Americans in general and Abraham Lincoln in particular had nothing but contempt for the repressive despotism of the Czar's government, and the antagonism toward a republican form of government was reciprocated by the Russian ruling class. And yet despite the incompatibility of their political principles the two nations were thrown into the strangest of alliances—an *entente cordiale*—which was to prove of supreme importance to both. Poles apart ideologically, the extremes nevertheless met in political collaboration.

The threads of the tradition of Russian-American friendship, spun through the years because the two nations had a common rival in Great Britain, wove naturally into the fabric of a political *rapprochement* which brought strength and encouragement to Lincoln and the Czar at a time when both governments were badly in need of friends. This friendly relationship between two nations, so remote and so unlike, excited much surprise. But it was realistic international politics in full play.

With the governments of Great Britain and France watching like vultures to intervene in the American conflict in order to make the sectional split permanent; with Spain sharing the official feelings of these two powers because of her own desire for a reconquest of Santo Domingo; with Austria who had furnished the puppet Archduke for Napoleon III's enterprise in Mexico, eager for the success of that venture; and with most of the other nations openly unfriendly or indifferent to the outcome of the American civil conflict, President Lincoln, in his desperate struggle to save a great nation from falling apart, could look to only one major power for help or active sympathy—Russia, "where they make no pretense of loving liberty."

Through the two years or more while the wily, scheming Emperor of France persisted in his efforts for concerted aggressive intervention by England, France and Russia in the American Civil War—a course intended to split the Union for all time—despotic Russia was the North's only dependable well-wisher among the European powers. While the outcome of the war of secession was still uncertain, Russia's attitude restrained France and England from proceeding with their plan of intervention which inevitably would have led to the recognition of the sovereignty and independence of the Confederate States.

Lincoln, striving with might and main to save the world's great experiment in democracy, quickly saw in Russia the one possible ally who might be counted on to help in the event of trouble with England and France. In his nation's hour of need, Lincoln eagerly clasped the only hand extended to him, even though it was the hand of a colossus of barbarism and reaction. Despite Stoeckl's reports expressing lack of confidence in Lincoln's leadership and in the Union's chances for survival, Czar Alexander II ranged himself openly and enthusiastically on the side of Lincoln and the Union. While France and England were waiting for the United States to break into two weak republics, Russian policy required the perpetuation of a united American nation as an essential element in the "universal equilibrium."

At a time when zeal for Russian participation in the French plan to intervene in the American conflict was gaining strength, the *Journal of St. Petersburg*, the official organ of the Czar's government, declared:

> Russia entertains for the United States of America a lively sympathy founded on sentiments of mutual friendship and on common interests. She considers their prosperity necessary to the general equilibrium. She is convinced that the American nation can only find in the preservation of the Union the conditions of power and prosperity which she wishes to see it enjoy.[2]

"We desire above all things the maintenance of the American Union as an indivisible nation," the Czar declared. For the imperial Cabinet was deeply concerned, for Russia's own good, that nothing should happen that would weaken the one powerful counterpoise to England. It was Russia that gave the United States government the first notice early in 1861 of the efforts of the French Emperor to effect a coalition of the three great European powers against the North.

In Secretary Seward's memorandum, *Some Thoughts for the President's Consideration*, he urged that an explanation be demanded from

Russia because of reports in Southern newspapers and in political circles in Washington that Russia was about to open diplomatic relations with the Confederacy. In marked contrast was his dispatch of May 6, 1861 to Clay, in which he stated that "that power [Russia] was an early, and it has always been a constant, friend."

While the specter of united intervention was haunting Lincoln and Seward, Prince Gortchakov dispatched a note to Baron de Stoeckl in Washington expressing the profound regrets of Czar Alexander II over the troubles that were befalling the United States—"a nation to which our August Master and all Russia have pledged the most friendly interest." The Emperor, wrote the Czar's Chancellor and Minister of Foreign Affairs, desired his Washington envoy to convey to President Lincoln his cordial sympathy and the assurance that the United States could continue to count on Russia's friendship. As a practical demonstration of this friendship, Prince Gortchakov had already assured U. S. Minister Clay that the North would be granted the right to carry prizes into Russian ports.

Gortchakov's message to Stoeckl, dated July 10, 1861, (Old Style), was intended for President Lincoln's eyes. Speaking for the Emperor himself, the Minister for Foreign Affairs said in the note:

> From the beginning of the conflict which divides the United States of America, you have been desired to make known to the federal government the deep interest with which our August Master has been observing the development of a crisis which puts in question the prosperity and even the existence of the Union.
>
> The Emperor profoundly regrets that the hope of a peaceful solution is not realized, and that American citizens, already in arms against each other, are ready to let loose upon their country the most formidable of the scourges of political society—civil war.
>
> For the more than eighty years that it has existed the American Union owes its independence, its towering rise, and its progress, to the concord of its members, consecrated, under the auspices of its illustrious founders, by institutions which have been able to reconcile union with liberty. This union has been fruitful. It has exhibited to the world the spectacle of a prosperity without example in the annals of history.
>
> It would be deplorable if, after so conclusive an experience, the

United States should be hurried into a breach of the solemn compact which up to this time has made their power.

In spite of the diversity of their constitutions and of their interests, and perhaps even because of this diversity, Providence seems to urge them to draw closer the traditional bond which is the basis and the very condition of their political existence. In any event, the sacrifices which they might impose upon themselves to maintain it are beyond comparison with those which dissolution would bring after it. United, they perfect themselves; isolated, they are paralyzed.

The struggle which unhappily has just arisen can neither be indefinitely prolonged, nor lead to the total destruction of one of the parties. Sooner or later it will be necessary to come to some settlement, whatever it may be, which may enable the divergent interests now actually in conflict to coexist.

The American nation would, then, give a proof of high political wisdom in seeking in common such a settlement before a useless effusion of blood, a barren squandering of strength and of public riches, and acts of violence and reciprocal reprisals, shall have come to deepen an abyss between the two parties to the confederation, to end definitely in their mutual exhaustion, and in the ruin, perhaps irreparable, of their commercial and political power.

Our August Master cannot resign himself to admit such deplorable anticipations. His Imperial Majesty still places his confidence in that practical good sense of the citizens of the Union, who appreciate so judiciously their true interests. His Majesty is happy to believe that the members of the federal government and the influential men of the two parties will seize all occasions and will unite all their efforts to calm the effervescence of the passions. There are no interests so divergent that it may not be possible to reconcile them, by laboring to that end with zeal and perseverance, in a spirit of justice and moderation.

If, within the limits of your friendly relations, your language and your counsels may contribute to this result, you will respond, sir, to the intentions of His Majesty the Emperor, in devoting to this the personal influence which you may have been able to acquire during your long residence at Washington, and the consideration which belongs to your character as the representative of a sovereign animated by the most friendly sentiments toward the American Union. This Union is not simply in our eyes an element essential to the universal political equilibrium. It constitutes, besides, a nation to which our August Master and all Russia have pledged the most friendly interest; for the two countries, placed at the extremities of the two worlds, both in the ascending period of their development, appear called to a natural community of interests and of sympathies, of which they have already given mutual proofs to each other.

I do not wish here to approach any of the questions which divide the United States. We are not called upon to express ourselves in this contest. The preceding considerations have no other object than to attest the lively solicitude of the Emperor, in presence of the dangers which menace the American Union, and the sincere wishes which His Majesty entertains for the maintenance of that great work, so laboriously raised, which appeared so rich in its future.

It is in this sense, sir, that I desire you to express yourself, as well to the members of the general government as to influential persons whom you may meet, giving them the assurance that in every event the American nation may count upon the most cordial sympathy on the part of our August Master, during the serious crisis which it is passing through at present.

Upon receipt of this message, Stoeckl hastened to have it translated into English and sent copies to President Lincoln and Secretary of State Seward.

On September 9, the Russian Minister reported the favorable reception of the note to Prince Gortchakov:

Both were deeply touched by this sympathetic appeal of our master. President Lincoln said to me, "Please inform the Emperor of our gratitude and assure His Majesty that the whole nation appreciates this new manifestation of friendship." The President and the Secretary of State told me that of all the communications which they have received from the European governments, ours was the most friendly, with the most good will, or in the very words of Mr. Lincoln, "the most loyal." I am persuaded that your message by carefully avoiding sectional partisanship, will produce the same effect throughout the nation and will prove as popular in the South as in the North.[3]

At the suggestion of President Lincoln, the Secretary of State asked the Russian Minister's permission to give wide publicity to this message of his country's friendship for the United States, to which Stoeckl readily assented.

Even while Russia was thus giving this conspicuous proof of its friendly feeling towards the United States, there was little confidence among the Czar's counselors of the ultimate success of Lincoln's striving to restore the Union. Stoeckl added in his September 9 report to Prince Gortchakov:

> Unfortunately, there is little hope that the wise counsel contained in the message of Your Excellency will be followed. Passions are too high to permit the voice of moderation to be heard. . . . Mr. Seward . . . treats the present crisis as a simple incident belonging to the past; "the international difficulties which for a time seemed to threaten the American Union." The Secretary of State is evidently deceiving himself, as the situation, far from improving, daily becomes more serious.[4]

When the *Trent* affair, which had brought the United States to the very brink of war with Great Britain, was amicably settled, Prince Gortchakov expressed his own warm satisfaction and instructed Stoeckl to convey the Czar's congratulations to President Lincoln on the adjustment of the controversy. The Russian Emperor ardently wished for an early restoration of the Union "not only because of the cordial sympathy which unites the two countries, but also because the maintenance of its power is essential in the highest degree to the general political equilibrium."[5]

In reporting to St. Petersburg concerning the favorable American reception accorded to Gortchakov's assuring message, Stoeckl wrote: "I can assure you, my Prince, that this country in its entirety appreciates the frank and loyal friendship indicated by the plain but sympathetic words of the overture of Your Excellency."[6]

In October 1862, perhaps the gloomiest and most desperate period of the rebellion, when Louis Napoleon was intensifying his pressure upon England and Russia to join him to stop the American war, there came to Bayard Taylor as Chargé d'Affaires of the American legation, following Cameron's resignation, a personal letter from President Lincoln which Secretary Seward instructed Taylor to transmit to Prince Gortchakov for delivery to the Czar. With France all set to force mediation in the American situation, waiting only the word from England, and with the British Cabinet debating the issue, a worried Lincoln wrote a personal letter to the Czar anxiously inquiring Russia's stand on Louis Napoleon's latest proposal.

The Czar and his Minister for Foreign Affairs read and discussed Lincoln's note of inquiry. Then on October 27, 1862 Taylor was summoned by Prince Gortchakov to the Foreign Office. The memorable conversation which ensued was reproduced "almost word for word" by America's Chargé d'Affaires and rushed to Lincoln and Seward by Taylor. This document, dated October 29, 1862, commenced with Prince Gortchakov saying:

> "You know that the government of United States has few friends among the Powers. England rejoices over what is happening to you; she longs and prays for your overthrow. France is less actively hostile; her interests would be less affected by the result; but she is not unwilling to see it. She is not your friend. Your situation," said he, "is getting worse and worse. The chances of preserving the Union are growing more desperate. Can nothing be done to stop this dreadful war? The hope of reunion is growing less and less, and I wish to impress upon your government that the separation, which I fear must come, will be considered by Russia as one of the greatest misfortunes. Russia, alone, has stood by you from the first, and will continue to stand by you. We are very, *very* anxious that some means should be adopted—that *any* course should be pursued—which will prevent the division which now seems inevitable. One separation will be followed by another; you will break into fragments."

Taylor's report of the remarkable interview continued:

> "We feel this," I replied, "the Northern and Southern States cannot peacefully exist side by side as separate republics. There is nothing the American people desire so much as peace; but peace on the basis of separation is equivalent to continual war. We have only just called the whole strength of the nation into action. We believe the struggle now commencing will be final, and we cannot, without disgrace and ruin, accept the only terms upon which the rebels would treat until our strength has been tried and failed."

> "You know the sentiments of Russia," the Prince exclaimed with great earnestness. "We desire above all things the maintenance of

the American Union as one 'indivisible nation.' We cannot take any part, more than we have done. We have no hostility to the Southern people. Russia has declared her position, and will maintain it. There will be proposals of intervention. We believe that intervention could do no good at present. *Proposals will be made to Russia to join some plan of interference.* She will refuse any invitation of the kind. Russia will occupy the same ground as at the beginning of the struggle. *You may rely upon it, she will not change.* But we entreat you to settle the difficulty. I cannot express to you how profound an anxiety we feel—how serious are our fears."

We were standing face to face during the conversation, and the earnest, impassioned manner of the Prince impressed me with the fact that he was speaking from his heart. At the close of the interview he seized my hand, gave it a strong pressure, and exclaimed, "God bless you!" I thanked him for his frankness and for the renewed declaration of the attitude of Russia.

I fixed in my memory at the time, and have reproduced almost word for word, the conversation that occurred between us.[7]

These heartening assurances brought comfort to Lincoln and Seward. The entire proceedings were regarded to be of such vast importance that by resolution of Congress they were ordered published and copies distributed throughout the nation.

Louis Napoleon's plan was to urge upon the Washington and Richmond governments "an armistice for six months, during which time every act of war, direct or indirect, should provisionally cease on the sea as well as on land, and it might be, if necessary, ulteriorly prolonged." Even if the attempt should fail, the French Minister said, it would still serve a useful purpose in encouraging public opinion to views of conciliation.

Napoleon's proposal precipitated a Cabinet crisis in England. Lincoln's secretaries, Nicolay and Hay, have written:

Many years elapsed before it became generally known how near the British government had come to accepting or even anticipating the overtures of France for mediation. On the 17th of October 1861, Lord John Russell had proposed a somewhat peremptory summons to the North and South to make up their quarrel, but Lord Palmerston had not thought it advisable. In September 1862

Lord Palmerston himself revived the proposition in a note to Lord Russell, who was in attendance on the Queen at Gotha. Lord Russell at once gave his adhesion to the scheme. "I agree with you," he said, "that the time is come for offering mediation to the United States government, with a view to the recognition of the independence of the Confederates. I agree further that, in case of failure, we ought ourselves to recognize the Southern States as an independent state." Lord Palmerston answered in the same vein.[8]

A few days later Russell wrote to Palmerston: "My only doubt is whether we and France should stir if Russia holds back. Her separation from our move would ensure the rejection of our proposals."

After days of bitter debate the British reply to the French government's overture was announced on November 13. In brief it declared that it was the Cabinet's belief that there was no ground at that moment to hope that Lincoln's government would accept the offer of mediation. Therefore, it would be better to wait for a time when there would be better hope for success.

The British decision had been influenced in no small degree by the telegram received by Lord Russell from Napier in St. Petersburg to the effect that Russia had already rejected Napoleon's proposal. Prince Gortchakov had advised Louis Napoleon's Minister for Foreign Affairs that it was "essential to avoid the appearance of any pressure of a nature to offend American public opinion, and to excite susceptibilities very easily roused at the bare idea of intervention." But although Russia, which "stood in peculiarly friendly relations with the United States," could not see its way clear to join a European coalition to interfere in American affairs, her Minister in Washington was nevertheless instructed to give his moral support to any conciliatory measures that might be taken—provided it would not cause irritation.[9]

In view of Russia's reluctance to intervene, Russell wrote to Palmerston: "We ought not to move at present without Russia."[10]

Thus Russia's attitude on the question of American intervention, to all intents and purposes, also determined the issue for the British government. Two days after Great Britain's decision not to accede to Napoleon's proposal, Bayard Taylor wrote to Secretary Seward:

> While I infer . . . that Russia would, to a certain extent, be inclined to take part in a movement which she foresaw to be inevitable on the part of England and France, rather than permit a coalition be-

tween these two powers from which she should be wholly excluded, the probable refusal of the English government announced today by telegraph relieves me from all apprehension of complications that might arise from the proposition. I stated to Prince Gortchakov, at our recent interview, my belief that England would not accede, and am very glad to find it so soon confirmed.[11]

Even though Russia was giving repeated conspicuous proof of her friendship for the North, the Confederacy hoped to win recognition from the Czar's government. Lucius Q. C. Lamar, appointed Commissioner to Russia by Jefferson Davis in November 1862, traveled to St. Petersburg to plead the South's case for independence. But Prince Gortchakov refused to give him any encouragement and delayed receiving him officially. At length Davis recalled Lamar, ending his hopeless mission.[12] Lamar had based his hope of eventual Russian recognition on the fact that there was "no party in Russia absolutely hostile to the South."

Lincoln and his Cabinet were elated over these repeated manifestations of Russian friendship. Whatever their real motive, they strengthened the hand of our government and made possible a firm attitude toward the persistent efforts of England and France to meddle in our affairs.

Secretary Seward invited Stoeckl to visit him and discuss the memorable meeting Bayard Taylor had held with Prince Gortchakov in St. Petersburg. He requested the Russian envoy to convey to his government the profound gratitude of America for the assurances of friendship which the Prince had given. "The Secretary of State said that the President was extremely grateful for the attitude taken by Russia in this question."

Stoeckl assured Seward that the Russian "reply to the French proposal was only the continuation of the frank and loyal policy followed by the imperial Cabinet since the beginning of the American crisis."[13] But Stoeckl added that his government felt that an effort should be made to conciliate the South:

> The federal government could not hope that the secessionists would surrender unconditionally . . . Why could not negotiations be launched to sound out the intentions of the authorities at Richmond to see if they would not be disposed to accept equitable terms?

Mr. Seward asked me "why I did not convey this question to the President and assured me that Mr. Lincoln would listen to me with the consideration due the representative of a friendly power. I replied to Mr. Seward that in my confidential conversation with him I could express myself freely, for I was speaking to a personal acquaintance of fifteen years standing, as much as to the Minister of Foreign Affairs. However, I could not be free to offer my opinions to the President without his asking me for them. I would have done it, except for the fact that it would have served no good purpose. Mr. Lincoln is President in name only. The demagogues surrounding him control him.[14]

Stoeckl was against Russian participation in any joint European action. "The rebellion in the United States is destined to go through different phases and we may be called on to lend our good offices as mediators or to be otherwise useful to a nation which has always had the most amicable relations with us. Therefore, it is essential that we should be free from all entanglements that might hurt us in American public opinion."[15]

On December 1, 1862 Stoeckl wrote to Prince Gortchakov of the "violent repercussions" created in the North by news of the "proposal made by France to our Cabinet and to that of London to offer collective mediation in the affairs of the United States." It had been expected here that England would take the initiative. "So the refusal of the cabinet of London was the subject of surprise."

The American press is arrayed not so much against the French government which initiated the move as against Emperor Napoleon, who is charged with being the personal enemy of America. But public opinion remains inflamed chiefly against England. The *New York Herald* declares, "Let us mistrust British neutrality. Her desire is only to see the two sections destroy each other so she may profit from the spoils." On the other hand the press is unanimous in its praise of imperial Russia's attitude.[16]

By April 26, Stoeckl was writing that strained British-American relations rendered collective mediation "in a friendly way" virtually an impossibility although he held out hope for an early cessation of hostilities:

As for France, it appears that she has equally renounced all idea of intervention. . . . If mediation was impracticable three months ago, it is even more so today. The military reverses suffered by the Americans will cause them more than ever to resent any attempt of foreign interference in their affairs, and more than ever offend their national pride. . . .

The war is being waged on too large a scale to continue indefinitely. It will have to end through negotiations, and in that case the good offices of a neutral nation will eventually become essential. I do not hesitate to assert that then Russia, more than any other power, will be in a position to render service to the Americans.

And in this respect I express the opinion of outstanding individuals, among others, [former] President Pierce, whom I met recently in New York. Mr. Pierce said that he read with the greatest satisfaction the communications that Your Excellency had ordered me to present to the federal government, and that he saw in them the sincere expression of frank and cordial friendship. "In the midst of our terrible experiences," Mr. Pierce said, "Russia alone has shown herself our disinterested friend and it is on her that we must count if ever we have need of an intermediary."

I spoke also with Mr. Pierce about the situation of the country. He said, "Our misfortune comes from the men who are in charge of affairs in the North as in the South. President Lincoln and the chiefs of the Republican Party as well as Jefferson Davis and the men who surround him are too deeply involved in this conflict to stop it and thus risk their political future. If affairs could be put back in the hands of the people they would quickly reach an agreement. A national convention composed of delegates named *ad hoc* would be able to arrive at a solution either by the formation of a new federal alliance, or by separation which, after all, would be more desirable than the prolonging of this Civil War. Moreover," he added, "at the end of the struggle, we shall find ourselves in a state of transition. We shall need time to find our equilibrium. If the separation takes place it cannot be more than temporary. With peace restored, the practical spirit of my countrymen will return. Both sides will become convinced that union has made strength, and a confederation on a new basis does not seem to be impractical. But to accomplish that the war must end. If it is prolonged we shall be exposed to new dangers whose symptoms are already too apparent. We shall be divided into three or four independent republics, jealous and naturally enemies of each other."

Since the expiration of his presidential term, Mr. Pierce has lived in retirement and has taken little part in public affairs, but he continues to exercise great influence on the conservatives. His views on the state of the nation seem so accurate that I have felt it my duty to submit them to Your Excellency.[17]

One of Bayard Taylor's last official acts as Chargé d'Affaires, while awaiting the arrival of Clay and Bergh, was to attend a reception given by Czar Alexander II on New Year's Day 1863. Here again the Emperor and Prince Gortchakov expressed "words so full of good will" for the United States. It was still another assurance that "the imperial Cabinet will not change in any way from the policies that it has followed since the beginning of the Civil War."[18]

Stoeckl, after describing a visit with Seward on Washington's Birthday, when this new expression of Russian friendship was discussed, added:

> On the part of England, the federal government is equally reassured. The speech of the Queen at the opening of Parliament and the debates that the speech caused proved sufficiently that for the moment at least the British Cabinet has no intention of intervening in the affairs of the United States.
>
> It is to be presumed that in the present circumstances, France will not renew her move, all the more since she must be convinced today that this proposal would have had no better reception in Richmond than the one made in Washington. The newspapers of the South which we received recently, are very clear on this point. They claim that the French proposition while constituting an indication of good will towards the seceded States, was not at all practical, and that the Confederate government will not consent to open negotiations except on terms of an armistice.[19]

This belief that "France will not renew her move" to bring about intervention in American affairs, was without foundation. Undaunted by the failure of his overture for joint mediation, the French Emperor now undertook to approach the government of the United States alone. This new solo attempt at "friendly mediation" by Louis Napoleon entailed the calling of informal conferences to be attended by representatives of the North and South where reciprocal complaints could be examined.

This new overture of French mediation, received February 3, 1863, was promptly and firmly rejected three days later by Secretary Seward under instructions from President Lincoln. Congress passed its admonishing resolution that any further attempt in the same direction would be looked upon as an unfriendly act.[20]

But insidious rumors of foreign intervention continued to circulate in the United States. On December 2, 1862, Seward had written to Bayard Taylor that though he was no longer worried about a change in Russian policy he would like to be certain about certain rumors which were coming to his attention:

> You may say to Prince Gortchakov confidentially that in British quarters it is said that Russia is verging towards a French convention, while in French quarters it is said that Russia, though reluctant, may yet be induced to join France if she should desire to interfere in the United States. This government gives no heed to any of these rumors. It has no apprehensions of British interference. It knows that no possible advantage, and only misfortunes, could result to France herself from any such interference or intervention; and it further believes that France sees the right and justice of our cause.
>
> In regard to Russia, the case is a plain one. She has our friendship, in every case, in preference to any other European power, simply because she always wishes us well, and leaves us to conduct our affairs as we think best.[21]

The rumors to which "this government gives no heed" were plainly worrying Seward. Early in 1863 he invited Stoeckl to visit him in the Department of State for a discussion of these rumors. Bluntly he told the Russian Minister that he had just been informed that a deal had been made between France and Russia providing that in exchange for concessions to be made by France to Russia in the affairs of Greece, the imperial government had promised to support the proposals of Emperor Louis Napoleon in favor of intervention in the American crisis. Were these rumors true or false?

The Russian Minister, in reporting this sensational conference to his chief in St. Petersburg, wrote, "I replied to him that these rumors were too absurd to be given any credence, and assured him again that the imperial government would abstain from all intervention and that it will offer its good offices only if called upon to do so."[22]

From St. Petersburg, Prince Gortchakov hastened to give added assurance: "Tell Mr. Seward that the policy of Russia in regard to the United States is fixed and will not be changed by the course adopted by any other nation. . . . We shall gladly proffer our services when they are mutually requested, but not until then."[23]

Despite these assurances and reassurances from Russia, the attitude of veiled hostility of the European powers remained a constant threat. The Cabinets of the Old World saw no hope of reconciliation between the North and the South, and were convinced that the restoration of the national authority was impossible. One sickening military disaster after another—Fredericksburg, Chancellorsville, Chickamauga—added to this belief in Europe and spread gloom and despondency throughout the United States.

The Russian Fleet Comes
to the United States

THE sickening and disheartening news of the bloody rout at Chick-amauga, (September 19-20, 1863) with its 16,000 federal casualties in killed, wounded and captured, had hardly reached the readers of the nation's newspapers, when another news item—more joyous and hope-ful—claimed their attention.

The imperial Russian navy had come to America and was standing ready to help us against any foreign power that persisted in meddling in our affairs. Just as the French had come in 1778 to help the strug-gling colonies win their independence from Great Britain, so now Russia was making common cause with us against England and France. Thus ran the reports that spread like wildfire from one end of the United States to the other.

For on September 24, four days after the military disaster at Chick-amauga, the imperial Russian navy's flagship, *Alexander Nevski*, a screw frigate carrying fifty-one guns, and the *Peresvet*, a frigate of forty-eight guns, sailed into New York Harbor. Two days later, the *Variag*, sloop of seventeen guns and 2,100 tons, and the *Vitiaz*, also a sloop of the same gun power and tonnage, dropped anchor in the port. And within another two and three weeks the *Almaz* and the *Osliaba* made their appearance. The latter, a screw frigate of thirty-three guns, 2,800 tons and manned by 450 sailors and marine artillerymen, had been sailing for three months since leaving its base in Greek waters in the Mediterranean, to keep its rendezvous off the coast of New York. The others had come from the roadstead at Kronstadt, where they had been in constant danger of being bottled up in the Baltic if Great Britain and France should join in a war against Russia. This very thing had happened to the imperial navy a few years before in the Crimean War. The Russian Atlantic fleet of frigates, clippers and corvettes, which cast anchor at the mouth of the Hudson River, was under the command of Rear Admiral Lisovski.

When Gideon Welles was officially notified by Stoeckl of the coming of the fleet, the American Secretary of the Navy wrote to the Russian Minister under date of September 23, 1863:

> The Department is much gratified to learn that a squadron of Russian war vessels is at present off the harbor of New York, with the intention, it is supposed, of visiting that city. The presence in our waters of a squadron belonging to His Imperial Majesty's navy cannot but be a source of pleasure and happiness to our countrymen. I beg that you will make known to the Admiral in command that the facilities of the Brooklyn navy yard are at his disposal for any repairs that the vessels of his squadron need, and that any other required assistance will be gladly extended.
>
> I avail myself of this occasion to extend through you to the officers of His Majesty's squadron a cordial invitation to visit that navy yard. I do not hesitate to say that it will give Rear Admiral Paulding very great pleasure to show them the vessels and other objects of interest at the naval station under his command.

Later Secretary Welles wrote in his diary concerning the arrival of the Russian warships: "In sending them to this country there is something significant. What will be its effect on France and the French policy we shall learn in due time. It may be moderate; it may exasperate. God bless the Russians."[1]

Lincoln told Senator James Harlan that in 1862 he had sought to learn the Czar's attitude in case England and France forced their unwelcome intervention. Lincoln stated that the Czar had replied to our Minister Simon Cameron, that in such a case the friendship of Russia for the United States would be shown in a "decisive manner." Was this unheralded arrival of the Russian naval squadron the "decisive manner" of demonstrating the friendship which the Czar had promised?

While Russia's Atlantic fleet was thus dropping anchor in the waters of New York Harbor, her Pacific squadron was also converging off

America's Pacific coast. On October 12, the Czar's Far East fleet, consisting of the corvettes *Bogatir, Kalevala, Rinda* and *Novik,* and the clippers *Abrek* and *Gaidamak,* sailed into San Francisco Bay; and its commander, Rear Admiral Popov, immediately put himself in touch with Minister Stoeckl in Washington. All the Muscovite ships bristled with gaping guns. The vessels, of wood construction, carried steam engines. But these were used only in cases of urgent necessity. At all other times the sail was the principal means of motion.

Harper's Weekly reported of the Atlantic fleet, "The two largest of the squadron, the frigates *Alexander Nevski* and *Peresvet,* are evidently vessels of modern build, and much about them would lead an unpractised eye to think they were constructed in this country." A reporter going aboard the *Alexander Nevski* thought its deck to be "large enough to accommodate a fair-sized army with an ordnance large enough to blow up Fort Sumter." He was told by a Russian officer that the flagship's guns "are of American make, being cast in Pittsburgh."

In its description of the other Russian warships anchored in New York Harbor, *Harper's Weekly* continued:

> The frigate *Osliaba* is unlike the other two; she has more the appearance of one of the first of the heavy screw ships built in the European dock yards. Her bluff bows and counter do not give evidence of great speed; but she is doubtless a fair goer and fine sea boat. The two steam corvettes, or sloops, as we term them, *Variag* and *Vitiaz,* are apparently very superior vessels. They are fully equal in tonnage to the steamers in our service of the class of the *Brooklyn, Richmond* and others, and carry very serviceable batteries. They are evidently constructed for speed, and have engines of full power. All these vessels are ship-rigged, and are heavily sparred, so much so that if their smokestacks were out of sight you would hardly suppose them to be propelled by steam.
>
> The batteries of these ships are of formidable character, although all smooth-bored guns. They are of one caliber, throwing a solid shot of sixty pounds' weight, and of two classes, the long and medium, weighing about sixty and eighty hundredweight.

The welcome accorded Admirals Lisovski and Popov and their officers and crews was extremely enthusiastic. Both on the Atlantic and Pacific coasts they were received with a warmth and cordiality that well reflected "the friendship which the nation cherishes towards Russia." New York City, gaily bedecked with American and Russian flags, bubbled over with sumptuous hospitality. Deputations came from surrounding States to pay their respects to the visitors from the realm of the Czar.

The Muscovite naval officers, wearing gold-laced chapeaux, were wined and dined wherever they went. They were cheered as they were being driven up Broadway in victorias, surrounded by American soldiers. The city's merchants and businessmen gave a banquet in their honor at the Astor House. There was a grand ball for the officers at the Academy of Music on November 5. According to the editor of *Harper's Weekly*, "It was undoubtedly the greatest ball ever given in this country, without excepting the ball to the Prince of Wales."[2] The brilliantly lighted Academy was draped in Russian and American flags and shields which bore the heraldic devices of the two nations. Quoting from an account in the *New York Herald*, *Harper's Weekly* described the affair:

> Immediately after the Russians arrived the dance began. . . . In truth it was a very wonderful and "indescribable phantasmagoria of humanity. . . ." Beautiful, bejeweled ladies vied with each other for dances with the bearded and uniformed visitors.
>
> Alas! for the Russians. It is known or should be, that these Sclavic [sic] heroes are not the largest of the human race—that they are small men in fact—and what is to become of small men in such a jam? Early in the night—indeed, very soon after the dance began—we saw several of them in the embrace of grand nebulous masses of muslin and crinoline, whirled hither and thither as if in terrible torment, their eyes aglare, their hair blown out, and all their persons expressive of the most desperate energy, doubtless in the endeavor to escape. What became of them we cannot tell.[3]

Supper of the *"Soirée Russe,"* prepared by Delmonico, was served in the adjoining Irving Hall. The tables were decorated with likenesses of Washington and Peter the Great, of Lincoln and Czar Alexander II.

A reporter for the *New York World* wrote: "As the ovation and ball is one which may leave its traces on centuries to come, we give, for the sake of history, an account of the principle edibles used, viz:

> *Twelve thousand oysters—10,000 poulette and 2,000 pickled*
> *Twelve monster salmon—30 lbs. each*

Twelve hundred game birds
Two hundred chickens
One thousand pounds of tenderloin
One hundred pyramids of pastry
One thousand large loaves
Three thousand five hundred bottles of wine[4]

Always the name of Czar Alexander II was cheered as the emancipator of the serfs and the friend of America. In their turn the Russian visitors drank toasts to President Abraham Lincoln and spoke eloquently about the historic friendship which bound the two nations.

Three Russian sailors who imbibed freely and became too boisterous on the streets had to be locked up as common drunks. They were booked as Russian No. 1, No. 2, and No. 3. But they were promptly set free the next morning by a police magistrate. He did not desire, he said pompously, "to do anything calculated to disturb the friendly relations which exist between the Emperor of Russia and the President of the United States."

Harper's Weekly in its Ocotober 17, 1863 issue painted this word picture of the civic parade conducted in honor of the Russians:

After the procession has passed Union Square, and wheeling fairly into the vast current of Broadway, the scene became splendidly animated. The moving pageant rolled in a glittering stream down the broad thoroughfare between banks of upturned human faces, the trappings of the equipages, the gold and silver epaulets of the Muscovite guests and the sabres, helmets and bayonets of the escort reflecting back in unnumbered dazzling lines the glory of the evening sun. The cavalcade advanced to the joyous time of exulting martial music like the vanguard of a conquering host returning to the metropolis of its power, and there was a proud and gratified feeling evident in the hearts of the vast concourse assembled to greet it, that would have been befitting to the most important triumphs at home. Far as the eye could reach down the great central avenue of our imperial city, the sidewalks were packed with human beings, and the balconies and windows—nay, in some instances, the very roofs of the buildings above them—were beset with eager multitudes, the general surface of this animated borderwork richly varied and enameled, as it were, throughout its length with groups of richly attired beauty. Above nearly every building gayly fluttered the Stars and Stripes, some in standards of immense size and others tricked off with scores of little Russian flags, waving and sporting in the breeze side by side with our own national colors. By-the-way, it may be remarked that the great *Autocracy* and the great *Republic* had the scene all to themselves, no other nation being represented even in bunting— a significant incident of the ovation.[5]

One Russian naval captain admitted he was thoroughly overwhelmed by the extreme cordiality of New York's men and the grace and love-liness of the fair dames and damsels. This caused a writer for *Harper's Weekly* to comment: "On the chill banks of the Neva, perhaps when far away on the boisterous billows of the Black Sea or the Caspian, he will recall, in his lonely midnight vigil, while he paces the stormbeaten deck, the sunny smiles that brightened the autumnal sunshine on the borders of the Hudson."[6]

The large sums of money spent in entertaining and staging demon-strations in honor of the Czar's navy officers and crew brought severe criticism from some New Yorkers. They protested that

> Such extravagant festivities were out of place when the Boys in Blue were dying in the trenches and when the government was having hard work to raise money for munitions. . . . The million spent on the "Ovation, Collation and Ball" should instead have been given to the Sanitary Commission.

But most New Yorkers were convinced that the Russian fleet had sailed thousands of miles across the ocean just to help the United States. They felt, therefore, that these demonstrations of welcome were the least they could do to show their appreciation.

The display was not altogether due to vanity. Its obvious purpose was to show the King of England that New York would make more fuss over a Russian admiral than it had over the Prince of Wales, and to prove to the Czar of Russia that the United States was an ally worth having. *Harper's Weekly* admitted that "The ceremony was intended to have, and had, a political significance. . . . Every citizen felt bound to do what in him lay to testify to the Russians our sense of gratitude for the friendly manner in which Russia has stood by us in our present struggle, while the Western powers have done not a little to work our ruin."[7] Other commentators also saw "a special significance" in the presence of the Russian warships in our ports:

During the late Crimean War, the Russian fleet was closely shut up at Kronstadt and in the Black Sea, and was unable to render any effective service. The Russians have now quite an effective naval force in the open seas. The experience of the *Alabama* and *Florida* shows how much damage may be effected by one or two armed vessels upon the commerce of an enemy.

Should a war break out, as still seems most probable, between Russia and France and England, the example set by the English government will afford a precedent for our dealings with the belligerents. The Russian vessels now at large, with such aid as we can give, in precise accordance with the course of the English government toward us, could render the commerce of England insecure.[8]

In December the Russian Atlantic fleet sailed up the Potomac and anchored near Alexandria. Secretary Welles ordered American naval personnel to show the visitors "all proper courtesy."[9] Steamboats carried excursionists from Washington on sight-seeing tours of the squadron. The Russian sailors with their outlandish whiskers and with queer lettering on their caps, wandered through the streets of Washington as on a holiday. "They have vast absorbent powers and are fiendishly ugly," John Hay observed.[10] The officers were entertained at banquets by Secretary of State Seward, by Navy Secretary Welles and by Russia's Minister Stoeckl.

Bayard Taylor, back in Washington from his stint as Secretary of legation in St. Petersburg, was delivering lectures on "Russia and the Russians." Lincoln had suggested to him that "a good lecture or two on serfs, serfdom and emancipation in Russia would be both interesting and valuable, could you not get up such a thing?" One lyceum audience, addressed by Taylor on the Russian situation, included Admiral Lisovski and several of his officers. John Hay noted in his diary that Lincoln also went one evening to hear Taylor's lecture.

It had been expected that President and Mrs. Lincoln would also receive and entertain the Russian naval visitors at a grand ball. But Lincoln had returned in poor health from Gettysburg where he had delivered a few remarks at the dedication of the famous battlefield.[11] For a time he was confined to his rooms with a bilious attack and later was advised he was suffering from a mild form of smallpox. Thus he was prevented from attending any of the functions in honor of the visitors. Secretary Seward wrote to Minister Clay:

I had the honor on the 5th inst. [December] to receive the Admiral and his associates and after bidding them a cordial welcome in behalf of the President, I presented them to my associates in the administration. . . . The President earnestly desired that their reception at the Capital might reflect the cordiality and friendship which the nation cherishes toward Russia, and thus far, I am happy to say, this wish has been realized. Indisposition of the President has, until now, prevented him from giving them a formal audience.

Not much attention was paid by the newspapers to this affair. But they filled endless columns concerning a shipboard reception on board the Russian frigate *Osliaba*, where General Dix and Mrs. Lincoln were reported to have drunk a toast to the health of the Czar. In response Russian Captain Boutakov toasted the President.[12]

The *New York Herald* seized upon Mrs. Lincoln's toast as an act that "will be heard with joy in the icy North and the steppes of Asia." And the *Richmond Examiner* commented sarcastically:

> The apparently trivial occurrence of a health being drunk by the wife of an Illinois lawyer should convulse with fear, or elate with joy, the people of Europe and Asia. Plain Mrs. Lincoln would never have made much of a noise in the world. Appendant to that extraordinary freak of nature, the President of the U.S., she can not only distinguish herself by the resplendent tints of her silks and possession of her jewels, but can frighten the world "from its propriety" by simply drinking a glass of sherry.

Then the Richmond editor tore into Lincoln himself by drawing a parallel between him and the Czar of Russia:

> The Czar emancipates the serfs from their bondage of centuries, and puts forth the whole strength of his empire to enslave the Poles. Lincoln proclaims freedom to the African, and strives at the same time to subjugate freeborn Americans. In this striking coincidence a similarity of character and feeling is denoted, which accounts for their close friendship, heretofore suspected, and now clearly displayed to the mingled admiration and awe of the world by Mrs. Lincoln's toddy.

Other anti-Lincoln papers like the *Chicago Times* reprinted the *Richmond Examiner's* comments and added a dig or two of their own.

San Francisco's welcome to Admiral Popov and his Pacific squadron officers and crew vied with New York's and Washington's hospitality in warmth and enthusiasm.[13] The Russians expressed their gratitude by deeds as well as by words. When, shortly after their arrival, a big fire broke out in San Francisco, Popov ordered his men to aid in putting it out. For this assistance they were voted the city's official thanks by the municipal council.

The Russian visitors demonstrated they were willing to do more. They stood ready to help fight America's battles if the opportunity presented itself. This they revealed when rumors were circulated in San Francisco in the winter of 1863-64 that the Confederate cruisers *Alabama* and *Sumter* were off the California coast and planning to attack the unguarded city. Excited citizens appealed to Admiral Popov for protection. Without consulting his superiors in St. Petersburg, the Russian commander decided to act on his own responsibility. He gave orders to his officers to prepare to prevent any attempt of the Confederates to attack the city. Should a Southern cruiser attempt an assault, they were "to put on steam and clear for action." It was Popov's belief that "the ships of His Imperial Russian Majesty's Pacific squadron . . . are bound to assist the authorities of every place where friendship is offered them, in all measures which may be deemed necessary by the local authorities, to repel any attempt against the security of the place."

The rumors concerning the *Sumter* and *Alabama* did not materialize. The Confederates did not appear and the attack against San Francisco did not take place. So it did not become necessary for the Czar's Pacific fleet to execute Admiral Popov's orders which would have made Russia the active ally of the United States in the Civil War.

Popov had acted without instructions. When Minister Stoeckl received a copy of the Admiral's orders he was shocked. He quickly dispatched them to Prince Gortchakov. Equally shocked, the Minister for Foreign Affairs instructed Stoeckl to reprove the naval commander for his unneutral stand and to urge upon him the strictest neutrality in the future. On March 13, 1864, Stoeckl sent Popov a scathing rebuke. As far as imperial Russia is concerned, he wrote, there is neither North nor South, but a United States. Therefore Russia had no right to interfere in the internal affairs of that sovereign nation. Consequently, he, Admiral Popov, must keep out of the sectional conflict.

From all the information to be obtained here it would seem that the Confederate cruisers aim to operate only in the open sea and it is not expected that cities will be attacked and San Francisco is in no danger. What the corsairs do in the open sea does not concern us; even if they fire on the forts, it is your duty to be strictly neutral. But in case the corsair passes the fort and threatens the city, you have then the right, in the name of humanity, and not for political purposes, to prevent this misfortune. It is to be hoped that the naval strength at your command will bring about the desired result and that you will not be obliged to use force and involve our government in a situation which it is trying to keep out of.[14]

The Russian Atlantic and Pacific squadrons remained in American waters approximately seven months. On April 26, 1864, Gortchakov notified General-Adjutant Krabbe of the imperial navy that the Emperor was of the opinion there was no longer any need for the fleet to remain in America. The departing Russian naval visitors were profuse in the expression of their thanks for the warm and wholehearted hospitality they had received wherever they had gone in the United States.

The officers of the Atlantic squadron on taking their leave of New York took up a voluntary subscription of $4,760. They presented the gift to Mayor Opdyke to be used for the poor of the city. It was intended as a token of appreciation for all the civic courtesies accorded them during their stay in the American metropolis. At the farewell banquet which the city of Boston tendered in honor of Admiral Lisovski and his officers in June 1864, one of the principal responses was given by Edward Everett.

When the Russians returned to Kronstadt they entertained Minister Clay and Secretary of Legation Bergh aboard the flagship as the Russian band alternated in playing *Yankee Doodle* and the Russian national anthem. And they requested our St. Petersburg representatives to convey to the American people the Russians' profound gratitude and appreciation for the welcome and hospitality they had received throughout their sojourn in the United States.

But what had been the real reason for the coming of the Russian squadrons to America's Atlantic and Pacific coasts? What was behind despotic, democracy-hating Russia's ostentatious demonstrations of friendship for Lincoln's government of the people, by the people, for the people?

The British navy had been watching the Russian fleet with great suspicion. At one time English observers were sure the Czar's navy was headed for Vera Cruz. The actual arrival of Muscovite men-of-war in New York and San Francisco Harbors came as a shock and surprise to London. Soon English newspapers were decrying Lincoln's "threats of war" against Great Britain.

English journalists poked fun at the fuss Americans were making over their Russian visitors. This caused *Harper's Weekly* to comment:

> John Bull thinks that we are absurdly bamboozled by the Russian compliments, and laughs to see us deceived by the sympathy of Muscovy. If one of the Russian officers, he says, were to express in St. Petersburg a tithe of the regard for American institutions which Americans recklessly attribute to them he would soon be in Siberia. But we are not very much deceived. Americans understand that the sympathy of France in our Revolution was not from love of us, but from hatred of England. They know, as Washington long ago told them, that romantic friendship between nations is not to be expected. And if they had latterly expected it, England has utterly undeceived them.

> Americans do not suppose that Russia is upon the point of becoming a republic; but they observe that the English aristocracy and the French empire hate a republic quite as much as the Russian monarchy hates it; and they remark that while the French empire imports coolies into its colonies, and winks at slavery, and while the British government cheers a political enterprise founded upon slavery, and by its chief organs defends the system, Russia emancipates her serfs. There is not the least harm in observing these little facts. Russia, John Bull will remember, conducts herself as a friendly power. That is all. England and France have shown themselves to be unfriendly powers. And we do not forget it.

The conspicuously friendly attitude of The Great Autocracy for The Great Republic gave rise to speculation in Europe of a secret Russo-American alliance. The French and British legations were greatly disconcerted by the rumors. They squirmed at the demonstrations given by the American people in honor of their Russian visitors. But John Hay noted in his diary: "The diplomatic body have all apparently stopped blackguarding and those who do not like have been forced to respect."[15]

What was the fact as to the existence of a Russo-American alliance? Clay in his speeches in the United States during the period between his two missions to St. Petersburg frequently referred to the Russian "alliance." Back in August 1861, Seward had actually signed a convention with Russia, but he never presented it to the Senate for ratification. It became known at the time of the *Trent* affair only through the fact that Minister Rudolph Schleiden of Bremen, in a report of November 14, 1861 to his government, stated that Stoeckl inquired of Seward

> whether the United States would equip privateers in case war should break out with England and France. Seward thereupon remarked, "that is a matter of course." Stoeckl then remarked that in any case no American privateer would be permitted to cruise in the northern part of the Pacific because Russia, which is the only state that has ports in these regions, would treat them as pirates in accordance with the convention of August 24. Mr. Seward exclaimed, "I never thought of that. I must write to Mr. Clay about it."[16]

Gortchakov gave much thought to the possibility of concluding a formal political alliance between his government and that of the United States. However, he finally decided that a formal alliance would not change anything in the existing position of the two nations. To Stoeckl he referred on October 22, 1863 to *"l'alliance existant des intérêts et les traditions politiques."* To which Czar Alexander II added his comment: *"Très bien."*

If no formal alliance with the Czar's government already existed, one ought to be negotiated, an editorial in *Harper's Weekly* of October 17, 1863 suggested:

> Times had changed greatly since Washington had warned his countrymen against entangling foreign alliances.
> When Washington lived, steam, telegraphs and railroads were unknown, and the United States were thirty days' distant from the nearest port of Europe. . . . Intelligence circulated slowly. One nation knew little of another; and peoples separated by an ocean were absolutely ignorant of the most common features of each other's idiosyncracies.

In his time the United States were so far separated from the rest of the world that their very isolation was ample protection against foreign attack. No European nation could hope to carry on war against them, at a distance of 3,000 or 4,000 miles from their base, with any reasonable hope of substantial success. So protected, we needed no foreign allies.

But three-quarters of a century have changed all this. We are now within fifteen days of almost any port of the coast of Europe. . . . Steam has placed Europe and America within easy striking distance of each other, and the ocean is no longer a protection against hostile attack. We are no longer isolated from the rest of the world. . . .

It seems quite doubtful, under these circumstances, whether we can possibly much longer maintain the position of proud isolation which Washington coveted. . . .

The alliance of the Western powers, maintained through the Crimean War and exemplified in the recognition of the Southern rebels by both powers conjointly—is in fact, if not in name, a hostile combination against the United States.

What is our proper reply to this hostile combination? . . . Would it not be wise to meet the hostile alliance by an alliance with Russia? France and England united can do and dare much against Russia alone or the United States alone; but against Russia and the United States combined what could they do?

The analogies between the American and Russian people have too often been described to need further explanation here. Russia, like the United States, is a nation of the future. Its capabilities are only just being developed. Its national destiny is barely shaped. Its very institutions are in their cradle, and have yet to be modeled to fit advancing civilization and the spread of intelligence. Like the United States, Russia is in the agonies of a terrible transition: the Russian serfs, like the American Negroes, are receiving their liberty; and the Russian *boiars*, like the Southern slaveowners, are mutinous at the loss of their property. When this great problem shall have been solved, and the Russian people shall consist of 100,-000,000 of intelligent, educated human beings, it is possible that Russian institutions will have been welded by the force of civilization into a similarity with ours. At that period the United States will probably also contain 100,000,000 educated, intelligent people.

To two such peoples, firmly bound together by an alliance as well as by traditional sympathy and good feeling, what would be impossible? Certainly the least of the purposes which they could achieve would be to keep the peace of the world. . . .

At the present time Russia and the United States occupy remarkably similar positions. A portion of the subjects of the Russian empire, residing in Poland, have attempted to secede and set up an independent national existence, just as our Southern slaveowners have tried to secede from the Union and set up a slave Confederacy; and the Czar, like the government of the Union, has undertaken to put down the insurrection by force of arms. In that undertaking, which every government is bound to make under penalty of national suicide, Russia, like the United States, has been thwarted and annoyed by the interference of France and England. The Czar, like Mr. Lincoln, nevertheless, perseveres in his purpose; and being perfectly in earnest and determined, has sent a fleet into our waters in order that, if war should occur, British and French commerce should not escape as cheaply as they did in the Crimean contest.

An alliance between Russia and the United States at the present time would probably relieve both of us from all apprehensions of foreign interference. It is not likely it would involve either nation in war. On the contrary, it would probably be the best possible guarantee against war. It would be highly popular in both countries. . . .

The reception given last week in this city to Admiral Lisovski and his officers will create more apprehension at the Tuileries and at St. James than even the Parrott gun or the capture of the *Atlanta*. If it be followed up by diplomatic negotiations, with a view to an alliance with the Czar, it may prove an epoch of no mean importance in history.[17]

If the United States entered into any secret alliance with Russia during the Civil War, Lincoln and Seward kept it so secret that not even the President's private secretaries, John Nicolay, John Hay and Noah Brooks, to whom he frequently imparted state secrets, had any inkling of it. Nor did Seward give the slightest hint of it to his bosom friend, Thurlow Weed.

But Weed's grandson, Thurlow Weed Barnes, relying on the inaccurate memory of his grandfather, has written:

Admiral David Farragut lived at the Astor House, where he was visited frequently by the Russian Admiral, between whom, when they were young officers serving in the Mediterranean, a warm friendship had existed. Sitting in Thurlow Weed's room one evening after dinner, Admiral Farragut said to his Russian friend: "Why are you spending the winter here in idleness?" "I am here," replied the Russian Admiral, "under sealed orders, to be broken only in a contingency that has not occurred."

He added that the Russian men-of-war were lying off San Francisco with similar orders. During this conversation the Russian Admiral admitted that his orders were to break the seals if, during the rebellion, we became involved in a war with foreign nations.

In Washington, a few days later, Secretary Seward asked the Russian Minister why his government kept their ships of war so long in our harbors, and the reply, in disclaiming any knowledge of the nature of the visit, was that it had "no unfriendly purpose."[18]

The utter incredibility of this account is evidenced by the fact that Barnes also quoted his grandfather as attributing the sending of the Russian fleets to the United States to our trouble with England over the *Trent* affair. Thurlow Weed is quoted:

The Russian Ambassador at London informed his government that England was preparing for war with America on account of the seizure of Mason and Slidell. Hence two fleets were immediately sent across the Atlantic under sealed orders, so that if their services were not needed, the intentions of the Emperor would remain, as they have to this day, secret.[19]

Actually the Czar's war vessels came to American shores in 1863, two years after the *Trent* crisis. The two events were entirely unrelated.

The myth of the Russian "concealed orders" crept into American historical writings when Thomas L. Harris repeated the Weed version almost word for word in his otherwise creditable book *The Trent Affair*. Harris also repeated Barnes' statement that:

A well-known American who was in St. Petersburg when the Rebellion began . . . during an official call upon Prince Gortchakov was shown by the Chancellor an order written in Alexander's own hand, directing his Admiral to report to President Lincoln for orders, in case England or France sided with the Confederates.[20]

Commander F. E. Chadwick of the U. S. Navy, and George Peirce, a Philadelphia lawyer, have written similar accounts. For many years Commander Chadwick was intimate with Governor Andrew G. Curtin, of Pennsylvania, who succeeded Cassius Clay as Minister to Russia in 1869.

Commander Chadwick stated that Prince Gortchakov personally showed Governor Curtin a copy of the orders that had been given to the Admiral commanding the Russian fleet sent to New York. These orders instructed the Admiral, in the event of the recognition of the Confederacy by France or England, to place his fleet at the disposition of the American government. "In other words, the recognition was to be the signal for the declaration by Russia of war against those powers. And there can be little doubt that the knowledge by the French and English Cabinets of these orders was the great leash which held them in check."[21]

All these traditional accounts giving Thurlow Weed or Governor Curtin as the source of their information are based on inaccurate memories or hearsay. No official documents have ever been published or undoubted evidence presented in verification.

10

The Myth of Russian Friendship

THE sensational, unheralded visit of the Russian fleet when the American future seemed so dark, was hailed with grateful rejoicing as an indication that, come what may, Russia—our old and staunch friend—was prepared to stand by the Union. The belief that the Czar had offered Lincoln the use of the Russian warships and that this gesture was responsible for stopping England's and France's efforts to recognize the sovereignty of the Confederate States, was to linger long in American memory.

The poet, Oliver Wendell Holmes, lyricized this legendary international friendship by singing the praises of the Czar "who was our friend when the world was our foe." Statesmen eloquently expressed America's undying gratitude for the support which came in our hour of trial and misfortune. It was a friendship, said Cassius Clay, which sprang from "a common cause in the advancement of our common humanity."

Actually, Russia's opposition to the British-French proposals for collective American intervention resulted from no concern or friendship for the United States. Rather it came from the necessity of being consistent in opposing foreign intervention in all domestic struggles; or to be more exact, in opposing threatened foreign intervention in Russia's own explosive Polish question.

The Czar's war vessels came to the United States not to aid the Union or to bolster up the morale of the North, but to escape the danger of being bottled up in European waters by the British navy, as had happened during the Crimean War. There were no "sealed orders" to go to the rescue of the United States in the event of intervention by European powers. If such mysterious orders existed they were kept secret even from President Lincoln and Secretary Seward. And no record of such orders has ever been found among the official archives of the United States or Russia.

Actually, the Polish crisis not only determined the Czar's attitude toward American intervention but was also responsible for his sending the empire's fleet to the United States. At the very time that France and England were endeavoring to induce Russia to join them in intervening in the American Civil War, they were also inviting the United States to join them in protesting against Russia's treatment of her Polish subjects. Russia, the most hated nation in Europe, was even more friendless than Lincoln's government. Her Polish policy was threatening to embroil her in another European war. She needed America's support for nonintervention in the Polish insurrection, as much as Lincoln's government needed Russian support for nonintervention in the rebellion of the Southern States. U. S. Minister Dayton wrote from Paris on February 23, 1863:

> The Polish revolt, which has been smoldering since 1861, broke into a fierce flame, and has driven American affairs out of view for the moment. A disturbance on the continent, especially in Central Europe, is so near at hand and touches so many of the crowned heads of these countries, that distant events fall out of sight until these more immediate troubles are settled.

Russia was ruthless in crushing the insurrection. Thousands of Poles were slain or incarcerated or deported to Siberia. The estates of numerous nobles were confiscated. And the last remnants of Polish autonomy were extinguished.

Europe was touched by Poland's plight. France, England and Austria decided to have recourse to diplomatic intervention, and invited the other powers who had signed the Treaty of Vienna to join in their remonstrance to persuade Russia to accord better treatment to her Polish subjects. But the Czar, emulating Lincoln's stand in the American rebellion, declared that the Polish uprising was a purely domestic affair and that foreign intervention was not acceptable.

Emperor Louis Napoleon, though thwarted in his scheme to intervene in the American conflict, had by no means lost his appetite for foreign meddling. Now he became the spearhead of the movement for collective intervention in Poland's insurrection. In May, 1863, Napoleon's Minister for Foreign Affairs, Drouyn de Lhuys, instructed Henri Mercier, in Washington, to invite Lincoln's government to join France, England and Austria in proposing a common *démarche* in St. Petersburg in favor of Poland. The Emperor appealed to the "historical sympathies" of the Americans for the Poles. The invitation stated:

> The good relations which exist between the government of the United States and the court of Russia cannot but give greater weight to the counsels presented in a friendly form; and we rely entirely on the Cabinet in Washington to appreciate the measure in which it will be able most satisfactorily to open its views to the Russian government.

In reality the invitation was an attempt to break the bond between the United States and Russia.

What should Lincoln do about Napoleon's appeal to help oppressed Poland? Years before, as a private citizen back in Springfield, Lincoln had not hesitated to take a leading part in protesting against Russia, "the foreign despot," who "in violation of the most sacred principles of the laws of nature and of nations" had, through unwarranted armed intervention, overwhelmed Hungary when she was striving to throw off the yoke of Austrian tyranny. He had subscribed to the principle: "That it is the right of any people, sufficiently numerous for national independence, to throw off, to revolutionize, their existing form of government, and to establish such other in its stead as they may choose." He had denounced Russia's interference in Hungary's struggle for freedom because of his firm belief that one nation had no right to interfere in domestic uprisings in other nations. "It is the duty of our government to neither foment, nor assist, such revolutions in other governments," he had written. By the same token that the United States "may not legally or warrantably interfere abroad to aid, so no other government may interfere abroad, to suppress such revolutions." He regarded "this mutuality of nonintervention as a sacred principle of the international law."[1]

Now as the responsible leader of the American nation engaged in a life and death struggle for survival because of the insistence of the Southern States to the right to national independence, Lincoln declared their claim to the right to secession as unconstitutional and sheer treason. Unflinchingly he combated the sophism of the secessionists who maintained that any State of the Union, consistently with the Constitution, might lawfully and peacefully withdraw from the Union without the consent of the Union or of any other State. Lincoln's answer was:

> The States have their status in the Union, and they have no other legal status. If they break from this, they can only do so against law and by revolution. The Union, not themselves, separately, procured their independence and their liberty. By conquest or purchase, the Union gave each of them whatever of independence and liberty it has. The Union is older than any of the States, and, in fact, it created them as States. Originally some independent colonies made the Union, and, in turn, the Union threw off their old dependence for them, and made them States, such as they are. Not one of them ever had a State Constitution independent of the Union.[2]

But on the question of foreign intervention in domestic affairs, President Lincoln remained consistent with his earlier views as a private citizen. His sympathies lay with the oppressed people of Poland, to whom Secretary Seward referred as "the gallant nation whose wrongs, whose misfortunes and whose valor have so deeply excited universal sympathy in Europe." But there was the principle of nonintervention by foreign powers in domestic affairs which Lincoln had once insisted to be a "sacred principle of the international law." As President of a nation torn by civil war, he opposed intervention by Europe in America. Consistency demanded that he also oppose interference by the United States with regard to the Polish uprising.

As a result of a consultation of Secretary Seward with President Lincoln, the Secretary of State on behalf of the administration declined to participate in the proposed collective anti-Russian action. The American answer expressed confidence that the Polish grievances would be righted by the liberalism, sagacity and magnanimity of Czar Alexander II. But the Secretary also pointed to the "insurmountable difficulty" in the way of American active participation with France, Austria and Great Britain in the Polish affair. Frequently the United States had seen fit to decline invitations to participate in the consultations held by foreign states for the common advantage of the nations:

Our policy of nonintervention straight, absolute and peculiar as it may seem to other nations, has thus become a traditional one which could not be abandoned without the most urgent occasion, amounting to a manifest necessity. Certainly it could not be wisely departed from at this moment, when the existence of a local, although as we trust only a transient disturbance, deprives the government of the counsel of a proportion of the American people to whom so wide a departure from the settled policy of the country must in any place be deeply interesting.[3]

America's refusal to join Russia's enemies caused the *Missouri Republic* to declare that "the pale corpse of Poland's murdered liberty" would haunt Lincoln in the days to come. *Punch*, in England, depicted Lincoln in grotesque garb conniving with the Russian bear. French journals likened the American Civil War to the Polish insurrection, and pictured Lincoln placing his hand in the bloody hand of Czar Alexander II. One French editor asked: "Is it right that fifty million Muscovites should unite to retain ten or twelve million Poles under a detested yoke? Is it right that twenty million Northern Germans and Irishmen should unite to impose on eight million Southerners an association they spurn?"[4]

But the American refusal to join the anti-Russian remonstrance produced such great satisfaction in St. Petersburg that Prince Gortchakov saw fit to give wide publicity in the Russian press to the expression of the Czar's appreciation of

the firmness with which the government of the United States maintains the principle of nonintervention, the meaning of which in these days is so often perverted; as well as the loyalty with which they refuse to impose upon other states a rule, the violation of which, in respect to themselves, they will not allow. The federal government gives thus an example of justice and political propriety which must increase the esteem which our August Master has avowed toward the America nation. . . .

His Majesty, the Emperor, has been sensibly moved by the sentiments of confidence which the government of the United States places in his views and designs in regard to the general well-being of his Empire. Such manifestation must strengthen the bonds of mutual sympathy which unite the two countries and constitute a consummation which too much accords with the aspirations of the Emperor, His Majesty, not to look upon it with pleasure.

Clay, from the American Embassy in St. Petersburg, applauded the administration's stand on the Polish situation. "It was due from us to be grateful for the past conduct of Russia toward us in our trouble, by a like moral support of herself, in defense of the integrity of her Empire."

Some American citizens had urged Lincoln to accept Napoleon's invitation to join the protest to Russia, because it would benefit the Union cause by diverting attention from the Civil War. To them Clay replied indignantly: How could it help the United States to weaken "our steadfast friend"? For should Russia suffer defeat it would open the way for our common enemies "to fall upon us."[5]

In the meantime neither Russia nor the Western powers would back down on their views on the Polish issue. France, England and Austria contended it was an international question—in accordance with the terms of the Congress of Vienna. On the other hand, St. Petersburg insisted that it was a purely domestic uprising and that foreign interference could not be countenanced. It looked as if the dispute would inevitably lead to a general European war.

The grave possibility of having to defend the Russian view by arms caused the Czar real worry about his navy. During the Crimean War the Russian fleet was bottled up in the Baltic and Mediterranean Seas. The present navy was weak and no match for the combined sea power of Great Britain and France. If it remained in European waters it would be blocked in at Kronstadt and rendered useless. It was imperative that the fleet be extricated from this potential danger in the event of a new war which now appeared inevitable.

General-Adjutant N. Krabbe, who directed the imperial navy while the Grand Duke Constantine was serving as Viceroy in Warsaw, urged the Czar to order the vessels out to the open sea where they could not be bottled up. Secret arrangements were, therefore, made to send the Russian fleet away to the ice-free waters of the United States. From the safe American coasts the Russians would be in a favorable position for cruising against British commerce in the Atlantic and the Pacific, should war suddenly break out over the tempestuous Polish question.

A note was dispatched to Stoeckl in Washington, outlining the Russian strategy and instructing him to make ready for the arrival of the warships. To Rear Admiral Lisovski, in command of the Atlantic squadron, Krabbe sent these orders on July 26, 1863:

Direct your course with the whole squadron to the shores of the United States of North America, not putting in to any port on the way; and upon arrival in America, you will drop anchor in New York. If it appears possible according to local conditions to remain in this port with the entire squadron, then you will there await the outcome of the negotiations on the Polish question. If our Minister in Washington, with whom you will immediately establish communication upon your arrival in America, should find that the sojourn of the entire squadron in New York might give rise to difficulties with the federal government or to other unpleasantnesses, then it is permissible for you to divide the squadron into two or three parts, and to scatter it among those ports of the North American coast which will be recognized by you as the most advantageous for this purpose.

In advance of a declaration of war, it is left to you to determine, according to the consideration of the locality and the circumstances of the moment, whether it is possible or advisable to remain with the squadron in New York or other North American ports until the actual outbreak of military activities or, leaving the anchorage upon the supplementing of supplies, or at a time when a declaration of war is becoming unavoidable and near, to put to sea so that at a known rendezvous, which has been previously determined, you will receive information of the declaration of war by means of a ship chartered expressly for this purpose by Counselor of State Stoeckl. It is understood that it will be necessary to preserve this arrangement with the greatest secrecy; and the place of rendezvous must not be divulged to anyone, excepting our Minister.

Following these orders, Krabbe gave instructions to be observed in the event of the outbreak of war. "Commence hostile action against the commerce of the enemy. You will distribute these ships with such consideration that they occupy the most frequented lanes on which are directed the most important and most valuable tonnage."[6] The Russian commander was told further that "these instructions are made purposely general in order to give you a free hand to act according to your judgment and discretion."[7]

To Rear Admiral Popov, in command of the Russian Pacific squadron, Krabbe issued similar instructions. "On receipt of news concerning the outbreak of warlike activities" he was to direct his ships toward the vulnerable places of enemy power, and likewise for the inflicting of injuries on antagonists on lines of trade communication. In 5,000 words of instructions to Lisovski and Popov, there is not a word about helping the North, or about "sealed orders," or about turning over the fleet to Lincoln in case of foreign intervention in the American conflict.[8]

Admiral Popov selected San Francisco Harbor because he considered it the safest and most favorable base for action by his squadron. On August 3, Popov wrote to the Russian Minister of the Marine:

> I took such a decision because I do not have here any other information besides my own views, which tell me that our [Far Eastern] ports are unfavorable for the concentration, just as they do not represent any fortunate means either for provisioning the squadron or for the indispensable repairs. . . . The republics of Central and South America do not seem inclined to turn us out of their ports, although they are indeed swamped with Poles. [But] they, too, as in Mexico, do not hinder either the French or the English from spying on our squadron in their roadsteads. There remains, therefore, the United States of America which England and France have worried to the utmost by their recent interference.[9]

Senator Charles Sumner, Chairman of the U. S. Senate Committee on Foreign Affairs, wrote to John Bright on October 6, 1863:

> At this moment I am more solicitous about France and England than about our military affairs. . . . Foreign intervention will introduce a new, vast, and incalculable element; it would probably provoke a universal war. You will observe the hobnobbing at New York with the Russian Admiral. Why is that fleet gathered there? My theory is that when it left the Baltic, war with France was regarded as quite possible, and it was determined not to be sealed up at Kronstadt; if at New York, they could take the French expedition at Vera Cruz.[10]

Badly needing friends, the people of the United States readily interpreted the arrival of the Russian naval squadrons as special proof of Muscovy's friendship for the Union in its hour of need, feted the Czar's officers and sailors, toasted the Emperor and praised his government.

But it is highly significant that the Russians, too, were most profuse in their expressions of obligation and of thanks and acknowledgment of courtesies and favors received from the American government and people during their sojourn in the United States. Clay, in his dispatch of November 8, 1863, had written of the genuine gratitude which prevailed in St. Petersburg toward the United States and her people for the warm reception accorded the Russian fleet.

> The Russian reception in American waters is the subject of conversation in all circles; and the gentry and the common people seem alike to understand and feel the friendly demonstration made at this time, when France, England and Austria are attempting, under the pretense of national justice, to put them under the ban of Christendom for defending the integrity of their Empire.[11]

Upon the fleet's return to Russia, representatives of the Czar made an official call upon U. S. Minister Clay, and amid pomp and ceremony formally expressed the profound gratitude of the Emperor of All the Russias for the help and cooperation granted to his navy and the favors and kindnesses bestowed upon the officers and crews.

After Clay met the Emperor at Peterhof Palace, where he received the personal thanks of the Russian ruler, the American Minister wrote to Secretary Seward on August 22, 1864: "His Majesty told me that he had allowed his officers lately in the United States to call upon me *en masse* and express their gratitude for the courtesies extended them in America, all of which was evidently as a national compliment."

Why—if the Russian warships had actually sailed to the United States to serve the Union in a grave crisis—would the Czar's government have felt itself under such obligation to Lincoln's government? Had the cruise of the Russian fleet been in fact for American benefit, the United States would have been under extraordinary obligation to Russia, and would have called for Lincoln or Seward to make an official public acknowledgment of American gratitude and indebtedness. No such acknowledgment was ever made by Lincoln's administration.

Moreover, if the Russians had in truth come on a mission of naval cooperation in actual war, the deal would have been a matter of official record both in Washington and St. Petersburg. Diligent research among Russian and American archives has revealed no record of "sealed orders" or of any other overture offering the use of Russia's warships to Lincoln in the event of Anglo-French intervention.

John Bigelow, who succeeded William L. Dayton as Minister to France upon the former's death in 1864, has commented that "it was not surprising" there was no official documentary record. "Flirtations between governments as between the sexes, are not apt to be proclaimed from the housetops, nor even made matters of record."[12]

Was Lincoln deceived by the "sympathy of Muscovy," and "absurdly bamboozled by the Russian compliments," as English journals asserted? Henry Clews, the New York banker, who served as an agent of the United States government in the marketing of bonds to finance the Civil War, and who enjoyed the confidence of the administration, has written:

> William H. Seward, the Secretary of State . . . afterwards told me that, when he heard of their [the Russian fleet's] arrival in American waters, he invited them to accept the hospitalities of the port of New York. He, of course, foresaw that their coming here would, or at least might, have a good moral and political effect in our favor both at home and abroad by depressing the South and encouraging the North, and causing any foreign powers that might have been considering the advisability of recognizing the Southern Confederacy to postpone action under the impression that we had or might have, Russia for an ally.
>
> He was astute enough to see that this visit of the Russian squadron might seem to be what it was not, particularly to foreign eyes. Appearances, we all know, are sometimes deceptive, yet they sometimes assert great influence. The visit of this squadron was a case in point. It was a splendid "bluff" at a very critical period in our history.[13]

A contemporary cartoon in *Harper's Weekly* depicts "Dr. Lincoln" prescribing Russian salve for Napoleon and John Bull. On the wall of his shop is a sign reading, "Dr. Lincoln's Specific for Confederate Rash—Russian Salve." "Dr. Lincoln" is shown talking to Seward, "the smart boy of the shop," who is carrying a basket filled with the salve. Lincoln, pointing to Napoleon and John Bull, across the way, instructs delivery boy Seward: "Mild applications of Russian salve for our *friends* over the way, and heavy doses—and plenty of it—for our Southern patient."

Lincoln was not "bamboozled" by the "sympathy of Muscovy." He realized that the Czar was acting for Russia's own interests exclusively.

He knew that Russia's "actions towards us . . . were but moves made by her upon the chessboard of European diplomacy."[14] But notwithstanding the real motive of Russian friendship, Lincoln took full advantage of the fortuitous circumstance and used it astutely for the best interests of the Union cause. Seward utilized the "sympathy of Muscovy" as a "splendid bluff" that a Russo-American alliance existed, and Lincoln used it as a "salve" with which to dose the seceded States and their would-be allies. As Clews has put it:

> Russia was friendly to the United States of course, but this friendship between the two countries was very different from an offer, or a willingness to help us by armed intervention in our favor. Russia has never intimated that she had any such intentions; and, indeed, such intervention on her part would have been folly, as her navy was then very small after the destruction of the Crimean War, and would have been powerless against England and France.
>
> Gortchakov repeatedly said to our Minister that Russia greatly favored peace and wished for a speedy return; but would never take sides in the controversy between the North and the South.

Professor Frank A. Golder in 1915, and Professor E. A. Adamov a little later, discovered in the Russian archives in St. Petersburg the documents which prove beyond doubt that the Russian fleet had been sent to the United States not to aid the North but for its own safety in anticipation of an Anglo-French intervention in support of the Polish revolt, and to put the vessels in a position where they might prey upon enemy commerce in the event of war. As Golder summed it up,

> It was a most extraordinary situation. Russia had not in mind to help us but did render us distinct service; the United States was not conscious that it was contributing in any way to Russia's welfare and yet seems to have saved her from humiliation and perhaps war. There is probably nothing to compare with it in diplomatic history.[15]

11

Alexander the Liberator and Lincoln the Emancipator

Just one day before Abraham Lincoln took the oath of office as the sixteenth President of the United States and assured the South that he would take no provocative step against slavery where it already existed, Czar Alexander II by one stroke of his pen set more than 20,000,000 Russian serfs free.

This epochal act of freedom, like a distant lightning flash, graphically illuminated the tragic predicament of the United States. Not that Russian serfdom was the same as Negro slavery in America. The white serf in Russia, his blood identical with that of the noblest Muscovite families, occupied a position only slightly comparable to that of the Negro bondsman in the South. Russian serfdom at the time of its extirpation was without the repulsive features of ordinary slavery. Many serfs had been able to purchase the privilege of exemption from work for their masters for a moderate payment. There were prohibitions against the sale of serfs at public auctions or the separation of members of the same family. In addition, the arbitrary rule of the landlords was held in check by defining the punishments they could legally inflict upon their serfs. Although there naturally remained much abuse of power there was less flagrant cruelty than in the slave States of America. Unlike the American slave who was of African and savage origin and held by the

Supreme Court to be an "inferior being," the Russian serf was one with his master in race and his potential equal.

But though the systems of Russian serfdom and American Negro slavery differed, the striking of the shackles from the millions of serfs of the Czar's domain gave new courage and impetus to all who were striving to destroy the institution of human slavery in the United States.

While all enlightened nations of the world were moving in the direction of emancipation, the United States of America—the nation which Lincoln believed to have been "conceived in liberty and dedicated to the proposition that all men are created equal"—was falling to pieces because one large section was insisting on the permanence and, if need be, the extension of the slave system. Void of shame, Alexander Stephens, Vice President of the Southern Confederacy, said of the Constitution adopted by the Confederate States:

> The new Constitution has put at rest forever all the agitating questions relating to our peculiar institution, African slavery. This was the immediate cause of the late rupture and present revolution. The prevailing ideas entertained by Jefferson and most of the leading statesmen at the time of the old Constitution were that the enslavement of the African was wrong in principle, socially, morally and politically. Our new government is founded upon exactly the opposite ideas: its foundations are laid, its cornerstone rests, upon the great truth that the Negro is not the equal of the white man: that slavery—subordination to the white man—is his natural and normal condition. This, our new government, is the first in the history of the world based upon this great physical, philosophical and moral truth. The great objects of humanity are best attained when there is conformity to the Creator's laws and decrees.

Equally frank and shameless was the convention of the State of Mississippi. "Our position," declared these Southerners, "is thoroughly identified with slavery."

Such was the stand taken by the South at a time when the conscience of civilized man had become intolerant of involuntary servitude, with the result that slavery had already withered away on three continents. Slave trading within the British dominions had been abolished by the Act of 1807, and the example of Great Britain had been followed by the other European nations—France, Prussia, Austria and the Dutch. In addition, the last vestiges of slavery had died away in Latin America. And now Russia—where one-third of the whole population was enslaved—on March 3, 1861 by autocratic decree inflicted the deathblow to serfdom in the domain of the Czar.

No Russian law had ever enslaved the peasantry in the Czar's realm. At the beginning of the seventeenth century through a decree of Boris Godunov, the lord who owned the soil was granted control of the peasants upon it, just as he owned the immovable boulders and ledges. When Godunov later followed this decree with a vigorous fugitive-serf law, he created a permanent serf-caste bound to the soil.

Already in the days of Peter the Great serfdom was recognized as a vicious evil. Peter himself stormed forth in protestations and invectives against what he stigmatized as "selling men like beasts—separating parents from children, husbands from wives—which causes many tears to flow." He declared that this inhuman practice should be ameliorated. But, preoccupied with the building of St. Petersburg—where in draining the marshes, he sacrificed one hundred thousand men in one year— he did nothing to improve the condition of the serfs. Actually the situation worsened. Serfage became practically undistinguishable from slavery; and a few years later, in the reign of Empress Anne, bloomed fully into slavery by reason of her decree permitting nobles to sell serfs apart from the soil.

Catherine II aroused hope when she issued a decree prohibiting the enslavement of serfs. She also encouraged the study of serf emancipation. But when she became embroiled in the crushing of Poland, the effort to improve the condition of the serfs stopped. Instead, her nobles prevailed upon her to issue an edict ordering the peasants of Little Russia to remain forever on the estates where the day of publication of the decree should find them. Court favorites, given advance information of this edict, enticed peasants by the thousands onto their estates. This edict was then sprung. "In an hour the courtiers were made rich, the peasants were made serfs, and Catherine II was made infamous forever."[1]

Alexander I, roused by the wrongs of the serf system, seized a cross and swore upon it that serfage would be abolished. He submitted to the nobles of the land a plan of gradual emancipation whereby during a period of twelve to fourteen years a serf could pass from serfage to personal freedom with ownership of his cabin and the bit of land attached to it. But serf-owners thwarted the plan everywhere except in three provinces. Alexander I, bitterly discouraged, dropped further efforts.

During the thirty-year reign of Nicholas I no less than 556 serious outbreaks by restless serfs took place. Nicholas, who became the world's greatest apostle of downright despotism and the very incarnation of re-action against revolution or liberalism, winced as he saw how serfage was keeping Russia weak, sluggish and stagnant—a land of dissolute lords and abject serfs. He vowed to improve conditions. But, like all his predecessors, he became appalled by the magnitude of the task. He dreaded the grave and perhaps fatal disturbances to the social and eco-nomic life of Russia. In 1842 he issued a ukase creating a moderate in-novation. Halfheartedly he established by decree the class of "con-tracting peasants." Masters and serfs were empowered to enter into contracts—the serf receiving freedom, the master receiving payments in installments.

But the revolutions which overran Europe in 1848 filled Nicholas with fear of all innovations. The outbreak of the Crimean War in 1854 ended even his feeble efforts to modify the iniquitous serf system. At his death in 1855, he bequeathed to his son, Alexander II, not only the war but a nation in bondage.

The breakdown of Russia following her ignominious defeat in the Crimean War made a general recasting of institutions imperative. Agri-culture and the industries were languishing because of the lack of free labor. The most fundamental of needed reforms was the complete abo-lition of the institution of serfdom.

When Czar Alexander II succeeded to the throne of his father, there were over 47,000,000 serfs in Russia. Of these, nearly 25,000,000 were crown serfs who enjoyed a large degree of personal freedom. They exercised local self-government, and administered their own affairs in communes through councils and tribunals which they themselves chose. Moreover, they were not restricted in their right to acquire or dispose of property or to remove from the place of their birth.

But the other 22,000,000 serfs, the "disposition" of approximately 100,000 nobles, were hardly better than slaves.[2] This enormous mass of human beings, more than one-third of the population of Russia, was in a state of bondage. They could be bought and sold with the property on which they labored. They were human chattels which were part of the estate of their master. Of the 100,000 Russian serf-owners, one Count Scheremetiev possessed more than 300,000 souls. There were a few others also whose possessions were enormous. However, more than 41,000 of the landed gentry owned less than twenty-one male serfs. A proprietor who was the owner of less than 500 serfs was not considered very rich, and there were about 4,000 of these.

Czar Alexander II realized that a serious general uprising of the serfs was inevitable unless a radical solution could quickly be achieved. No moderate amelioration would do. It had to be complete liberation accompanied by a land settlement. But he realized that so radical a revolution was fraught with danger to the entire economic and political structure of Russia. Like his predecessors, Alexander II began by urging the nobles of the realm to take the initiative in solving the problem. It was better, he pleaded again and again, to abolish serfdom from above than to wait until it begins to abolish itself from below.

In March 1856 the determined young Emperor invited his "faithful nobility" to consider what steps were necessary to bring about emancipation. He himself proposed emancipation during a period of transition from serfage to freedom lasting twelve years. At the end of that time the serf was to be given his full freedom and ownership of his cabin with an adjoining piece of land for cultivation. He asked the ruling nobles to work out the details of a fair indemnity to themselves. Committees of emancipation were set up in many areas. But the nobles refused to cooperate and fought Alexander at every step. The Czar concluded that the critical situation would no longer permit temporizing. He decided to take matters into his own hands. By autocratic decree his predecessors had foisted serfdom upon the land. Now by autocratic decree the new Czar determined to abolish serfdom throughout his domain.

In February 1860 Alexander, in anticipation of granting general freedom, liberated the crown serfs. On March 3, 1861 he issued a manifesto setting all serfs of Russia free. By this action he raised 22,000,000 human chattels to the rank of free men. He had struggled long and in vain to work out satisfactory arrangements for gradual emancipation. Now he forced immediate emancipation upon the unwilling nobility. Detailed arrangements would have to be worked out afterwards.

The manifesto was read in all the churches. These were its fundamental principles: The serfs should at once receive the civil rights of the free rural classes, and the authority of the proprietor should be replaced by communal self-government. The rural communes should as far as possible retain the land they actually held, and should in return pay the proprietor certain yearly dues in money or labor. The government should by means of credit assist the communes to redeem these dues, or in other words to purchase the lands ceded to them. The domestic serfs should continue to serve their masters two years for wages and thereafter become completely free. But they would have no claim on the land.

Against the strong opposition of the majority of nobles, the reform was carried out by the autocratic sovereign in cooperation with a few enlightened bureaucrats. A change so radical was naturally accompanied by many local disturbances and much bloodshed. For three years a fierce struggle went on over the terms of emancipation. No one was completely satisfied. The peasantry was disappointed because they were compelled to pay dues on land which they believed to be their own by right. But liberation was ultimately achieved without civil war and without widespread violence.[3]

The removal of the shackles from the peasants of Russia heartened the antislavery leaders in the United States and gave impetus to their efforts to strike the fetters from the 4,000,000 Negroes held in slavery in the Southern States. They contended that now that despotic Russia had liberated her millions of serfs by "perhaps the greatest single legislative act in the history of the world," how could America, professing freedom and equality, justify her own moral position in the world? So long as the barbaric institution with its odious conception of human property remained the law of the land, America, they contended, would be stigmatized with a foul blot that would enable Europe to point the finger of scorn at her professions of liberty.

From the very outset of Lincoln's administration, impatient abolitionists importuned him to bring about the immediate destruction of slavery by emancipation. Lincoln hated slavery with every fiber of his being; he fervently wished that all men everywhere might be free; he had been the outspoken antagonist of the slave power. While serving in Congress, he had introduced a bill to abolish slavery in the District of Columbia. It provided for gradual emancipation with compensation to the owners. The bill was buried in committee.

But despite his personal inclinations as a citizen, now as the President of the nation with powers and duties prescribed by a fixed Constitution whose provisions he had sworn to obey, his personal feelings had to be sacrificed to his sworn obligation. It was his duty to uphold the Union and the laws. The barbaric institution of slavery was a part of the law of the land countenanced by the Constitution and sanctioned by the courts. It had existed even before the Constitution itself and had been accepted by the creators of that great instrument as an unavoidable evil. Congress, he believed, had no right to interfere with slavery in the States where it existed. As a lawyer and constitutionalist he took the stand that slavery could be abolished only through means compatible with the Constitution.

He believed that the abolitionists' rash disregard of the constitutional rights of the slave States tended only to drive more States out of the Union and make the disruption permanent. Slavery, he concluded, could be abolished only by saving the Union. For it was clear to him that if the Confederate States—whose government "rests upon the great truth that . . . slavery—subordination to the white man—is his [the Negro's] natural and normal condition"—were victorious in the war—abolition would be impossible.

So with all his sympathy for the downtrodden slave, with all his opposition to the extension of slavery, he took the anomalous position of supporting, defending, and preserving the Constitution, which forbade interference with that institution. His task was to save the Union—with or without slavery. To this end he devoted his energies to hold the border States. To this end he repudiated the orders of military emancipation by General Frémont commanding in Missouri, and General Hunter commanding in South Carolina.

Yet while professing these policies he earnestly pressed his plan of compensated emancipation upon the loyal slave States. He pointed out that the cost of freeing the estimated 430,000 slaves in the border States of Kentucky, Missouri, Delaware and Maryland, was about $120,000,-000—the cost of carrying on the war for two months. And although Congress adopted Lincoln's recommendation the border States refused to take a single step toward emancipation.

However, in April 1862, Congress did abolish slavery in the District of Columbia, and, as compensation, paid the owners three hundred dollars for each liberated slave. Stoeckl, reporting to Prince Gortchakov about this event, wrote that

> abolishing slavery in the District of Columbia . . . will not be a heavy burden on the treasury because out of a population of 10,-000 Negroes, there are hardly 2,000 slaves in Washington and environs. This emancipation should have been completed a long

time ago. It was demanded by the dignity of the republic as much as by considerations of humanity.[4]

But impatient abolitionists accused Lincoln of temporizing with the slavery question. They refused to accept his theory that the supremacy of the Constitution and the preservation of the Union were the only and the paramount issues. They demanded the immediate emancipation of the slaves. Those who had been Lincoln's friends and supporters now criticized and censured him with the vehemence of his bitterest enemies. These radical abolitionists—many of whom even welcomed disunion because the Union sanctioned slavery—attributed the President's failure to liberate the slaves immediately by a military edict to his weakness and unsteadiness of purpose.

On August 20, 1862 Horace Greeley, in an editorial entitled *The Prayer of Twenty Millions*, bitterly attacked the President for failing to take immediate steps for abolishing slavery by some sweeping proclamation of emancipation. With all the humility of a private citizen, the President who had acquired a power that never before had been wielded by a ruler of this nation, forgot the might and dignity of his office and penned a reply to Greeley.

It was a reiteration of his whole creed, so far as emancipation and the preservation of the Union were concerned. His personal wish, he declared, was that all men everywhere could be free. But now his paramount object in this struggle was to save the Union, and not either to save or destroy slavery.

> As to the policy I "seem to be pursuing," as you say, I have not meant to leave anyone in doubt. I would save the Union. I would save it the shortest way under the Constitution. The sooner the national authority can be restored, the nearer the Union will be "the Union as it was." If there be those who would not save the Union unless they could at the same time save slavery, I do not agree with them. If there be those who would not save the Union unless they could at the same time destroy slavery, I do not agree with them. My paramount object in this struggle is to save the Union, and is not either to save or destroy slavery. If I could save the Union without freeing any slave, I would do it; and if I could save it by freeing all the slaves, I would do it; and if I could save it by freeing some and leaving others alone, I would also do that. What I do about slavery and the colored race, I do because I be-

lieve it helps to save the Union; and what I forbear, I forbear because I do not believe it would help save the Union."5

Though President Lincoln subordinated the question of the overthrow of slavery to the paramount issue of saving the Union, eventual emancipation never for a moment left his mind. He knew that beneath the preservation of the Union, was the preservation of the democratic way of life. As he said, "slavery must die that the Union might live." For how could the republic keep its integrity and shelter it while the iniquitous institution of slavery was sanctioned by the supreme law of the land?

Through all those soul-torturing struggles of the first two years he was reading the signs of the times, calmly waiting, patiently waiting, for the propitious moment when circumstances would permit the fulfilment of his devout wish that all men everywhere might be free. Bravely he bore the criticism of impatient friends and the hostility and calumny of open and avowed enemies. He had registered an oath in heaven to preserve, protect, and defend the Constitution. The rights of the individual States in regard to their slave property must remain inviolate until the safety of the Union demanded their forfeiture in favor of the higher obligation. He alone was to be the judge of when that exigency had arrived. His alone was to be the awful responsibility.

He waited until slavery's extinction became an imperative duty—until further temporizing would prove disastrous to the cause of the Union. Convinced that the propitious moment was at hand, without further hesitation, without consultation, simply, undramatically, he struck the deathblow to slavery.

Unknown to Greeley when he published his famous *Prayer* on August 20, was the fact that a month earlier, on July 22, Lincoln had secretly called his Cabinet into session and informed them that he had drafted an Emancipation Proclamation, declaring free the slaves in all the States still in rebellion on the first of January ensuing but commending once more to the loyal slave States his plan of compensated abolition. He told his surprised ministers that he did not require their opinions as to the competence of the edict. He had already made the irrevocable decision himself. He assured them that his mind was clear and set. But Secretary Seward spoke up to question "the expediency of its issue at this juncture." The Secretary of State believed "the depression of the public mind, following upon recent reverses, might make it viewed as the last measure, a cry for help—the government stretching forth its hands to Ethiopia, instead of Ethiopia stretching forth her hands to the government." Accordingly he advised deferring its issue until supported by some military success.

The President regarded this view as sound counsel. So he put the document away, waiting for a victory on the battlefield. The Emancipation Proclamation already lay in a drawer of Lincoln's desk when Greeley penned his famous editorial reproaching the President for his apparent failure to do something about abolishing slavery.

On September 22, 1862, five days after the battle of Antietam, Lincoln again summoned the Cabinet. "I made a solemn vow before God, that if General Lee was driven back from Pennsylvania, I would crown the result by a declaration of freedom to the slaves," he told Secretary Chase. The battle of Antietam, though not a great victory, was a distinct gain for the Union since it stopped Lee's invasion of the North for the time being.

"I think the time for acting has now come," Lincoln told his ministers, "and I have got you together to hear what I have written down." Calmly and solemnly he read his death warrant for slavery:

I, Abraham Lincoln, President of the United States of America, do proclaim that on the first day of January 1863, all persons held as slaves within any State, or designated part of a State, the people whereof shall then be in rebellion against the United States, shall then be, thenceforth and forever, free; and the executive government of the United States, including the military and naval authorities thereof, will recognize and maintain the freedom of such persons, and will do no act, or acts, to repress such persons, or any of them, in any efforts they make for their actual freedom.

Upon this momentous and most beneficent military decree of history, and by Lincoln "believed to be an act of justice, warranted by the Constitution," he invoked "the considerate judgment of mankind and the gracious favour of Almighty God."

The Confederacy treated Lincoln's Proclamation as an idle threat. On New Year's Day of 1863, none of the rebellious States having returned, the Emancipation Proclamation went into full force and effect. Automatically, all slaves within the territory then held by the Confederate armies were declared thenceforth and forever free.

The Proclamation did not completely abolish slavery. It was made applicable only to those States or part of States in open rebellion. But with its pronouncement "that the executive government of the United States, including the military and naval authorities thereof, will recognize and maintain the freedom of such persons," the mortal blow to the hated institution, as events proved, had been inflicted, and its absolute extinction through the length and breadth of the land became only a matter of time.

The Emancipation Proclamation, which takes rank with the Declaration of Independence as the second great charter of American freedom, was a military measure—an act of war based on imperative necessity and deemed helpful in a military way to the Union cause. For Lincoln concluded that to strike at slavery was to strike at the very heart of Southern military strength. By virtue of his power as Commander in Chief of the army and navy in time of actual armed rebellion against the authority of the government, and as a fit and necessary war measure for suppressing said rebellion, Lincoln justified his act. It had no sanction as a constitutional provision. Congress had not approved it as a statute and no court had pronounced it as a binding rule of law.

In normal times he was convinced that the President could not interfere with slavery in the States, nor had he legal power to liberate a single slave. But now, with the nation engaged in a life-and-death struggle with public enemies, he was just as convinced that his wartime powers authorized him to use against the rebels every expedient countenanced by public law. Among these powers was the confiscation of the enemy's slaves.

He was frank to admit the legal weakness of the Proclamation and its insufficiency as a permanent means of destroying slavery. But it was a step in the right direction from which he would never retreat. He was determined never to retract or modify this edict. Not one slave liberated under its provisions must ever be returned to bondage. "If the people should, by whatever mode or means, make it an executive duty to re-enslave such persons, another and not I must be their instrument to perform it," he declared.

If the Emancipation Proclamation, as a permanent and universal remedy for the evil, was futile, then the next step was to change the Constitution itself to confer upon Congress express power to enlarge the field of personal liberty and restore to the four million human beings the God-given right of freedom so long denied them. This could be accomplished by confirming President Lincoln's beneficent edict of freedom by embodying the Emancipation Proclamation in the organic law of the land by constitutional amendment. The Proclamation had at least theoretically destroyed slavery in the rebellious States. Now it remained for a constitutional amendment to make its effects practical and permanent, not only in those regions but also in States not included in the Proclamation. Such an amendment would not only destroy the legal existence of the cursed institution, but would forever prohibit its re-establishment. In urging the immediate passage of a proposed constitutional amendment, the President said:

> A question might be raised as to whether the Proclamation was legally valid. It might be added that it aided only those who came into our lines, and that it was inoperative as to those who did not give themselves up; or that it would have no effect upon the children of the slaves born hereafter; in fact, it could be urged that it did not meet the evil. But this amendment is a king's cure for all evils. It winds the whole thing up.

In 1864 a measure to submit a constitutional amendment abolishing slavery came before the Thirty-Eighth Congress. Lincoln's friend from Illinois, Senator Trumbull, reported the Thirteenth Amendment from the Committee on the Judiciary and led the fight in its behalf in the Senate. "This amendment adopted," he declared, "not only does slavery cease, but it can never be re-established by State authority, or in any other way than by again amending the Constitution." By a large majority it was approved by the Senate; but in the House the necessary two-thirds vote could not be obtained.

However, when Congress reconvened after Lincoln's re-election, the President in his Message pointed out that the victory of his party clearly demonstrated that it was the will of the majority that the amendment be ratified. Therefore, "May we not agree that the sooner the better?"

On January 6, 1865 debate on the question was reopened. Powerful, eloquent, and elaborate speeches covering both sides of the proposition were made. On the last day of January a vote was finally reached, the roll call proceeded, and amid the deepest excitement, enthusiasm, and fervid rejoicing the Speaker of the House declared the amendment approved.

To a body of citizens who marched to the Executive Mansion the night following the passage of the measure, to congratulate the President, Lincoln in his characteristic homely fashion declared the "great job" was completed. "The occasion," he said, "is one of congratulation to the country, and to the whole world. But there is yet a task before us—to go forward and have consummated by the votes of the States that which Congress so nobly began yesterday." The necessary ratification by twenty-seven of the thirty-six States was not to be accomplished until December 18, 1865, months after the madman's bullet had taken Lincoln's life. But the "great job" was virtually finished. His cherished hope that all men, everywhere, might be free would soon be made good by law. The Thirteenth Amendment reduced to law, as it were, Lincoln's life and creed.

Alexander the Liberator and Lincoln the Emancipator were the subjects of the toasts proposed at the reception given in Kronstadt in honor of U.S. Minister Clay by the officers of the Russian fleet which had returned from its memorable visit to American ports. Rear Admiral Lisovski in proposing his toast to the President of the United States, said that he paid tribute to "a name, which the possessor has already rendered immortal by the exercise of high moral courage in opposition to erroneous popular prejudice, and by the practice of a sublime humanity in the emancipation of the slave." Clay responded with a toast to the Emperor as "Alexander, not Emperor but Liberator," whose deeds belong not to "Russia but to the world." Jubilantly, Lincoln's Minister declared Emancipation to be "a new bond of union with Russia."

12

The Czar Criticizes Lincoln's Proclamation

EMANCIPATION changed the course of the Civil War. Thenceforth the cause of liberty was to be bound up with the cause of the Union.

In his own heart Lincoln was confident that his Proclamation "will commend itself to the enlightened judgment and moral approbation of not only all Christian states but of mankind." The world could now see that the American conflict was no simple political rebellion, but a battle between slavery and freedom. It was now a war dedicated by Lincoln to the destruction of human bondage—a crusade for liberty. With the injection of this great moral issue, the Union's friends in Europe could now uphold Lincoln's hand with zeal and courage.

The result was a turning point in America's foreign relations. The danger of intervention by European powers began to vanish. From London, Henry Adams wrote, "The Emancipation Proclamation has done more for us here than all our former victories and all our diplomacy. It is creating an almost convulsive reaction in our favor all over this country." This despite the fact that Earl Russell, Britain's Foreign Minister, did not like Lincoln's edict of freedom. He declared it left him puzzled as to what the President was trying to do. To Lord Lyons, in Washington, he wrote:

> The Proclamation *professes* to emancipate all slaves in places where the United States authorities cannot exercise any jurisdic-

180

tion nor make emancipation a reality; but it does not *decree* emancipation of slaves in any States or parts of States occupied by federal troops. . . . There seems to be no declaration of a principle adverse to slavery in this Proclamation. It is a measure of war of a very questionable kind. As President Lincoln has twice appealed to the judgment of mankind, in his Proclamation, I venture to say I do not think it can or ought to satisfy the friends of abolition, who look for total and impartial freedom for the slave, and not for vengeance on the slave owner.

But with the promulgation of the Emancipation Proclamation it became clear that government heads of Great Britain would find it less easy to interfere with the United States or lend aid to the South. The England of Wilberforce, a nation that had taken the lead in the world movement for ending slavery and which for decades had been holding America up to scorn for supporting this barbaric institution, could hardly be expected to support a rebellion being fought for the perpetuation of slavery. And any Cabinet that took sides openly with the effort to perpetuate human bondage would not have remained in power twenty-four hours.

From St. Petersburg, U.S. Minister Cameron wrote: "Now the constitutional nations which have hitherto regarded the friendship which exists between Russia and the United States as wanting a foundation in common principles and sentiments, must, hereafter, admit that this relation is as natural as it is auspicious to both countries in its results."

Bayard Taylor sent an article from the *St. Petersburg Journal* which praised the Proclamation as just and sagacious. It expressed confidence in Lincoln's opinion that it would never produce a "servile insurrection" as the South feared. Taylor stated that in a conversation on American affairs at an imperial ball the Emancipation Proclamation was characterized as the equivalent of many battles by Emperor Alexander II.

"Friends of America" in France were wildly enthusiastic in their approval of Lincoln's act. Their message to him stated: "We declare that we have never hoped nor wished for a more steady, rapid and resolute progress. We have understood the difficulties which surrounded Mr. Lincoln. We have honored his scruples of conscience with regard to the Constitution of his country which stopped his path. We have admired the courageous good sense with which he moved straight on, the instant he could do so, without danger to his cause or violation of the law."

The fighting Italian patriot, Giuseppe Garibaldi, who had expressed a desire for a federal army command—providing the war would be fought for emancipation of the slaves—rejoiced over the Proclamation. "Let free men religiously keep sacred the day of the fall of slavery," he declared. "Prosperity to you, Abraham Lincoln, pilot of liberty; hail to all you who for two years have fought and died around her regenerating banner; weal to you, redeemed sons of Ham—the free men of Italy kiss the glorious marks of your chains."

Garibaldi's followers, the republican liberals of Italy whose red shirts had become symbols of freedom, added their lavish praise in these exuberant phrases: "If in the midst of your titanic battles, our voice can yet reach you, let us, O Lincoln, free sons of Columbus, send you a word of good wishes and admiration for the great work that you have begun. Heir of the aspirations of Christ and of John Brown, you will pass to posterity with the name of the Emancipator, more enviable than any crown or any human treasure."

It was clear that the emancipation of the slaves would thenceforth be regarded as the crowning act of Lincoln's eventful career—the act with which his fame would most indissolubly be linked.

But in Washington, Stoeckl expressed deep regret that the Emancipation Proclamation had been issued. In a conference with Seward, the Russian Minister told Lincoln's Secretary of State that he regarded the Proclamation "as but a futile menace," because "it set up a further barrier to the reconciliation of the North and South—always the hope of Russia."[1]

In a lengthy report to St. Petersburg shortly after Lincoln issued the preliminary Proclamation, Stoeckl charged that radical Republican leaders had forced Lincoln into this extreme measure in a desperate effort to maintain their waning political powers. "Their program called for immediate and unconditional emancipation; the arming of the slaves against their masters; the confiscation of all property belonging to the insurgents; and finally the inauguration in the North of a reign of terror to silence the protests of the timid conservatives."

Stoeckl described Lincoln as vacillating and resorting to half measures because "he does not dare to go along" with the radicals, nor does he possess the courage to break with them:

He signed the confiscation bill. He authorized wholesale arrests in the North and even suspended the writ of habeas corpus. But he would not consent to their demands for placing the entire country under martial law. These half measures fail to satisfy the radicals. So they attack the administration, oppose the President in Congress, and climax it all by conspiring openly against him.

Some twenty prominent political leaders of New York have organized a permanent committee to prosecute the war in accordance with their program. Without legal authority this committee undertook to arm 50,000 men under the command of General Frémont, one of the extremists of the radical party who, after his disastrous campaign in Virginia, left the active service. The chairman of the committee wrote to President Lincoln to demand his approval of the committee, declaring that if this authorization were refused they would nevertheless put their plan into operation. Governor Morgan of New York State had already sanctioned it. The President replied that such a step was illegal and that Governor Morgan, a Republican, would not dare to assume the responsibility for this drastic act.

Another committee organized in the same manner in the West sent a deputation here to ask the President that he give to Governor Morton of Illinois, an ultra-radical, the chief command of affairs of war in the West, and delegate to him in this part of the Union all of the powers which the Constitution invested in the Chief Executive of the Republic. The conference between the deputation and the President, who naturally refused the request, was a stormy one. Mr. Lincoln having said to one of the delegates that Providence had betrayed the cause of the Union, the latter answered, "It is the administration that has betrayed the people, and you will be held accountable." I have been told on good authority that this deputation demanded the President's resignation.

All these committees are affiliated with one another and work hand in hand. They have skilfully employed the nation's press to spread their doctrines and attacks upon the government. Their newspapers have attributed the recent defeats of the federal army to the weakness and incompetence of the government. They have maintained that the generals placed in command of the army, and McClellan in particular, were too weak to meet the exigencies of the moment and that the country could not be saved except by replacing them with more aggressive men, that is to say, radicals. Some meddlers have gone still further in that they have threatened Mr. Lincoln with political destruction if he didn't openly accept the dictates imposed by the radicals.

The President, intimidated by these intrigues and violent attacks, decided to publish the Proclamation emancipating the slaves in all States which by January 1, 1863 have not returned to the Union. This Proclamation settles the question only halfway; slavery will continue to exist in the States which recognize the Union, like Maryland, or in those which return to the Union before the end of the year. Slavery would not be abolished except in the States which at that time still remain in rebellion, and where the decrees of the President could not be executed.

According to this act, the protection of the government is offered as a premium to the owners of slaves who will remain faithful to the Union flag, and emancipation is not accorded to Negroes except as a punishment imposed upon their masters. In brief, emancipation is used by President Lincoln as a military weapon to subdue his enemies and is not at all a proclamation of human liberty.

Whatever it may be, the President's act is untimely and unwise. The course which Mr. Lincoln should have taken in the present difficulty was to have complied with the will of the people, the vast majority of whom are conservative, and who while desiring emancipation, want to achieve it in such a manner as to avert a servile war. Several well-intentioned leaders have counseled the President to take this step. Unfortunately, he adopted an entirely different course of action and yielded to the radicals who today are the masters of the situation. They will not stop with the recent Proclamation. They will demand the dismissal of all Cabinet officers and all army commanders who do not share their radical views. Mr. Lincoln will be forced to submit to all their wishes, even to his own abdication, for which the radicals have already formulated secret schemes.

Yesterday I conferred with the Secretary of State about the

President's Proclamation. He did not want to commit himself on this act. He said only, "It is a *coup d'état*; let us see what results it will produce." He did not express his usual confidence. His influence on the President has diminished, but he still exercises enough power to give offense to the radicals who will spare no effort to have him ousted. Mr. Seward can well become the victim of the edict at the bottom of which he affixed his signature.

We are thus threatened by a revolutionary anarchy, the consequences of which will be even more disastrous than the Civil War itself.

A new proclamation issued by the President suspends the writ of habeas corpus and establishes martial law in the entire United States. It is a new concession wrung from Mr. Lincoln by the radicals.[2]

Throughout the Civil War, Stoeckl persisted in his belief that the Emancipation Proclamation was but a futile gesture. And what was worse, he declared, was the continuous grave prospect of inciting servile war in the South. If only the Proclamation had been made universal in its application, then he would have regarded it as "a great triumph for the principle of universal freedom."

Perhaps the glaring failures of the liberation of the Russian serfs caused Stoeckl to continue reporting about the weaknesses of American emancipation. Misery loves company, so Stoeckl believed that reports of Lincoln's troubles with a kindred problem might prove comforting to the Czar Liberator.

The Russian Emperor's edict had satisfied neither peasants nor gentry. On the contrary it had aroused murderous animosity among both classes. Indeed, the Czar's ukase had granted a bare freedom in which the lot of the liberated peasants did not at once seem improved. True, no man was now the property of any other man. But the masses of redeemed serfs were to remain for decades in a state of abject poverty and economic thralldom.

Andrew Dickson White, the first president of Cornell University, who lived in Russia, first as Secretary in the U. S. legation in St. Petersburg in 1855, and from 1892-94 as Minister Plenipotentiary, has written:

> I do not deny the greatness and nobleness of Alexander II and the services of the men he then called to his aid; but I lived in Russia both before and since that reform and feel obliged to testify that,

thus far, its main purpose has been so thwarted by reactionaries that there is, as yet, little, if any, practical difference between the condition of the Russian peasant before and since obtaining his freedom.[3]

Stoeckl reported to the Czar that the situation of the freed Negro slaves of the United States was even worse than that of the freed serfs.

He wrote about the establishment of a Freedmen's Bureau as a branch of the War Department in March 1865, shortly before Lincoln's death. Its purpose was the general supervision of the liberated slaves. It was to act as their advisor in respect to their new status in society, and to look after their rights in the courts and elsewhere.

But within a few months, Stoeckl was also able to report that the Southern legislatures were already passing stringent laws—"black codes"—for the regulation of the freed black men. Not that he criticized these laws. Their manifest purport was to keep the Negro subservient and inferior to the whites. He could sympathize with the white people of the South in whose midst millions of blacks were suddenly turned loose; and he could understand their perplexity as they undertook to deal with these illiterate ex-slaves, most of whom had not the slightest conception of what it was all about.

The misery which the whole South was to experience during the tragic era of reconstruction was the unavoidable consequence of a revolution so radical. A massive old oak like slavery could not be uprooted without causing tremendous upheaval to the entire surrounding terrain.

But the Czar, reading such reports on American conditions as Stoeckl dispatched to the Russian Foreign Office in St. Petersburg, asserted "the time must come when many will question the manner of American emancipation of the Negro slaves in 1863." He boasted that he did far more for the Russian serfs than America did for the slaves emancipated by President Lincoln. Czar Alexander II made this claim to Wharton Barker, a Pennsylvania banker who was serving as the financial agent in the United States of the Russian government. For his services on behalf of Russia, Mr. Barker was made a Knight of St. Stanislaus by the Czar.

In August 1879 the American financier was the guest of Grand Duke Constantine, the Czar's younger brother, at his palace in St. Petersburg. He had made the trip to Russia at the request of the Grand Duke and some of the Czar's Ministers to advise them regarding several large and important railroad, coal, iron and steel enterprises about to be launched in southern Russia. Mr. Barker has written that he was about to take his leave upon the completion of the conference when the Grand Duke bade him to remain as the Czar was expected at the palace, and he had expressed a desire to speak with his American banker.

"The Emperor is coming," Grand Duke Constantine said. "He wishes to talk with you in a somewhat informal way—a way in which he could not talk if you were presented to him at a formal audience by the United States Minister." In Mr. Barker's words:

> The Grand Duke left me at the window and went to meet his brother at the doorstep. With no escort of servants, no bodyguard of armed men, the Emperor, mounted on a brown horse, came into the yard. . . . He was followed by a one-horse phaeton, in which were two ladies—the Empress of Russia and the Queen of Greece, daughters of the Grand Duke Constantine. There was no pomp, no display—nothing to mark the distinction of the little party of great people who had driven through the park that summer morning. . . .
>
> On his entering, I was presented without any formality or delay to the Emperor by the Grand Duke, as "Mr. Barker, Your Majesty's American banker."
>
> The Emperor's first remark was incisively inquiring: "Mr. Barker, is your American system of banking, in your judgment, adapted to meet the needs of Russia?"
>
> There was then for a few minutes a general talk on economic and financial questions that satisfied me the Emperor had been a student of those questions that pressed upon his own country and upon other countries as well.
>
> He spoke of the liberation of his serfs; of his efforts to educate them; of how and why those efforts had largely failed. He referred with earnestness to the conditions he met in the course of discussions with the landowners; of how he went through the provinces, appealing to the conciliation spirit and the devotion of his nobility, reprimanding those who hung back, reminding them that reforms come better from above than from below. He even disclosed frankly the manner in which he had packed the Imperial Commission with men devoted to the principles of emancipation. The

commission declared for the immediate abolition of serfdom and urged the most effectual measures to prevent the re-establishment of the seignorial authority under other forms; and it decided, also, that the peasant should become a proprietor on the payment of an indemnity.

It is important to remember that the manifesto of March 3 1861 declared these fundamental principles. The peasants were to be invested with all the rights of free cultivators of the soil. In consideration of certain quit rents, they were to obtain full enjoyment of their inclosures and also a quantity of arable land. More than nine acres of land were given to every male peasant. The government made loans so that the peasants could immediately liberate themselves from their lords, yet remain debtors to the state. More than one-half the land was thus taken from the lord and given to the peasant.

After fully discussing what he had achieved for his serfs, the Czar, according to Mr. Barker, declared "in earnest, aggressive, but sad tones":

> I did more for the Russian serf in giving him land as well as personal liberty, than America did for the Negro slave set free by the Proclamation of President Lincoln. I am at a loss to understand how you Americans could have been so blind as to leave the Negro slave without tools to work out his salvation. In giving him personal liberty, you gave him an obligation to perform to the state which he must be unable to fulfill. Without property of any kind he cannot educate himself and his children. I believe the time must come when many will question the manner of American emancipation of the Negro slaves in 1863. The vote, in the hands of the ignorant men, without either property or self-respect, will be used to the damage of the people at large; for the rich man, without honor or any kind of patriotism, will purchase it, and with it swamp the rights of a free people.[4]

Mr. Barker, who became the presidential nominee of the Anti-Fusion Populists in the election of 1900, concluded:

> The hopes and dreams of the Emperor Alexander, and of the great men who helped him free the Russian serfs, and the hopes and expectations of Lincoln, Garrison and the thousands of Amer-

icans who gave their lives and fortunes to the cause of Negro emancipation, have not been realized. But the fears of Alexander have been realized. The Emperor was right in thinking the solution of the Negro slave question would debauch our people and bring serious trouble to America.[5]

"Lincoln's War"

John Hay, writing to Nicolay in August 1863, said of Lincoln: "The Tycoon is in fine whack. I have rarely seen him more serene and busy. He is managing this war, the draft, foreign relations and planning reconstruction of the Union all at once. I never knew with what a tyrannous authority he runs the Cabinet till now. The most important things he decides and there is no cavil."[1]

The Civil War had in truth become "Lincoln's war." The history of the Union after the assault upon Fort Sumter had virtually become one with the history of Abraham Lincoln himself. He had become the personification of the Union's struggles, aspirations and hopes. Lincoln's unique personality and the trend of national history had become inextricably interwoven. The slow shifting political aim from rescuing the Union to the abolition of slavery was his decision alone. He took all the strings of the government into his own hands—making political appointments, creating armies, selecting generals, making historic decisions. He was everywhere. He personally wrote to the Governors of the States to supply more and more troops. He visited the battlefields. He participated in war councils. He interviewed subordinate military leaders as well as chiefs. He toned down Secretary Seward's irritating diplomatic notes. Seward wrote to his wife: "There is but one vote in the Cabinet and that is cast by the President . . ." Everything that happened and everything that did not happen for the moment depended on

Lincoln's judgment. When things went right the credit was his. When things went wrong he bore the blame.

But of all this Stoeckl seemed unaware, although as the representative of the most friendly foreign power he was accorded opportunities for information which no other members of the foreign diplomatic corps in Washington received. On June 19, 1862 the *London Times* complained editorially about "the partiality in favor of the Russian ambassador at Washington."

Stoeckl was able to walk into Seward's office almost at will. He conferred with President Lincoln frequently. He offered suggestions to General Scott. He met and talked to General McClellan and other commanders about military strategy. He asked Secretary of War Cameron about the numerical strength of the federal armies, and did not hesitate to dispute Cameron's figure as "an exaggeration." He obtained information about Union army enlistments from General Halleck, while he was Commander in Chief. Even Secretary of War Stanton took the Russian envoy into his confidence on occasion. He obtained plans of battles, fought and to be fought. He procured the designs and blueprints of the ironclad *Monitor* and sent them to St. Petersburg. He reported on secret maneuvers of federal troops and inferred that he knew more about the Confederate armies than Lincoln did. He saw, heard and reported on everything.

Although Stoeckl's dispatches were frequent, detailed and voluminous, he seldom mentioned President Lincoln in them. On occasion he would write: "Lincoln himself told me," or "Today I saw the President." But there were months at a stretch when Lincoln was not even mentioned and, so far as the Russian Minister was concerned, was of no importance to the events he chronicled. From the infrequent reference to Lincoln, the Czar and Prince Gortchakov, reading Stoeckl's dispatches, could conclude that Lincoln was playing but an insignificant role in the epoch-making drama which was then convulsing the American continent.

Stoeckl persisted in his belief that the North could never subjugate the South. The Union, he felt, could not endure. He was sure it was divided forever. "In my opinion, the permanent separation of the North and South will be the inevitable consequence of the American crisis. It is difficult to witness events without being convinced that a return to the old system is impossible."

A born aristocrat, Stoeckl blamed the plight and tragedy in which the nation found itself on the "ultra-democratic system." He pointed out that "only a handful of demagogues were able to accomplish this work of destruction." He never ceased deploring the "rule of the mob." This tragic "result of democracy" should be a warning to Europe, he declared.[2]

"I regret to say it," he wrote on another occasion, "separation is inevitable. As sad as this necessity may be, the North will be compelled to submit to it." He hoped the North would accept the inevitable and seek co-operation with the South. The sooner the bloodshed could be ended the better for all concerned. He never overlooked an opportunity to offer his services as conciliator.[3]

After the federal forces commanded by General Grant had won notable successes at Fort Henry, Fort Donelson and Nashville early in 1862, Stoeckl asked Seward "if it was not time now that the national pride of the North was sufficiently satisfied to have recourse to means of conciliation to bring about peace. He replied that nothing would please him more, but the feelings were still too bitter even to think about conciliation at the present time."[4]

While Admiral David Glasgow Farragut was successfully conducting a momentous naval campaign to open the Mississippi from the mouth, capturing New Orleans, Baton Rouge and Natchez, the Confederate ironclad, the *Merrimac*, was inflicting terrible damage upon ships of the North in Chesapeake Bay. Covered with heavy armor made by joining railroad rails together, the *Merrimac* attacked a federal squadron in Hampton Roads. She rammed the *Cumberland* and sank her, fired the *Congress* and forced her crew to surrender, and ran the *Minnesota* and other vessels into shallow waters. The *Merrimac* resumed her destruction of the federal fleet early on the following morning. It was feared that this strange sea monster would soon be bombarding Washington, and might even sail to Philadelphia and New York. But during the night an even stranger craft had entered the scene of conflict. The *Monitor*, built by John Ericsson, and looking like an ironclad cheesebox on a raft, sighted the *Merrimac* and immediately engaged her in battle. Ericsson had equipped the "Yankee Cheesebox" with a revolving gun turret which gave her a greater range of action than any warship hitherto built. The shot and shell poured by the *Merrimac* against the *Monitor's* turret and deck inflicted but slight damage. After a battle of several hours the *Monitor* withdrew to shallow water and the *Merrimac* returned to Norfolk to repair her own injuries, her victorious career at an end.

Excitedly, Stoeckl reported the exploits of these ironclads which had revolutionized naval warfare:

> I regret that no Russian naval officer was present to study the battle. It marks an epoch in naval history because it is the first serious engagement between armor-plated vessels. The battle shows beyond a doubt the superiority of armor-plated ships over wooden ones. . . . These floating batteries have given new impetus to the American inventive genius.

Stoeckl hurried to the United States Navy Department to see what he could find out about the construction of the *Monitor*. He requested Assistant Navy Secretary Gustavus Vasa Fox to furnish the Russian government with detailed plans and specifications. Fox replied "this ironclad was not constructed by the government but by private interests under the direction of John Ericsson, an engineer, who alone possesses the plans." Ericsson was contacted, and he promised to furnish the designs of his invention to Russia's Minister. Stoeckl hastened to apprise Prince Gortchakov, "As soon as I get these plans I will forward them to you in the hope that they will be of some interest to His Imperial Highness."[5]

After Grant's victory at Donelson, a fearful bloody battle was fought at Shiloh or Pittsburg Landing in Western Tennessee. It was one of the most hotly contested engagements during the entire war. It cost the opposing armies twenty-four thousand men, killed, wounded and missing. Among the slain was General Albert Sidney Johnston, the Confederate commander. The indomitable courage and stubborn obstinacy of General Grant turned impending defeat into a tremendous victory— a victory which opened the Mississippi to Union vessels. But Stoeckl complained in his dispatch to St. Petersburg that he could report only a fragmentary account "as the government has clamped down a rigid censorship to such a point that it is impossible even for the diplomatic corps to remain well informed."[6]

The government was also repressing news of an expedition against New Orleans. But on May 5 the Russian Minister was able to confirm the capture of New Orleans. Stoeckl regarded this as the "most important blow to the South since the beginning of the war."[7] "Nothing will now stop the federals from becoming master of the entire Mississippi, thus cutting the Confederacy in two. This development gives new hope for the early end of the war. The President and the Secretary of State should now advance steps for peace and conciliation. But they are controlled by the radicals who demand complete destruction of the South."[8]

Stoeckl's dispatches throughout May and June dealt with the failures of Generals McClellan and Halleck to take aggressive steps against the rebels, "although Lincoln issues order after order to attack the enemy":

> McClellan is seven or eight miles from Richmond. He will not venture an attack without more re-enforcements. But President Lincoln does not want to strip the Capital of its troops, some 12,000 to 15,000 in number. The President, without waiting for sanction from Congress, issued a call to the Governors of the States to raise more troops, organize them into regiments and to send them without delay to the various army corps.
>
> The situation is deplorable. Congress wastes its time in demagogical debates. The administration possesses no overall military plan and the President vacillates from one course of action to another. The generals quarrel among themselves, each acting according to his own dictates. Such is the present situation. God alone knows the extremes to which this rebellion will lead this country.[9]

Stoeckl's dispatches during the summer of 1862 continued to speak of the inactivity of the federal generals, the inept direction of the government and the vacillating policies of Lincoln. "Lincoln and the Secretary of War are rarely informed about the movements or the strength of the enemy. They believed that Stonewall Jackson was commanding a large force which after repulsing General Banks could advance upon and capture Washington." Actually Jackson with bold strategy mysteriously left the Shenandoah Valley and after a series of brilliant victories which sent the federal armies in full retreat, rode into Richmond for a conference with Lee.[10]

"Considering the vastly superior resources of the North, Lincoln should have brought about a speedy suppression of the rebellion," Stoeckl asserted on June 23.[11] "All eyes are centered on Richmond where the best troops of the North and the South face each other. A great battle is expected which will vitally affect the outcome of the war."

Before the battle, Stoeckl saw Secretary of War Cameron and asked him how many men were in the armies of the North. "Mr. Cameron . . . assured me that 750,000 volunteers have been enrolled. This is probably an exaggeration, but it can be said with some accuracy that the number of troops in active service has not been less than 600,000 men."[12]

Seven days of fierce fighting from June 26 to July 2, 1862, around Richmond from the Chickahominy to the James, created tremendous excitement throughout the country. The losses on both sides were terrific. "The President and the Secretary of War are not to be seen much these days," the Russian Minister wrote. He added that the government was issuing no report on the military operations with the result that national anxiety was intensified. "Uncertainty is worse than the worst news." However, Stoeckl wrote that he had

> learned from some Senators who contacted the President that on June 26 the Confederates attacked the right flank of General Mc-Clellan and after a bloody battle forced him to cross over the Chickahominy and to retreat to Harrisons Landing where he was within reach of his gunboats and transports. McClellan's position seems to be in jeopardy. Surely the silence on the part of the government does not indicate that results are favorable for the federal troops.[13]

The government's ironclad censorship did not stop the Russian Minister from procuring details of the battle. Stoeckl learned them from Prince de Joinville, a brother of the deposed King of France, whom Lincoln had appointed to McClellan's staff. This scion of the House of Orleans, which Napoleon had succeeded, had just arrived from McClellan's headquarters. He described to Stoeckl how McClellan, after a bloody battle, retreated from his position in front of Richmond:

> It appears that the army of McClellan is completely disorganized as a result of the precipitate retreat. From what Prince de Joinville said, the carnage was frightful. The Southerners fought with diabolical ferocity. The disorder was so serious that even at general headquarters the true situation of the army was still not known.
>
> The nation had a right to expect much more from the Army of

the Potomac, consisting of its best organized regiments and commanded by supposedly the most skilful general.[14]

With Washington again in danger of attack, "General Halleck has been ordered to Washington to take charge of military operations."[15] Stoeckl wrote that Lincoln was experiencing great difficulty in replenishing the depleted military ranks. "The government has been compelled to offer a premium of twenty-five dollars a man." Later he reported that premiums up to fifty dollars have been offered, yet there are few volunteers. Two weeks later, Lincoln had issued another call for volunteers, with premiums of up to $300.

The government was compelled to resort to conscription. Lincoln decreed that all men twenty to forty-five years of age were to be drafted for military service:

Mr. Lincoln told me himself one day that in case of necessity he could count upon two or three million men. Experience has demonstrated that such estimates are inaccurate. . . . At the outset the armed services absorbed the adventurous types, the poor, the unemployed laborers and the foreigners who filled the large cities. Not many of these classes remain. The new recruits must come from the farmers, businessmen and, in general, the prosperous classes who are opposed to the war.

Those who volunteered at the outset never dreamed of the dangers and privations which awaited them. It was generally believed that the mere presence of the Northern army would coerce the South into rejoining the Union. I saw New York regiments leave in a spirit of gaiety in the belief that they would be gone less than three months. But events have shown how wrong they were. The ever-increasing number of mangled, sick, crippled or maimed soldiers who have returned to their homes has opened the eyes of Northerners to the horrors of war.

Men no longer volunteer for military service. Bonuses of $250 to $300 are being offered to volunteers without spurring enlistments. As a result, the government was forced to resort to conscription. But it is doubtful if the government will succeed in recruiting the number Lincoln has fixed in his call. General Halleck, now in command of federal forces, admitted to me that not more than 300,000 to 350,000 men can be recruited, the majority for a term of nine months. . . .

The decision of the government to limit the term of service to nine months is a tacit avowal that the conflict will not last beyond that time. That is what the Secretary of State told me in trying to convince me that everything would end with the subjugation of the South. I agree with Mr. Seward that the conflict will not last long but I do not share his opinion as to the outcome. In my opinion, and I regret to say it, separation is inevitable. Sad as this necessity may be, the North will be compelled to submit to it.[16]

After General Pope led the Army of the Potomac to a second disastrous defeat on the old battlefield of Bull Run on September 1, Stoeckl wrote that "the President and his Cabinet cannot cope with the situation. Everything is in a state of confusion and indecision." He praised the military genius of Stonewall Jackson, and continued:

The Union generals are torn with dissension and hatred for one another. Last week General McClellan was in disgrace and was relieved of his command in favor of General Pope. Now McClellan has been recalled to take command of the army. There is no accord between McClellan, Halleck and Stanton—McClellan accuses the Secretary of War of being an enemy of the country. In short, the disorder is complete among the men in charge of affairs. Not one is capable of forming a plan or giving counsel in a crisis. . . .[17]

The principal cause of all of these disasters must be attributed to the intrigues and petty jealousies as much as to the incompetence of the men who direct the affairs of state. The more serious the situation becomes, the more intense becomes the discord. Mr. Stanton, Secretary of War, who represents the ultra-radical party in the Cabinet, places only those officers who are faithful to his Party in command of the army, and ousts the conservatives from these posts. He holds an unrelenting hate for General McClellan, whose temperate policies provoke him. Unable to dismiss him, he gradually withdraws his troops from his command and assigns them to Pope, whose incompetence is notorious but whose policies are in agreement with those of the Secretary of War. The last disaster which the Union army suffered is a direct result of these intrigues. . . .

Lincoln does not possess the moral courage to do anything. The President was obliged to restore General McClellan as Commander

in Chief of the army despite the fact that McClellan has yet to
prove any great military skill. By reason of his affability and because of his concern for the welfare of his men, he has won the
deep affection of his troops. But in making this concession to the
army, Mr. Lincoln did not have the moral courage to dismiss
Stanton. How can satisfactory results be expected from military
operations when the control is entrusted to two men who detest
each other?"[18]

Again Washington was imperiled. "We are expecting a bloody
battle," Stoeckl wrote. On the night General McClellan left Washington to re-assume command of the Army of the Potomac, Stoeckl
conferred with him about the new crisis. "He assured me that he had
taken all necessary precautions, and he felt confident that he would be
able not only to repulse General Jackson, who was supposed to be
marching on Washington, but also to cut off his retreat."[19]
The Battle of Antietam, a fierce contest in which the Union forces
lost more than 12,000 men and the Confederates nearly as many, was
claimed as a victory by McClellan. But, Stoeckl reported:

the Confederates did not suffer a defeat, as next day they crossed
the Potomac carrying with them their equipment and wounded.
It was not until two days later that McClellan pursued them into
Virginia but was repulsed. . . .[20]
On November 4, McClellan, pressed by the President and public
opinion, decided to cross the Potomac for a decisive campaign to
end the war this fall, but finding the enemy in great numbers, he
stopped. The offensive campaign was postponed until spring.[21]

McClellan's failure once more to take action caused Lincoln to re-
move him again. On November 5, General Burnside was named com-
mander. With the appointment came the order to move on Richmond.
Burnside obeyed—reluctantly. He pushed vigorously on the enemy.
The result was the massacre at Fredericksburg on December 13, 1862.
Could nobody beat Lee?

Now all who had a part in directing the military operations are
blaming one another. A congressional committee is visiting the
Army of the Potomac to investigate the causes for the military

disaster. These investigations are made here after every engagement, but produce absolutely no results. With the disorder and
confusion which prevails in Washington it is impossible to fix
responsibility.[22]

Thus the year 1862 ended on a note of gloom and disaster for the
North. The "Horror of Fredericksburg" led to Burnside's removal on
January 26. The command of the Army of the Potomac now went to
"Fighting Joe" Hooker, chief of Burnside's critics. Stoeckl's dispatches
for the month of January 1863 were filled with detailed reports of
United States military plans and operations. He met the new commander and wrote, "General Hooker hopes to do better than his predecessors."[23] But the Russian Minister added that the true situation,
which the government was endeavoring to conceal, was actually most
critical. "We hear that the troops are not being paid and discontent
prevails everywhere."[24]

"With the federals inactive, the secessionists baffling in their activity,
and the incompetency of the Northern generals continuing, anything
seems possible to me.[25] So critical is the situation that ruin of the administration along with what still remains of the Union is imminent.

"But of all the difficulties which assail the federal administration, the
most alarming is the state of the treasury." The Russian Minister
pointed out that Secretary of the Treasury Chase and Congress were
at odds how to raise the countless millions of dollars necessary to
finance the war:

> Last week Mr. Chase went to New York to consult with the
> bankers but he could obtain no relief. The value of government
> bonds has been falling as rapidly as paper money. Government
> bonds are now being discounted at 50 percent. . . . Congress will
> probably end up by authorizing Mr. Chase to raise money as best
> he can by selling treasury bonds at any rate he can obtain and by
> issuing more paper money. . . .
> Another great problem confronting the government is the diffi-
> culty of procuring men for the army. The terms of these volun-
> teers who had enlisted for two years and those who later enlisted
> for nine months, will expire next May. Thus the army ranks will
> be reduced by 250,000 men, without taking into account the losses
> from battle casualties, sickness and especially desertions. This will

make necessary a new call for men, but considering the opposition which prevails throughout the land, the success of such a call seems impossible.

So far, the North has been more or less united and the government has been able to raise immense resources in men and money. But today, the States which have remained loyal are divided into two factions which seem to have sworn implacable hatred to each other. We already see proof of this in the legislative assemblies of the States of New York and Pennsylvania which met a few days ago. The Republicans and the Democrats resorted to acts of violence and they debated the issues with revolvers in hand. In addition to this bitterness between the Republicans and Democrats are the sectional quarrels between the West and the East.

The Republicans demand the subjugation of the South without realizing the obstacles which two years of fighting have demonstrated so clearly. The Democrats contend that a compromise based on the federal pact is today more possible than the conquest of the South. So, the Americans seem to be rushing blindly into a state of anarchy which will be the inevitable consequence of the war if it continues much longer [26]

Washington was filled with rumors about the Union campaign against Charleston. The Russian Minister sought more authentic information. He received it from an officer of the United States navy:

Commander Goldsborough, one of the most distinguished naval officers of the Union, told me that Charleston is so well fortified that they hesitated to attack it and that the federal expedition will probably go to Savannah and Mobile where the defenses are not so strong.[27] . . .

The attack upon Charleston will have special interest from the point of view of military technique. It is the first time that armor-plated steamships will attempt to overwhelm shore batteries. I regret that our war clipper *Arriazr* has not yet arrived so her commander could observe the effect of the new armament which has been introduced into naval warfare.[28]

Weeks before the actual launching of the Charleston and Vicksburg campaigns, Stoeckl observed: "The attack against Charleston and Vicksburg was to have begun two weeks ago. But so far, nothing has been achieved. . . . The struggle will be bitter, the bloodshed terrific, unfortunately without any hope that victory, whichever side may win it, will solve anything."[29]

Later when the Spanish Consul at Charleston came to Washington, Stoeckl learned from him that the federal fleet sent to attack that Confederate stronghold had not accomplished its mission. The Spaniard told the Russian Minister "that if the federals had made the attack six weeks ago, they would certainly have succeeded. But the Confederates have taken advantage of the North's failure to act and have installed new defenses which make it almost impossible for them to take Charleston, at least not without paying a terrific cost." From a letter written by an officer commanding one of the ships of the federal squadron, Stoeckl was able to report that "the armor-plated monitors are excellent for defense, but not suitable for offensive operations."[30]

Stoeckl attributed the loss of the gunboats *Queen of the West* and the *Indianola*, "the best of the fleet of Admiral Porter at Vicksburg, to the negligence of the commanders and to the halfhearted fighting of the crews."[31]

When the House of Representatives passed a bill authorizing the President to arm 150,000 Negroes, Stoeckl reported that "the Democratic Party regarded this measure as humiliating for the nation" since it was an admission that "an army of a million men cannot win without the help of some 100,000 Negroes":

> Mr. Stevens, author of this measure, said that the federal army . . . far from being a million strong scarcely numbered 500,000 men under arms; that half of these troops were scheduled to return home soon since their term of service expired next May; that volunteers are no longer enlisting; and that conscription was so unpopular that the government hesitated to invoke it again.

Once again Stoeckl expressed the view that "the political separation of the North and the South with the maintenance of commercial relations was the most favorable solution of the Civil War."[32]

From conversations he had with Congressmen from the Western States, Stoeckl learned that

> conditions in that part of the country were pitiable; that the hatred between Republicans and Democrats was as bitter as between the North and the South. Both factions are arming themselves and any day now fierce fighting may be expected. . . .

Peace, no matter what the terms, is the only means of resolving this situation. But leaders in charge of affairs do not want it. Their slogan is all-out war. Any compromise would endanger their political existence. They are politicans of low caliber—men without conscience, ready to do anything for money, individuals who have achieved rank in the army and others who still have hopes of obtaining high commissions. They constitute the swarm of speculators, suppliers of material, war profiteers through whose hands pass a large portion of the millions of dollars spent daily by the federal government.

Aside from these and some fanatics, practically everybody else desires the cessation of hostilities. But unfortunately, few dare to protest, and those who have the courage and patriotism to express their opinions, are too few in number to make their influence felt.[33] . . .

Domestic affairs continue to worry the government as much as military failures. The people are becoming more and more concerned. The hatred between the parties gets more bitter especially in the West where several towns have been the scenes of bloody riots.[34]

In New York Stoeckl conferred with some officers of the French and Spanish warships who had arrived from Charleston, and gained more information as to the dark state of affairs:

They confirmed all the reports which had previously reached us about the fortifications of that port, and about the improbability of destroying them. The monitors, according to these officers, are not as effective as they claim here in Washington. It is apparent that the commanders of the federal forces have not sufficient confidence in their armor-plated ships, for they have been hesitating for two months to begin the attack in spite of the repeated orders of the federal government to take Charleston at any price. On the Western front the federals have made several attempts to take Vicksburg but without success. Some fairly serious engagements have taken place, but judging from the silence of the government the advantage has not been with the federals.

Thus the winter campaign ends without any result, and the spring campaign is not being launched under very favorable conditions. The heat has already set in on the lower Mississippi, and on the coasts of South Carolina, and in a few weeks the federal government will be obliged to withdraw its troops from Charleston and from Vicksburg unless it wants to see them decimated by the pestilential climate of these regions. Domestic affairs, far from improving, become more threatening every day.

The jealousies and dissensions among the men in authority keep growing. The Democratic opposition is similarly torn with dissension. As the peril increases, the confusion grows. In fact, the entire nation seems to be carried along by the torrent of events towards a future which is uncertain and full of dangers.[35] . . .

It is doubtful whether the attack will be renewed at least for some time in the near future.[36] . . . The President and the majority of his Cabinet desire the immediate renewal of the attack, at any price at all. But they had to yield to the naval commanders who were consulted.[37] . . .

In North Carolina, General Foster who commands the troops stationed on the coast, wanted to make an excursion into the interior. After a march of two days his corps of 4,000 men was surrounded by the Confederates and it is feared that he was forced to surrender.

The news from the West is equally bad. After a siege of six months the federals have had to abandon Vicksburg. The army of the North retired, having lost 20,000 to 25,000 men, of whom three-fourths succumbed to sickness.

I scarcely need to tell you how much these successive disasters have discouraged the federal government. All its hope is now centered in the Army of the Potomac which must proceed vigorously towards Richmond. It remains to be seen if General Hooker who commands it, will be any more fortunate than General McClellan last year. In any event, it will meet with desperate resistance on the part of the Confederates.[38]

Thirteen days later, on April 26, Stoeckl noted that the new commander was proving no less dilatory than his predecessors:

General Hooker, who commands the Army of the Potomac, was to have started moving three weeks ago, but so far he has done nothing except to throw some detachments of cavalry onto the other side of the Rappahannock, to make reconnaissances.

The Confederates, realizing the importance of stopping the ad-

vance of General Hooker on Richmond, have massed, so it is reported, all the forces which they have been able to find, on the
left bank of the Rappahannock. If that is so, the two armies will
meet almost equally matched. The struggle will be one of the
fiercest and perhaps the bloodiest of this war.[39]

At length, on April 30, General Hooker led the Army of the
Potomac out of its camps, and fought his first—and last—great
battle, at Chancellorsville. "This army," wrote Stoeckl, "was destined
to add a new defeat to all those it has suffered, always due to the poor
leadership of its commanders."

When the anxiously awaited news finally arrived from the battlefield, it was another terrible blow to the cause of the Union—the
greatest defeat the Union armies suffered in the Civil War.

"What will the country say? Oh, what will the country say!" Lincoln moaned.

Stoeckl hastened to give the Russian Foreign Office a detailed account of this new Union disaster:

> After the reverses suffered by the federals during last winter, all
> the hope of the nation was concentrated on the Army of the
> Potomac, the best organized and the best disciplined in the Union.
> General Hooker, who commands it, started out on April 22. He
> avoided committing the fault of his predecessor by attacking
> Fredericksburg from the front. He ordered the Rappahannock
> crossed by a company of 25,000 men, a few leagues below that
> town. And he himself crossed the river with the main part of his
> army twenty-five miles above Fredericksburg. The plan of Gen-
> eral Hooker was to upset the fortifications of the enemy and cut
> his communications with Richmond.
>
> The Confederates put up no resistance to the crossing of the
> Rappahannock and fell back on their entrenchments.
>
> On April 30 General Hooker issued a bulletin in which he said
> that he had succeeded in maneuvering the enemy into the position
> of either fleeing or leaving its entrenchments to fight a battle on
> its own ground, and thus expose itself to certain defeat.[40] . . .
>
> General Hooker has proved no more skilful and no more fortu-
> nate than his predecessors, and instead of destroying Confederate
> General Lee as he announced in his bulletin of April 30, he himself
> was defeated by Lee who has demonstrated unusual military skill.

It was on May 2 that the armies met at Chancellorsville, a little village twelve or fifteen miles from Fredericksburg. After a battle which lasted all day, the federal army was driven from its position. On the next day—May 3—they fought again with the same result; the federals again lost ground. Then Hooker gave the order to General Sedgwick, whom he had left with a corps of 30,000 men close to Fredericksburg, to come to his aid. Sedgwick crossed the Rappahannock on May 4 to join the army of Hooker. The latter did not move the whole day. Lee, profiting by this inactivity on the part of Hooker, drove a large part of his forces against Sedgwick and threw him back across the Rappahannock. During May 5 there were only a few skirmishes, and at nightfall the federal army recrossed the Rappahannock without much resistance from the enemy. Thus Hooker saved the greater part of his artillery, but he left behind his wounded and much equipment.

The losses of the two sides have been immense. The Confederate losses have been estimated at 18,000 to 20,000 men put out of action. The federals admit 12,000 to 15,000 killed and wounded, but some officers who have arrived here from the army report numbers higher than 30,000. The regiment of Sedgwick alone lost 9,000 men—almost one-third of its strength.[41]

Gathered so soon after the end of the fighting, it is not surprising that Stoeckl's figures differ from those later released officially by the government, which state that the Union lost 17,287 killed, wounded and missing, the Confederates 12,764. But in general his report depicted the magnitude of the disaster suffered by the Union. Stoeckl wrote:

The federal army is at present in its initial positions on the left bank of the Rappahannock, with a strength of 120,000 men. It is reported that it will take the offensive again, and that together with Hooker's force, two other army corps will advance on Richmond, one from the Monroe fortress and the other from Washington. These three armies will have the strength of 180,000 men against whom the Confederates will hardly be able to muster 100,-000. But if the federals possess the advantage in number, their rivals have the advantage of fighting on their own territory and of being commanded by generals of superior ability.

In spite of all these disasters, the federal government refuses to

modify its policy with regard to the army. All the generals are
politicians. McClellan is the only exception, so he has been removed from his command. Burnside, Pope and Hooker owe their
positions to their political connections. As for the division and
brigade chiefs, they are for the most part lawyers and journalists
whose only merit is that they made some contribution to putting
the present administration into power.[42]

Chancellorsville was to Lincoln the darkest hour of the Civil War.
His critics became savage in their denunciations. Discontent manifested
itself everywhere.

Hooker began to reorganize the Army of the Potomac. Lee planned
an invasion of Maryland and Pennsylvania to take away the pressure
from the Confederate forces besieged by Grant at Vicksburg. On June
2 Stoeckl reported:

> After the failure of the Army of the Potomac under General
> Hooker, all the efforts of the government have been concentrated
> on Vicksburg.
>
> In my preceding reports I told of the unfruitful attempts made to
> capture Vicksburg during last winter and spring by the federal
> army and gunboats. However, General Grant was not discouraged
> and conceived a bold plan which promised a happy result. He sent a
> force of 40,000 to 50,000 men down the river and disembarked at
> Grand Gulf, a little village fifty miles from Vicksburg. From there
> he advanced towards Jackson, the Capital of the State of Mis-
> sissippi, and cut communications with Vicksburg. Then without
> stopping at Jackson he went on towards the Confederate fortress,
> thinking he could easily take it from the rear. Grant accomplished
> this march with great speed, and without much trouble overthrew
> the small detachments which he encountered on his way. But
> when he arrived behind Vicksburg he found that the fortifications
> of this town on the land side were as formidable as those which
> face the river. Grant, who is said to be a man of energy and who
> commands veteran troops, decided to assault the enemy positions.
> The soldiers marched forward boldly but they were driven back
> each time with losses estimated at from 10,000 to 15,000 men. The
> last assault took place on the 25th of May.
>
> The state of affairs on the Mississippi has changed for the worse.
> A week ago everyone was rejoicing in the impending fall of

Vicksburg which they considered more or less accomplished, but this certainty has given way today to serious concern about the fate of the Army of McClellan threatened in turn by the Confederate General Johnston, who is commanding the Department the West. It appears that Johnston has received reinforcements from many sources, even from South Carolina, and he has sent a message to the garrison of Vicksburg that if it could hold out for two weeks he would arrive with sufficient forces to save it. At the latest reports Johnston had re-occupied Jackson and his outposts were on the Black River bridge, seventeen miles from Vicksburg. Two divisions of the strength of 10,000 men each have rejoined Grant to face Johnston. We are momentarily expecting the news of a bloody battle.

Vicksburg is one of the most important points. If the federals succeed in capturing it, they will be masters of the whole Mississippi, and will cut the Confederation of the South into two.[43]

As regards the political situation, it is still deplorable. The quarrels and the rivalries between the members of the Cabinet, and, in general, between the men in power, continue as in the past. The administration is proceeding without any plan, and the end of the struggle is more uncertain than ever.

The booming guns at Vicksburg were temporarily forgotten by Washington as startling rumors flew through the Capital that Lee was marching north to attack the city. The rebel cry, "On to Washington" echoed up from Richmond. And the residents of the nation's Capital listened in fear to the cannon fire rumbling ominously from the direction of the Blue Ridge. In describing the new peril to Washington, Stoeckl wrote on June 16:

A month ago the federal army with the strength of 150,000 men crossed the Potomac to march on Richmond. Today, following reverses due to the inability and intrigues of the men who direct military affairs, it is the federal Capital which is in danger of falling into the hands of the enemy.

After the Battle of Chancellorsville, and the disastrous retreat of Hooker, this general remained inactive in the presence of his adversary who, more skilful and bolder than he, prepared to take the offensive. General Lee, whose army was reinforced to 120,000 men, on June 12 directed General Ewell, at the head of 25,000 men, to advance up the Potomac. With a rapid movement, Ewell surprised the federal garrisons occupying Winchester, Martinsburg and some other points, and thus made himself master of the Shenandoah Valley.[44]

This movement finally brought Hooker out of his inactivity. On June 13 he left Falmouth and withdrew on Washington, closely followed and harassed by the main part of the forces of General Lee.

In the meantime the Confederate corps of Ewell crossed the Potomac and seized Hagerstown and Fredericksburg in Maryland, crossed the borders of Pennsylvania, and according to telegraphic news received last evening, he was already occupying Chambersburg.

The administration, caught off guard by this rapid movement, called on the militias of Pennsylvania, Maryland, Ohio and West Virginia for 100,000 men.

The President has said that he must rely on the State militias for the defense of the area, as he could not, at this moment, release a single regiment of the Army of the Potomac. As a matter of fact, this army is hardly in shape to face Lee.

It appears that yesterday there were some serious engagements, and at the moment of writing we can clearly hear the boom of the cannons on the other bank of the Potomac. The federal authorities are in consternation and various departments of state are hastily packing up archives so that they may be sent away on gunboats in case of necessity.

Yesterday there was a Cabinet meeting to decide whether to leave Hooker in command of the army or replace him. But nothing has been decided. Hooker has shown himself incompetent. But they hesitate to dismiss him because he is supported by the radicals whose willing tool he has become.

The diplomatic corps is, as last year, in an embarrassing position. We have sent our families to the North and we are ready to follow the government. I have taken all precautions to put our archives in a place of safety in case of danger and I shall take with me the most important papers of the imperial legation.[45]

In his next dispatch, Stoeckl reported:

The principal forces of the two enemy armies are facing each other on the right bank of the Potomac at a distance of a few miles from Washington. Skirmishes take place every day and yesterday a serious engagement must have taken place for we distinctly heard cannon fire the whole day long. But we do not know the result of it, for the government continues to maintain its usual silence.

Such is the position of Washington on the southerly side. We are similarly threatened by a Confederate division of 15,000 men which occupies the upper Potomac thirty miles from here. This armed force has seized the railroad which links the Capital with the West. If, as is feared, the Confederates also manage to seize the railroad of the North, all communications from Washington will be interrupted and the federal Capital will be completely isolated from the other states.[46]

The days following were ones of terrible suspense for the North. With panic beginning to overtake the residents of Washington a clamor arose for the reinstatement of McClellan to the Potomac command. But on the morning of June 28, 1863 a messenger from the President arrived at the headquarters of General George Gordon Meade, commanding Hooker's Fifth Corps, and handed him a dispatch from Lincoln. It was an order to take immediate charge of the Army of the Potomac.

Three days later (July 1) the newly led Army of the Potomac and the advancing forces of Lee met head-on at the little village of Gettysburg. For three days the epochal battle raged. When it was over the hitherto invincible army of Lee, decimated by 20,000 slain and wounded, had lost one of the decisive battles of history. "They fought bitterly on both sides and with equal courage," Stoeckl stated in his account of the "terrific battle."

> Finally, on the evening of the 4th, the Confederates withdrew in the direction of Maryland, probably with the intention of crossing the Potomac and returning to Virginia.

> Meade says that his cavalry was pursuing the enemy. Everything depends now on the skill of Lee's retreat to Virginia. If he can do it without having his army seriously disorganized, the situation will be as it was before the invasion. But, if Meade should succeed in cutting off the retreat of the Confederate troops, the result will be disastrous for them. The losses have been terrific. They are estimated at from 20,000 to 25,000 men on each side.

This morning I saw the President and Mr. Seward whom I complimented on the success of the federal army.[47]

While Lincoln bemoaned Meade's failure to pursue Lee and cut off his retreat, Stoeckl wrote:

As always happens in this war on one side or the other, General Meade was not able to press the advantage gained at Gettysburg. He followed Lee, but only after a lapse of two days after the battle. This gave the enemy time to complete his retreat without much trouble.

The two armies are again facing each other and we are awaiting a clash at any moment. The federal government has done everything to reinforce General Meade. They sent him all the troops which could be spared and his forces must be up to 175,000 men, among whom there are 25,000 to 30,000 militia on whom he cannot rely for much help.

General Lee has been reinforced and his army today may be up to 100,000 men, but this time he will have the advantage of being on the defensive and of encountering the enemy in a country that is wooded, mountainous and cut through with ravines.[48]

Meanwhile the star of a great general was rising in the West. For two years U. S. Grant had been hammering away at the "hard nut" of Vicksburg. On this fateful July 4, while Lee was fleeing from Gettysburg, Confederate General Pemberton finally surrendered the stronghold to Grant. Stoeckl reported:

While the blood was flowing so freely on the plains of Pennsylvania . . . the federal forces won a victory on the Mississippi of the greatest importance. The stronghold of Vicksburg which has been besieged for almost two years fell into the hands of the federals. After having exhausted all their provisions and munitions the Confederate General Pemberton capitulated. The garrison with a strength of 12,000 men was taken prisoner. The officers and the soldiers have been sent home on parole. With the fall of Vicksburg it is improbable that Port Hudson, the last fortified point of the Confederates on the Mississippi, can hold out much longer.

It is the first time since the beginning of the war, apart from the taking of New Orleans, that the federals are gaining any real and important advantages.[49]

Only ten days after the great victories at Gettysburg and Vicksburg—while for the first time during the Civil War, Lincoln found real cause for rejoicing—draft riots broke out in New York City over the enforcement of the conscription act of 1863. The draft riots were confined to a district of New York largely inhabited by foreign laborers. A slogan: "Rich man's war and poor man's fight," repeated over and over again by antiwar agitators, had made a great impression upon them. It arose from the permission to escape service by the payment of $300—at the outset, the equivalent of the cost to the government of a substitute. But it ceased to be so owing to the rise in prices and wages due to the depreciation of the currency. The New York riots did not reflect the spirit which animated the North generally. But the Czar's representative advised his Foreign Office:

> New York, the metropolis of the nation, with a population of nearly 1,000,000, has been the scene of disorders more than once, but never before to such a degree as this. For the first time the people rose up against the duly constituted authorities. A mob invaded the main recruiting office, drove out the officers and set fire to the police station. Several men were killed by the troops who interceded. This is an indication of the confusion and demagoguery which prevails in the North. . . . The government is very uneasy and has ordered the suspension of recruiting at Philadelphia where riots are also feared.[50]

Stoeckl also observed that as a result of the Union successes a new split had resulted in the ranks of Lincoln's administration. The clash was over future policy.

> The conservatives want peace. They say that now that Northern honor is saved, the time is at hand to start negotiations with the Confederates for their re-entry into the Union on an equal footing with the Northern States. On the other hand the radical Republicans are demanding that the government should continue the vigorous prosecution of the war and that it should not lay down arms until the South is completely subjugated.
>
> Unfortunately the administration is completely dominated by

the radicals. A recent incident is proof of this. Mr. Stephens, Vice President of the Southern Confederation, came to Fort Monroe in a government vessel, and requested permission to come to Washington to deliver a letter and to convey a verbal message to President Lincoln from Jefferson Davis. Mr. Lincoln, after having consulted with his Cabinet and several Republican senators present in Washington, who were known for their extreme views, refused to see Mr. Stephens.

Mr. Seward, with whom I spoke about this matter, said to me: "I was of the opinion that Mr. Stephens, whom I have known for many years and who I know is still attached to the Union, should be received by the President, but the President decided otherwise, and I did not insist."

The radicals who control the Republican Party want no compromise. They noisily demand continuation of the war in the hope of assuring that one of their Party will become the Chief Magistrate of the Nation in the next presidential election. The conservatives who constitute the majority of the population are opposed to all extreme measures, but they are afraid to speak up.

At the outset of the conflict the North took its stand fighting for liberty as against slavery. As a result public opinion was on their side. Later the edicts of confiscation, the threats of inciting a servile war, and the arbitrary acts of some of their generals, purposely exaggerated by the English press, have damaged their cause, particularly in Eastern Europe. They now have the opportunity of showing themselves magnanimous towards their former countrymen, and thus regain the ground they have lost in the eyes of the world.[51] . . .

In spite of the recent successes of the federal armies, the general situation has not improved noticeably. The ranks of the federal army must be replenished. . . . Conscription goes on very slowly. . . . The government will be fortunate if it can obtain 150,000 of the 300,000 required.[52]

Writing almost two months later, on September 23, 1863, Stoeckl expected a long continuance of the contest, and wondered what it would settle:

It is impossible to foresee the end of the Civil War in the near future. The areas captured and occupied by the federal troops are situated either on the Atlantic coast or along the Mississippi River. The task still remains to advance into the interior of this vast territory and it is there that the Union troops will meet with the greatest difficulties because they will be deprived of the support of the gunboats which played such an important part in winning the recent victories. The Southerners, in spite of their reverses, do not appear demoralized, and the tenacity with which they defend themselves at every point proves that they are not yet ready to surrender.

In the event that the South is subjugated, a difficult but not impossible task, the question will arise as to what policy should be assumed towards these States: Should they be occupied by the army as some parts of Tennessee and other Southwestern States are occupied today, or should they be admitted to the Union in their former status? If the first possibility should come into reality it would become necessary to maintain a permanent army of thousands of men. The other alternative seems to be as impractical as the first. Actually, how can it be expected that States which have waged a long and fierce war can rejoin the Union and live in peace and harmony with the loyal States? In addition, the North itself is disunited and torn by partisan strife. The hate between the Republicans and the Democrats is as bitter as that between the North and the South.

These are very grave difficulties and I cannot share Mr. Seward's optimism in seeing a quick re-establishment of the old Union. In time the nation will be reunited. I have the firm conviction that the American nation will regain its prosperity and greatness. But having endured a cataclysmic revolution, the nation will be reconstructed in a different form and under new conditions.[53]

Having thus expressed his opinion regarding the political situation and future reconstruction policies, Stoeckl went back to reporting the military situation:

The military operations in the West which had been stopped for a time after the fall of Vicksburg have started up again. General Rosecrans, who is Commander in Chief of the Department of the West, set out two weeks ago and has occupied Chattanooga, a very important military position on the boundaries of Georgia, and continued forward with the intention of seizing Atlanta, one of the principal cities of that State. When he arrived at Fayetteville, twenty or twenty-five miles to the south of Chattanooga, he met the Confederate army of Generals Bragg and Johnston, which had been reinforced by a division of the army of General Lee on orders from General Longstreet. The two armies came upon one another and fought one of the fiercest battles during September 19-21.

Mr. Seward, whom I saw this morning, has confirmed the news of the defeat of the Union army at the Battle of Chickamauga. He told me that Rosecrans was forced to withdraw to Chattanooga, where he hoped to remain until the arrival of reinforcements from the North.

The siege of Charleston continues but with less intensity. The federals are meeting much more stubborn resistance than they expected.[54]

On November 7 the Russian Minister reported that as a result of Rosecrans' defeat by Bragg at Chickamauga he had been replaced by General Grant "who has acquired an enviable reputation since his capture of Vicksburg."[55] He added:

The federal armies are feeling the losses they sustained last summer. I have been assured that these losses ran as high as almost 300,000 men, two-thirds of whom were lost on the banks of the Mississippi and on the coasts of the South regions whose pestilential climate is fatal to the men of the North. The government is doing all it can to procure recruits, but it is meeting great obstacles. This is not surprising as the country has already provided almost a million fighters from a population of 20,000,000. The conscription of 300,000 men decreed by the President last summer has so far produced only 40,000 to 50,000 men at the most. A new decree recently published calls to arms 300,000 volunteers. They will get only a fraction of this number but not without difficulty and by paying bounties in certain localities as high as $1,000 a man.

Placed in charge of all the forces between the Alleghenies and the Mississippi, Grant's first task in his new command was to save Rosecrans and the State of Tennessee. On October 23, he advanced upon Chattanooga, and after waiting for the arrival of General Sherman and his troops, attacked Bragg's forces. After one of the war's decisive battles, Grant—with Sherman, Thomas, Sheridan and Hooker as his lieutenants—succeeded in dislodging Bragg's army from its seemingly invulnerable positions and put it to rout. As a result, the entire State of Tennessee was won for the Union. The Confederacy had again shrunk in territory and resources.

Lincoln was elated. Had he at last found in Grant the leader he had been searching for all these months?

What Can Be Expected from a Democracy?

In a series of dispatches written in late November and December of 1863, Baron Edouard de Stoeckl presented to his government a detailed review of the historic events he had been witnessing in America.

He had formed certain definite opinions and impressions about the United States, its institutions and its leaders. The importance of these personal impressions lay in the fact that they were generally accepted by the Czar, Prince Gortchakov, and the Russian nation as a whole, in the formulation of Muscovite opinion regarding America, her people, statesmen and institutions.

First of all was Stoeckl's conclusion that the foundations of true democracy, as they existed in the United States before the Civil War, had been completely undermined. With the President as Commander in Chief usurping so much power, the Constitution had become an empty shell, he declared.

"The republican form of government, so much talked about by the Europeans and so much praised by the Americans, is breaking down." Democracy in the United States had become "irresponsible," he believed,

> owing to the rising streams of radicalism and universal suffrage at home, to the influx of socialists and anarchists from Europe, and to the rise of such men as Garibaldi and Bakunin. What can be expected from a country where men of humble origin are elevated

to the highest positions, where honest men refuse to vote and dishonest ones cast their ballots at the bidding of shameless politicians? This is democracy in practice, the democracy that the European theorists rave about.[1] . . . If they could only see it at work they would cease their agitation and thank God for the government which they are enjoying.[2]

He had rejoiced that "the crumbling of the American system" would prove to be "a salutary lesson for European anarchists and visionaries" who "preach limitless freedom and who are convinced that they have found in America the realization of their theory of free will." They "will necessarily become convinced that self-government, like all other human institutions, has its weak points." Here in the United States it had "operated under uniquely favorable conditions and seemed to be absolutely secure." Failure of the ultra-democratic system under these circumstances was to him convincing proof that it could not succeed anywhere.[3]

Second only to the Russian Minister's disdain for American democracy was his continued low opinion of President Lincoln as a national leader in time of crisis. He considered Lincoln to be personally honest, kind, courteous and possessed of a fine character. But as a leader he believed him to be weak, inexperienced and lacking in moral courage. He had neither an immediate plan nor a long-range policy. He was the tool of unscrupulous intriguers who had made him their candidate for President for the very reason of his weakness. They were sure they could bend him to their will and have him do their bidding. Now he was forever vacillating between the conservatives and radicals and always yielding to the extremists. Stoeckl declared: "Considering the vastly superior resources of the North, Lincoln should have brought about a speedy suppression of the rebellion." However, "the great trouble with Lincoln was that the task was too great for him."

Stoeckl, however, had nothing but admiration for the American people. "Nothing is impossible for this extraordinary people, nothing is too difficult for them," he wrote. One of their chief characteristics was their confidence in their nation and its destiny. Strangely, they believe their form of government to be "the best government God ever saw," and that it will last forever.

But the Russian envoy had no confidence in the leaders of democracy. They appeared to him as a noisy, fanatic and ignorant lot of mediocrities. He looked on most members of Congress as demagogues and intriguers, ignorant of the fundamentals of government.

With the start of the session of Congress which meets on December 6, we are entering the fourth year of the American revolution, for this revolution will date from the opening of the federal legislature which preceded the inauguration of President Lincoln. In fact, it is to the politicians of the two parties, Republicans and Democrats, who were then sitting in Congress, that we owe the Civil War.

No one at that time, neither the heads of the parties nor the nation at large, could foresee the disastrous consequences of these political dissensions which took place in Washington. The men of the South believed that the Democrats of the free states would sustain their cause and would prevent war. In the North they were persuaded that 40,000 to 50,000 men would be sufficient to put down the insurgent States. They were mistaken on both sides. The Democrats of the North, far from opposing the war, made common cause with their political rivals and did not draw back from any sacrifices in support of the struggle.

On the other hand, the federal government found on the part of the secessionists a resistance which it hardly expected.

I shall not speak of the military operations of the last three years. I shall only deal briefly with the causes that have paralyzed the efforts of the federal armies and which have prevented them from profiting from their successes each time that the fortunes of war were in their favor.

The movement of the armies was directed from Washington by the President as supreme head of the land and sea forces, by the Secretary of War and by General Halleck, Commander in Chief. The first two are lawyers by profession and naturally have no knowledge of military art. The third is a former officer but in the position which he occupies has already shown himself to be a mediocrity. Never have these three individuals been able to agree. Each one had his plan and each one issued orders. The commanders of the army corps constantly received conflicting instructions and did not know whom to obey. In addition, Congress named a committee of senators to supervise the progress of military operations. The members of this committee visited the camps and assumed the

right to give orders which the generals had to comply with under
pain of dismissal. From these facts one gets some idea of the confusion that this state of affairs produced in the army.

Military operations have always been subordinate to political
needs. Whenever it became necessary to influence the elections of
the States they gave the order to certain generals to advance and
wage battle without any concern whether they were prepared or
not. Often it resulted in a defeat instead of a victory. . . . Finally
the jealousy and the mistrust of the politicians towards the military chiefs were equally important factors which hindered the
progress of operations. General McClellan is the object of deep
hatred of the radicals and the Secretary of War. Toward the end
of 1861, General McClellan could have captured Richmond if they
had not taken away part of the army which was to have joined
him. Last May McClellan was besieging Richmond. McDowell, at
Fredericksburg with 40,000 men, was to march on Richmond to
join McClellan. At that time the Confederates had but a very
small defending force which could not possibly resist McDowell.
Richmond would doubtless have fallen. But the politicians inter-
fered. They did not want McClellan to get credit for capturing
Richmond. As McDowell set out for Richmond, President Lincoln ordered McDowell to take the greater part of his army into
the Shenandoah Valley. McDowell replied to the President that
he would obey but that such a maneuver would be fatal. "This is
a crushing blow to us," he said. The President answered that he
regretted the necessity of having to assign him to the new destina-
tion but that circumstances demanded it. McDowell, in comply-
ing with the order of his superior, felt it his duty to tell the President that it would take him ten days to reach the upper Potomac
and by that time General Jackson would have withdrawn.

The secret explanation for this maneuver is that McClellan had
always been the object of hate of the radicals and Secretary of
War Stanton who is their tool in the Cabinet. They couldn't permit McClellan the honor of taking the Confederate Capital.

General McClellan was gaining the affection of his soldiers to
an ever-increasing degree, and they were afraid he might become
powerful enough to become a candidate at the next presidential
election.

According to the report of the Secretary of War at the beginning of the present year, the federal army numbered more than a million men. Now it must be reduced by at least half by battle, desertion and above all by sickness.

I have had an opportunity to discuss things with several officers who have returned from the armies stationed along the Mississippi and on the coasts of the secessionist States. They admitted to me that fever and other sicknesses carried off the staggering number of 200,000 men.

In considering the progress of events in domestic affairs during the last three years, one will find the same disorder and the same confusion. The President has vacillated constantly between the conservatives and the radicals, and has always yielded to the pernicious advice of the latter. Mr. Seward, without doubt the only capable man among those in power, has always been motivated by the best of intentions, but has never had enough power to make himself heard. No strong leader has been found to direct affairs of state. In the administration as in the federal legislature, no one up until now has had any set plan. No one has proposed a single practical measure.

The condition of the treasury is more satisfactory than one might believe after three years of tremendous expenditures. The public debt at this moment must be at least a billion and a half dollars, if not more. In spite of that Mr. Chase, Secretary of the Treasury, is not at the end of his resources. True, government bonds have to be issued at a huge discount. However, Mr. Chase continues to dispose of them, and succeeds by this method in raising revenues needed to meet government expenses, which are roughly two million dollars a day.

It is believed that for next year the budget of Mr. Chase will rise to $1,000,000,000. Thus if the war continues two more years, the debt of the United States will reach the size of the English debt, with this difference, that here the interest rates are double, and that in addition to the federal debt, the States and the municipalities have their own separate debts. Up to this point interest has been paid by floating new loans. But this state of affairs can hardly continue and it remains a question how the government can later fulfill its obligations, especially if the struggle results in a separation of the Southern States. A leading banker of New York with whom I conversed on this subject, said to me: "We will be able to pay the interest of the debt, no matter how heavy, if we succeed in restoring the Union in such a way as to be able to profit from the rich products of the South, as in the past. If not, bankruptcy is inevitable." He added, "Since we have no foreign debt, we of the United States will be the only people to suffer from it. The people would rather see the government repudiate the public debt than be overburdened with taxes."

Such, sir, is the military and political situation of the country. The revolution has already been going on for three years and it is impossible to foresee an end to this conflict. More than ever a conciliation based on compromise has become impractical. The nation wants it. The American people remember the benefits of peace which they have enjoyed so long. They regret the loss of their past prosperity and the high position that they occupied among the nations of the world and of which they were so justly proud. They find themselves today in the midst of a dreadful fratricidal war and cannot deceive themselves on the dangers of the future. The great majority of the nation would be ready to compromise, but the voice of the conservatives is stifled among cries of vengeance uttered by the radicals in their newspapers, on the public streets, and even in religious gatherings.

The war will, therefore, have to continue. The resources of the North have been strained, it is true, but not exhausted. There is difficulty in procuring men, and public credit is no longer as firm as it once was. Nevertheless, the government, with the great powers it possesses today, will find the means of continuing the struggle for another two or three years. The exhaustion of the South is the only hope of seeing an early end to the war.

We have little contact with the seceded States. We do not know their true condition, but it is certain that they are suffering the greatest misery and distress. In spite of this they continue to defend themselves with the utmost vigor. They have the advantage of waging a defensive war, in a vast, widespread area which is difficult to invade. They have had the good fortune of possessing military leaders more skilful than their adversaries. Through well-planned maneuvers they frequently succeeded in defeating the federals who always outnumbered them. But the most effective weapons which the Southerners have used to prolong the struggle have been given them by their adversaries. The secessionist leaders have skilfully exploited the threats of conquest and extermination uttered by the extremist party of the North. They have persuaded the people of the South that they have no other alternative than to conquer or be exterminated. They thus succeeded in creating among these people a fanaticism which alone can explain this desperate resistance.

But if it is still impossible to foresee the outcome of the struggle, there are two things which can already be considered as a part of history. The first is that the institution of slavery has received a blow from which it will never recover. In the border States— Maryland, Kentucky, Missouri and a large part of Virginia and Tennessee—occupied by the federal troops, slavery no longer exists except in name and will disappear completely with the end of the war. If the separation does take place this institution may still be able to be maintained in the cotton States but under new and less solid conditions.

In the second place, this revolution has undermined the foundations of pure democracy as it existed in the United States. The Constitution is now no more than an empty shell. Step by step the President has assumed more and more discretionary powers. He was led to this by the pressure of events rather than by his own will.

Universal suffrage is practised here today more or less as it exists in certain parts of Europe. The writ of habeas corpus has been suspended. The rights of the States have been almost annulled, and military authority is absolute in every part of the country.

There is a strange contrast as to what is happening at this moment on the two continents. In Europe the revolutionists, the Utopians and the other restless spirits are agitating to upset the whole order of things and to substitute for them democratic institutions. In America these same institutions seem to have run their course. The military regime is taking root more and more, not only in governmental affairs but even in the day by day activities of the American people.[4]

In a subsequent letter Stoeckl continued:

No one believed at the beginning of this struggle that the North would be able to stand for such a long time the staggering expenses of war and yet, after three years, the treasury continues to meet the necessities of the situation, and in spite of an enormous debt, public credit has not been greatly disturbed. Mr. Chase has proved to be a skilful financier. He has procured the co-operation of all the banks of the North by convincing them that the nation's financial ruin would undoubtedly also result in their own bankruptcy. Supported by the financial interests, Mr. Chase will be able to furnish the funds for prolonging the war until a crisis which is inevitable shall upset this procedure.

The difficulty of procuring men is even greater. In June the President issued a call for 300,000 men by conscription. Later he issued a decree calling 300,000 volunteers to arms. With difficulty, 40,000 to 50,000 conscripts and almost as many volunteers were obtained. At the beginning of the war men came forward in large numbers. Two or three weeks were enough to form a regiment. But it is not so today. It is difficult to procure volunteers even by offering them bounties of $700 to $800. This state of affairs is not surprising. The States of the North have a population of 20,000,-000. They have already furnished over 1,000,000 troops. All the adventurous spirits that there were—all the unemployed in the great cities—immigrants brought here from Europe by poverty, have been absorbed by the army. Next, conscription will draft the agricultural, industrial and commercial classes. Only force will be able to drag men of these groups away from their homes, and it is doubtful whether they will submit willingly to it. Congress has already discussed this question. Several measures have been proposed, but none has been judged practicable. In the ultimate, conscription will have to be enforced, no matter how unpopular it may be.

However, with the almost limitless powers which the federal government possesses it will manage to surmount these obstacles up to a certain point, and the war will be prolonged still further, intensifying the poverty and bloodshed which have overwhelmed this country for three years."[5]

Later, in February 1864, he wrote:

The President has just ordered a new conscription of 500,000 men which forms with the two drafts of 300,000 men each, decreed in the months of June and of October, 1,100,000 called to arms in nine months. The two drafts of 600,000 men produced at most

200,000 and it is improbable that the new order will produce a larger number.

They have always tried here to delude themselves on the true state of the South which the newspapers, especially those of the ruling party, represent as being reduced to the last extremity. But the federal government thinks otherwise, and the new draft of 500,000 men is proof of this.

According to the information that we have about the South, the seceded States seem to be more determined than ever to continue the struggle and are making tremendous efforts to resist the invasion by the North. All men between the ages of twenty and forty have been called into active service and those between forty and sixty have been organized into garrisons in the towns. These people, whose hatred against their former fellow countrymen is growing daily, are truly answering the new appeal of Jefferson Davis.

It seems that the plan of the coming campaign is to seize and occupy the ports of Mobile and Savannah and to advance from those two points towards the interior of the States of Georgia and Alabama and Mississippi. These operations are to be combined with a similar movement of two army corps which would leave Chattanooga and Vicksburg also to converge towards the interior. These different corps are to join in the center of the Confederate States. It is a bold plan and there is no doubt that if it succeeds, the Confederate army will be destroyed.

But the distance that the federal armies have to cover, the lack of good roads and the difficulties of procuring provisions and of transporting munitions make the success of this enterprise problematic, to say the least.

In the meantime, they are getting ready on both sides. The armies are starting out and a month from now military operations will begin seriously.

All the advantages are now with the North. Their troops are more numerous, better equipped and better armed. They command the sea and all the waterways and thereby have a powerful aid in their warships and their gunboats. But what they lack is unity of action and the strong will to organize military operations. I must also say that among their generals there has so far been found not a single outstanding leader. In this respect, the leaders of the South are infinitely superior. Because of this situation there remains an element of doubt as to successful operations. But what is not doubtful is that the bloodshed will be terrific, and that the losses in life will surpass all losses to date, as large as they have been.[6] . . .

This war is a duel which, it now appears, will end only after the resources of both sides are drained.[7]

It Is Thus Lincoln Wages War

AN ELECTION of a President was due to take place in the autumn of 1864. The Russian Minister, accustomed to a government where the Czar ruled by divine right, thought it strange that a popular referendum to select a Chief Magistrate should take place in the middle of a war for national survival, especially since Lincoln, the incumbent, had already assumed dictatorial powers which perhaps not even the Czar wielded. How could an orderly election be held amid such chaos, turmoil, bitterness and partisan strife? No doubt it would be another example of the "rule of the mob" in America.[1]

In March, Stoeckl advised his superiors in St. Petersburg that he had just learned that Salmon P. Chase, Secretary of the Treasury, had refused to be a candidate for the presidency. "I regret this very much," wrote the Minister, "because of all the men in power, Mr. Chase is without doubt the most capable of pulling the nation out of the dangerous crisis in which it finds itself."[2]

Chase was actually engaged in open intrigues for Lincoln's overthrow, while remaining a member of his Cabinet. While asserting that he had no wish to be President he encouraged a campaign on his behalf to develop. But the Chase-for-President movement soon collapsed, and Lincoln accepted the resignation of his disloyal Cabinet officer.

All through the early months of 1864 politicians were actively planning the defeat of Lincoln in the coming election. The antislavery cabal could not tolerate his moderate and magnanimous views on reconstruction and treatment of the vanquished. They wanted a President of their own faction who would carry out their vengeful program of abolition and subjugation of the seceded States.

Confederate leaders, seeing only extermination of all they stood for, unless they conquered, would not recognize their impending defeat and refused to try to make terms with the magnanimous Lincoln. Feeling had become too bitter to permit that. They would struggle on as long as resistance was possible.

In frightening and convincing words Jefferson Davis exhorted the soldiers of the Confederate States to fight on. The eventual triumph of the South, he declared, was inevitable, yet the Northerners insisted upon continuing the conflict. "Their malignant rage aims at nothing less than the extermination of yourselves, your wives and children." He warned that the homes of the Southerners were to "be partitioned among the wretches whose atrocious cruelties have stamped infamy on their government."[3]

The most terrible devastation, suffering and loss of life of the war was now about to start as the armies of the North prepared to invade the South in a wide sweep of desolation. Atrocities were to be answered by counter strokes. An all-out effort to strike the Confederates on all fronts through simultaneous advances, was launched by the Union forces in February 1864. The plans were laid in strict secrecy, but the Russian Minister learned the details. To Prince Gortchakov in St. Petersburg he wrote on March 7:

> Military operations began sooner than we expected, an unusual spring having allowed the armies to start out in February. In order to prevent the Confederates from reaching points threatened by the federal government forces, they had decided to attack them on all sides at once—both on the Atlantic coast and on the Western front.
>
> Either this strategy was poorly planned or the generals were unskilful in carrying it out. The fact remains that the results have been unfavorable everywhere to the armies of the North.
>
> General Sherman, at the head of 20,000 to 25,000 men, left Vicksburg and, abandoning his communications, went towards Meridian from where he was to march to Mobile and encircle that town by land, while Admiral Farragut was to attack it by sea. Another army corps composed principally of cavalry troops under the command

of General Smith, entered the State of Mississippi near Memphis. This army was to join up with Sherman at Meridian and accompany him to Mobile. General Grant, commanding the main army of the West, advanced at the same time against the Confederate General Johnston. And lastly an expedition was sent by sea to Florida to occupy that State.

Unfortunately none of the federal commanders succeeded in fulfilling the mission which had been entrusted to him. General Grant advanced on Johnston, but after two or three days of bitter fighting, returned to his former quarters at Chattanooga. Scarcely had this news been received in Washington than it was learned that General Smith had also failed in his enterprise. In the report that this General sent to the Secretary of War, he said that for three days he drove the enemy ahead of him, but when he arrived at Pantatoc, he met a large Confederate force and in the struggle which followed, two of his regiments weakened and adversely affected the rest of his troops. He had to return to Memphis after losing a great many men. But it was the Florida expedition which was the most unfortunate. General Truman Seymour, who commanded it, disembarked at Jacksonville with eight or ten thousand men. He immediately set march towards the interior without taking any precautions. When he arrived at a village called Alegator [*sic*] he ran head-on into a Confederate force. It appears that the federal troops put up only weak resistance. They were routed and pursued as far as Jacksonville with a loss of 2,000 men killed, wounded and captured. General Seymour was put under arrest and is to be tried before a court martial.

The Army of the Potomac was also scheduled to participate in this general movement, but it was delayed for two or three weeks by preparations and only lately became ready for action. A detachment of from 5,000 to 6,000 horsemen under the command of General Kilpatrick succeeded by a bold maneuver in reaching the rear forces of the army of General Lee. It is reported that they advanced within ten miles of Richmond, but having no support, General Kilpatrick had to retreat, after suffering a loss of several hundred men.

There is no direct news from General Sherman, but it has been learned from the newspapers of the South that he had reached Meridian. It is doubtful that he will reach Mobile and we suppose that he will return to Vicksburg.

The result of these military operations is unfavorable. But the federal armies are too large to be seriously affected by a loss of 10,000 or 12,000 men. However, the moral effect has been strong and the North has had to realize more than ever the obstacles that it will meet in its invasion of the South.

In Washington, they were all the more disappointed because they had been so confident about the success of this combined movement of the armies. They accuse the President, Mr. Stanton, Secretary of War, General in Chief Halleck, in fact, all those who directly or indirectly participate in the numerous military councils. Mr. Stanton, with whom I spoke the day before yesterday, told me that the future lay with the generals commanding the different corps. But whose fault is it if not of those who direct affairs? The administration, in order to retain partisan control of the armed forces, appoints only those commanding officers who are loyal to it. When it comes to naming a general, they give greater consideration to his politics than to his military ability. It is, therefore, not surprising that the federal armies have frequently suffered defeats when they should have been victorious. Unfortunately it is unlikely that this will change now while the parties are waging bitter political warfare—one group to retain its power, the other to attain it.[4]

In the latter part of March, Stoeckl advised the Czar's government of what was to be the final and decisive change in the high command of the Union forces:

General Grant, who had distinguished himself last year by the capture of Vicksburg on the Mississippi, has been appointed Lieutenant General and Commander in Chief of all the armies of the Union. He is replacing General Halleck who is staying on in Washington as Chief of Headquarters.

It is hoped that General Grant, whose vigor and perseverance are well known, will give new drive to the federal armies in the campaign which is about to start. The new head of the army has asked for an increase in federal troops and the President has just issued a proclamation drafting 200,000 men. This call, together with the preceding drafts, increases the number of men whom the President has requested from the country in the last nine months, to 1,300,-000.

In his proclamation the President assigns to each State a quota that it must furnish, with the power of obtaining voluntary enlistments if that is possible; and if not, by conscription. But it is feared they will have to rely on this latter method, which is very unpopular. The government has, therefore, been compelled to rely on volunteers whose number has fallen far below the number requested by the President. At most, 200,000 recruits have enlisted. The total number today must be from 550,000 to 600,000 active men. This constitutes a strong force against a comparatively weak adversary. The country has the right to expect favorable results from the approaching campaign, and if this expectation is not realized the fault, as in the past, will be due to the confusion which prevails in the councils of the administration and in the incapacity of the generals.[5]

One of these "improvised" generals, according to the Russian Ambassador, was General Banks. "He always held high rank among politicians, but he possesses no military ability." Yet he was placed in command of an army of 25,000 men to invade Louisiana and take Shreveport.

His army was advancing, stretched out on a line of thirty miles. When they reached within two days of Shreveport, the federals met the Confederate General Kirby Smith at the head of 12,000 or 15,000 men. Smith massed all his forces and broke up the federal divisions one after the other, compelling Banks to retreat sixty miles. The federal defeat was complete. They lost 5,000 men killed and wounded and 4,000 were taken prisoners. In addition, they left in Confederate hands thirty pieces of artillery, two hundred wagons and the military treasury containing a million dollars.

The government has sought to keep secret as far as possible the extent of this disaster, but the details have gradually leaked out, and the effect on the country has been most painful. From all sides complaints have been lodged against General Banks, but as he has great political influence, the President has not dared to remove him. They try to appease public opinion by court martialing several lesser generals. It is thus that the administration of President Lincoln wages war.

The federal armies have also suffered defeats on the coasts of North Carolina, in Kentucky and Tennessee, always through the failures of the generals and the mismanagement of the government.

But all these preliminary operations have only secondary importance compared with the events about to take place on the banks of the Potomac and in the immediate vicinity of Washington. General Grant has collected an army of 180,000 men. Of these, 60,000 are to march on Richmond from Fort Monroe at the entrance of Chesapeake Bay, and 120,000 under the personal leadership of General Grant are going from Washington to the Capital of the South. General Lee seems to have taken all measures for putting up a desperate resistance. The strength of his army is not known, but it is estimated at 100,000 men. The delay by the federal government, necessitated by the extensive preparations for the campaign, has enabled Lee to fortify not only the outskirts of Richmond, but also all the principal strategic points on the road leading to this Capital.

I recently obtained permission for Lieutenant Colonel Struve, who is here on a scientific mission for the imperial Ministry of War, to visit the Army of the Potomac. When he returned he gave me some interesting information about this army. The troops were in good condition but discipline was not perfect. The commanders gave great praise to the soldiers who have been in the service since the beginning of the war, but they admitted that they had little confidence in the new recruits. Colonel Struve found the two armies stretched out for a distance of forty miles, the sentinels in sight of each other. We are thus at the eve of a new and frightful sacrifice of men, without any hope that the result, whatever it may be, will bring this terrible struggle to an end.

Washington has been converted into a vast hospital. Besides the 12,000 wounded already here, they have prepared 25,000 beds for the maimed and wounded who will be brought here from the battlefields.

The Secretary of State, whom I saw this morning, told me that General Grant was expecting to be able to start on a campaign today or tomorrow. It is, therefore, possible that before you receive this report, you may be informed by telegram of the result of the battle which is about to take place.[6]

On May 13, 1864, Stoeckl wrote of the desperate fighting taking place between Grant's and Lee's huge armies in the tangled wooded district called the "Wilderness," the outcome of which "will have great effect upon the result of the war":

General Grant set out on May 4 with his entire army and sent it across the Rapidan. General Lee was waiting for him at Chancellorsville. On the 5th they fought from dawn till evening on even terms. On the 7th the fight was renewed all along the line and again lasted the whole day without either side gaining any real advantage. The two armies held their respective positions. During the night of the 7th to the 8th, Lee left the battlefield and withdrew a few miles. The news of Lee's retreat spread at once and caused a great sensation in the country. It was believed, and the government shared this opinion, that the enemy was in full retreat, but they were not long in learning they were mistaken. The retreat of Lee was only a strategic move. In fact, this General retired to Spotsylvania, a position which he had fortified in advance, six miles beyond Chancellorsville. General Grant followed him and the two armies continued fighting on the 8th, 9th and 10th, but we have no official news about these battles.

The reports which we received from General Butler are as obscure as those we have of the Army of the Potomac. This General, who was to cooperate with Grant in the capture of Richmond, went up the James River and disembarked his troops at City Point, eighteen miles from the Confederate Capital. The day before yesterday he sent a report to the government in which he states: "I am now well entrenched in City Point protected by many gunboats," which proves that he has done nothing so far to create a diversion in favor of Grant.

Butler became a general only during the war. Grant protested against the order which entrusted the command of such an important expedition to an inexperienced man, but they did not follow his advice, for Butler is a politician of great influence in the North, and the President is afraid he might be against him at the next election.

Fierce as previous battles have been during this war, the losses suffered in the battles of the last five or six days have surpassed all others. According to the most authentic reports that we have, the army of Grant was reduced two days ago by 35,000 men, of whom 25,000 were killed or wounded, and 10,000 were taken prisoner or deserted. Five generals have been killed and seven or eight wounded. The federals have taken 2,000 prisoners but they admit having lost a larger number. Three of their generals have fallen into enemy hands. We do not know about the losses of the Confederates, but it is to be assumed that they are equal to those of the federals.

Mr. Seward and the Secretary of War, with whom I talked, told me that nothing is decisive yet. But the situation looked as though there could be no doubt about final success.[7]

Unable to pierce Lee's defenses at Spotsylvania, General Grant wrote his famous dispatch that "I propose to fight it out on this line, if it takes all summer." Lincoln was pleased with Grant's resoluteness. Future historians were to declare, "The great and winning strategy of the war was created by Grant." Military experts were to acclaim him "a really great soldier" whose "Vicksburg campaign was a master-piece." And a recent writer dealing with Lincoln's troubles in select-ing winning generals was to state, "Grant was, judged by modern standards, the greatest general of the Civil War. He was head and shoulders above any general on either side as an over-all strategist, as a master of what in later wars would be called global strategy. . . . He was a brilliant theater strategist, as evidenced by the Vicksburg cam-paign, which was a classic siege operation."[8] But Stoeckl, giving full weight to the charges that Grant's incompetence, lack of precaution and shortcomings as a tactician had been responsible for the heavy Union losses at the Battle of Shiloh, wrote to Prince Gortchakov on May 23, 1864:

General Grant has so far given no proof of being a great strategist. It appears that he undertakes no maneuvers, and that he simply drives his masses of men against the fortified positions of Lee trying to crush him by sheer superiority of numbers.

Continuing his report of May 23, Stoeckl added:

On the peninsula, General Butler advanced with the intention of attacking Fort Darling, an important place situated a few miles from Richmond, but he was driven off and is today bottled up in City Point where he landed three weeks ago.

But most important has been the defeat of the federal General Sigel, who, at the head of 12,000 or 15,000 men, was advancing in the Shenandoah Valley in order to outflank the position of Lee and cut his communication with Richmond. Sigel was advancing, as often happens here, without taking any precautions. He suddenly found himself face to face with a Confederate division which defeated him with considerable losses in men and equipment.

This General Sigel is the same man who, in 1848, participated in the revolution of Baden. Appointed general at the beginning of the war, he has proven himself altogether incapable, but as he is very popular among the German radicals of the North, and as the administration needs their votes, the President has given him a command.

The news from the West is better. General Sherman, who commands the main body of the federal army, has left Chattanooga and advanced towards Atlanta, one of the most important cities in Georgia, without meeting any strong resistance on the part of the Confederate General Johnston.

The government continues to express confidence and considers the fall of Richmond a certainty. However, it admits that it needs time and immense sacrifices of life to achieve this goal. The losses so far have been terrific. They have already transported to Washington more than 18,000 wounded and 12,000 others are at present in the temporary hospitals set up not far from the battlefield.[9]

During the ensuing weeks, while the military situation was causing profound anxiety, the political campaign was producing intense excitement. On May 31 Republican bolters met in convention in Cleveland. They shouted their disgust for "the imbecile and vacillating policy" of Lincoln, and demanded "immediate extinction of slavery . . . by congressional action." They named as their presidential candidate John C. Frémont who asserted that Lincoln's administration was "politically, militarily and financially a failure." But the Frémonters struck no responsive chord among the people, and during September Frémont withdrew from the race.

Republican malcontents endeavored to persuade Lincoln to stay out of the contest. They predicted that he could not be re-elected. But on June 7 the National Union convention at Baltimore unanimously renominated Lincoln for President. As his running mate they selected

Andrew Johnson, an energetic and aggressive war Democrat from Tennessee.

The Democrats were to wait until the end of August before naming their candidate. Confident of victory, they nominated General George B. McClellan as their standard-bearer. He ran on a platform which stigmatized Lincoln's war policy a failure, and cried for peace and a settlement.

Amid this political excitement Stoeckl kept writing about the military campaigns of the frightful conflict which, in its fourth year, was devouring men and money without stint. On June 13, he reported to his government:

> To judge by the few details that we have regarding the movement of the armies in the West, it appears that the victories have been equally divided between the two sides, and that so far nothing has been decisive has happened. What is certain is that the losses continue to be immense. It is now a question of what the government will do to fill the gaps caused by these last battles. This question is being discussed in Congress, but so far nothing has been decided. The country has already supplied too many men to be able to give any more. It is perhaps fortunate, for the exhaustion of the two sides alone may put an end to this devastation and bloodshed.[10] . . .
>
> The very day that I sent my last report on military operations, we learned that the Confederates had crossed the Potomac and entered Maryland. The government believed it at first to be an invasion of guerrillas and did not take any steps. But they were not long in realizing that the matter was very serious. Actually Lee had detached a fairly considerable force whose number is not known but is estimated at 20,000 to 30,000 men, in order to make a demonstration against Washington, with the probable intention of forcing General Grant to raise the siege of Richmond and come to the help of the federal capital.
>
> The Confederates first attacked Harpers Ferry, a town situated on the Potomac, and carried off or destroyed munitions and provisions to the value of some millions. They then crossed the northwest of the State of Maryland and even entered Pennsylvania. General Wallace, commanding the Union troops in Maryland, gathered together 10,000 or 12,000 men and went against the

enemy. A very fierce battle took place on the River Monacacy. General Wallace was defeated and had to withdraw to Baltimore. The Confederates advanced on Baltimore and Washington, and at the moment are only about eight or ten miles from here. What is strange and what characterizes the federal government, is that Lee has been able to send a fairly considerable force from Richmond to the Potomac without the authorities of Washington having the least knowledge of it. It was only when danger was imminent that they began to take precautions against invasion. The President appealed to the Governors of the States of the North for 25,000 or 35,000 militia, but this appeal was not received with enthusiasm, and so far not a single man has appeared. At the same time, Grant was given the order to send troops here. I have been assured that 30,000 men are already here; that several more divisions were going up the Potomac and were to keep on arriving; and that the Capital was properly protected from attack. Nevertheless, the Confederates continue to occupy the positions that they had taken two days ago to the northwest of Washington.

We find ourselves again in the same danger which we ran into two years ago. The city is in a state of consternation. The President and the members of the Cabinet have a gunboat ready to take them away if the Confederates should succeed in entering the city. We cannot hope that the government, in case of danger, will assume responsibility for the diplomatic corps, and we shall have to provide our own means of reaching safety.[11]

However, two days later Stoeckl was able to write:

The federal Capital has just been saved for the fourth time during this war from the danger of being captured by the enemy.

In my report of the day before yesterday I informed you that the Confederates were besieging Washington. During the night of the 12th to the 13th, the federals, having received reinforcements from General Grant, made a reconnaissance and an engagement took place without advantage to either side. Yesterday morning the Confederates had disappeared. All kinds of rumors were circulating in the city. They said that the Confederates had withdrawn in order to make the federals leave their entrenchments and engage in battle. At the same time, reports were circulating that a corps of 25,000 men from the South had crossed the Potomac about ten miles from here and was coming to reinforce the troops which were besieging Washington. The government had no positive information and several generals with whom I spoke yesterday in the Department of War, admitted to me that they were in complete ignorance of the whereabouts of the enemy. Nevertheless, it appears probable that the Confederates have abandoned the siege and that they are recrossing the Potomac to go back to Virginia. But there is nothing certain about this.

It is impossible to describe the consternation which has prevailed and which still prevails in Washington. And the alarm has been equally great among the federal authorities. The roads are blocked with wagons of the residents from the outskirts who sought refuge in the city. The department offices are closed and the clerks, organized into companies, are drilling on the public square. The fear was so great that arms were supplied to a crowd of government workers, tramps, and Negroes without considering that these people might be altogether useless for defense purposes, and that they would be the first to pillage the city on the approach of the Confederates.[12] . . .

As the European press has probably been filled with exaggerated accounts about the invasion of Maryland and the siege of Washington by the Confederates, I feel it my duty to give you some details about this event and the military operations which preceded it.

While Grant was crossing the James River to attack Richmond on the South, General Sheridan with 7,000 or 8,000 horsemen was advancing towards Lynchburg situated 60 miles to the southwest of the Confederate Capital. General Hunter, who was in the Shenandoah Valley at the head of 20,000 men, received similar orders. These two divisions were to meet at Lynchburg, a railroad center, to cut communications and entirely isolate the Confederate army. This expedition which promised such important results, failed completely.

Within a few weeks the fearless young General Sheridan was to launch his brilliant campaign in the Shenandoah Valley. His decisive victories over General Early at Winchester (Sept. 19), Fisher's Hill (Sept. 22), and Cedar Creek (Oct. 19) were to shut forever the dangerous "backdoor to the North." But now Stoeckl in reporting the failure of the Lynchburg campaign, advised Prince Gortchakov:

> Sheridan was forced to withdraw. Hunter advanced as far as Lynchburg but did not succeed in taking it. It appears that lack of munitions and provisions compelled him to withdraw before engaging Confederate General Early, who had been sent after him with a division of Lee's army. Instead of returning through the Shenandoah Valley and protecting Washington, Hunter headed towards the West and has not been heard from since. Early took advantage of the mistake of his adversary and invaded Maryland by forced marches up the Potomac. He then scattered his army to launch attacks on several points at once and thus gave the impression that he was in command of considerable forces. The authorities at Washington were in fact made to believe that the invasion force was 40,000 to 50,000 men strong, while in reality it scarcely numbered 15,000. After threatening Baltimore, the Confederates advanced towards Washington, and besieged it for two days, in the presence of an army of 30,000 men, of whom 20,000 were veteran troops sent here by General Grant.

> But what is most surprising is that the Confederates, after wandering around Maryland for two weeks and destroying the railroads and carrying off a considerable number of horses and cattle, retired with all their booty to Virginia without even being hindered in their withdrawal.

> The success of this invasion by the Confederates is due to the confusion which prevails in the councils of the federal authorities, and to the insubordination and lack of skill of the military leaders. The troops defending Washington were under the orders of two generals each claiming to be in command, and neither wanting to obey. General Hunter, who was the chief cause of this humiliating invasion, is a politician. He has experienced nothing but reverses wherever he has gone. But they kept him in the service and during this campaign the President gave him an important command only to please the radicals whose protege he is. Finally, General Wallace, who commands at Baltimore, is only a lawyer of second rank. They have just removed him from his command.

> In the light of this, it is not surprising that Early, who is re-

ported to be a skilful general, succeeded so well in his bold enterprise. He counted on the ineptitude of his rivals and was not mistaken.

The reports which we have from the West are more favorable
to the Northern cause. General Sherman is only a few miles from
Atlanta, one of the most important cities of the South. Grant is
still occupied with the siege of Petersburg.[13]

The people of the United States had become weary of the war.
Sagacious Party leaders, observing this discouragement in their own
neighborhoods, reported it to Party headquarters. Most of them agreed
that there was no chance of winning the election with Lincoln heading
the ticket. From one quarter after another came the suggestion of setting aside Lincoln and inviting Grant to be a candidate. In the middle
of August, Thurlow Weed, shrewdest of the Republican Party man-
agers, told Lincoln point-blank that his chances for election were hopeless. A few days later the distraught President received a similar report from the central Republican Committee, through its Chairman,
Henry J. Raymond.

Lincoln, watching the straws in the wind all pointing toward defeat,
admitted that the only chance for his winning in November lay in the
occurrence before that time of a military success—one great enough
to convince the people that there was no cause to despair of the war.

In the meantime advocates of a peaceful adjustment of the conflict
were insisting that a commissioner be appointed with authority to
negotiate with representatives of the Confederacy for peace. Lincoln
replied to Horace Greeley, the noisiest of this group: "If you can find
any person, anywhere, professing to have authority from Jefferson
Davis, in writing, embracing the restoration of the Union and the
abandonment of slavery, whatever else it embraces, say to him that he
may come to me with you."

Lincoln authorized the patriotic but erratic editor to act as a commissioner. Greeley went to Niagara Falls to hold an interview with
two rebel emissaries, Clement C. Clay and Jacob Thompson, who had
served as Secretary of the Interior in the Cabinet of President Buchanan.

It soon became apparent that Jefferson Davis' representatives had
no authority to negotiate for peace. They were interested only in such

propositions as were consistent with the independence of the Confederacy. The failure of Greeley was most humiliating, and for a while he was effectually silenced.

As the terrible summer of 1864 dragged to an end, the autumn began with surprising good news. The black clouds over the North suddenly disappeared when on September 2, General Sherman electrified the Nation by telegraphing: "Atlanta is ours, and fairly won." Only a few days before, Admiral Farragut had defeated the Confederates in the dramatic naval battle of Mobile Bay. The victory closed the Gulf port, tightened the blockade, and greatly increased the isolation of the South from the outside world.

To Lincoln the news of these victories was as welcome as a day of warm sunshine in a winter month. Almost overnight the despondency of the North gave way to hope. There was now a chance for Lincoln's re-election.

Although Sherman had captured the important city of Atlanta after besieging it, both his position there and his future movements were by no means safe because of his precarious line of communications. Stoeckl, reporting this situation to his government, wrote:

> General Sherman has advanced into Georgia and has occupied Atlanta, but he has had to stop there since he is too far from his base of operations. The Confederates, not being strong enough for a frontal attack, came in from the rear and cut his communications. Sherman has had to withdraw, and according to the latest reports, was in a very difficult position.
>
> The same is true of General Sheridan who invaded Virginia through the Shenandoah Valley. His communications have also been cut and while he was almost one hundred miles to the south of the Potomac, a thousand guerrillas crossed that river and came within twenty-five miles of Washington. Sheridan was obliged to withdraw.
>
> General in Chief Grant came to Washington recently to consult with the President and the Secretary of War. Until a short time ago, he continued giving the most positive assurances that Richmond, the Confederate Capital, would soon be in his power. But it appears now that he no longer is so confident and according to information I possess, it is doubtful that the federals will succeed in entering Richmond before winter.

At this moment a great naval expedition against Wilmington, the principal port of North Carolina, is being prepared. It is a daring enterprise, for according to reports, Wilmington is defended by fortifications as strong as those that the federals found before Charleston. Several people with whom I have discussed the matter, among others the Secretary of State, have admitted to me that its success was doubtful.

Actually this expedition has no other aim than to appease public opinion and especially to influence the presidential election.[14]

The election campaign continued in an atmosphere of military excitement. On November 6, two days before the people of the North went to the polls, Stoeckl reported that the various campaigns of the all-out drive against the Confederacy were not succeeding at all. Grant had met with a setback before Petersburg and Richmond. Sherman was threatened at the Tennessee border by General Beauregard, the new Confederate commander of the Army of the West. And Missouri, depleted of her troops who had been sent to re-enforce Grant and Sherman, was invaded by Southern guerrillas.

In spite of all the efforts which the administration is making to conceal the true state of affairs from the public, these last defeats have not failed to produce an unfavorable impression about the party in power. However, Mr. Lincoln and his adherents are sure of winning the forthcoming presidential election.[15]

Democrats denounced the War Department for turning its power into the service of Lincoln's re-election. They claimed that thousands of Republican soldiers were furloughed to return to doubtful districts and vote, while few Democrats were granted leaves. This caused the Russian Minister to write: "If the vote were free, the chances would certainly be in favor of General McClellan, but with the powers which the government possesses, it will find the means of controlling the election. Universal voting is as easily managed here as anywhere else."[16]

Now That Lincoln Has Been Re-elected

THE PEOPLE of the loyal States went to the polls November 8, 1864, to elect a President of the United States. Never before in history had a nation, embroiled in a civil war and fighting for its very life, risked a national referendum.

Despite the opposition of the politicians to Lincoln, the people demonstrated their confidence in his administration. Every loyal State excepting only three—New Jersey, Delaware and Kentucky—gave him its electoral vote. In response to public congratulations, Lincoln said:

> I am thankful to God for this approval of the people. But while deeply grateful for this mark of their confidence in me if I know my own heart, my gratitude is free from any taint of personal triumph. It is not in my nature to triumph over anyone; but I give thanks to Almighty God for this evidence of the people's resolution to stand by free government and the rights of humanity.

Stoeckl, who had expressed amazement at the phenomena of a strife-torn nation conducting a national election while fighting for survival, could have found his answer in a little speech which Lincoln made to a party which came to "serenade" him. The re-elected President said:

> It has long been a grave question whether any government not too strong for the liberties of its people can be strong enough to

maintain its existence in great emergencies. On this point the present rebellion brought our government to a severe test, and a presidential election occurring in regular course during the rebellion added not a little to the strain. But we cannot have a free government without elections; and if the rebellion could force us to forego or postpone a national election it might fairly claim to have already conquered and ruined us. But the election along with its incidental strife has done good too. It has demonstrated that a people's government can sustain a national election in the midst of a great civil war. Until now it has not been known to the world that this was a possibility. But the rebellion continues, and now that the election is over may not all have a common interest to reunite in a common effort to save our common country?

The people's mandate was clear: the war should be fought to the end. Now the attention of the entire nation was focused on Sherman's invasion of the South. He had been unable to maintain his line of communications, and rumors were being spread that his army, surrounded and starved, was in danger of capture. As Stoeckl wrote:

> Public anxiety is all the greater because since the advance of Sherman already twenty-two days ago, there is very little news of this expedition. The Richmond newspapers which we receive here fairly regularly have decided to remain silent on the movements of the invading army. The federal government on its part is also silent. The Secretary of State told me that all was going well, and that there was no apprehension about the result of this campaign. About twenty transports loaded with provisions and munitions are cruising along the coast of Georgia and South Carolina ready to help Sherman as soon as he arrives on the Atlantic Coast.[1]

By the middle of December the Russian Minister was able to report to his government that the suspense over Sherman was relieved. In fact, the entire military situation had taken a favorable turn for the federals.

> General Sherman, who left Atlanta to cross Georgia, reached the Atlantic coast and got into communication with the fleet stationed along the Georgia coast. In a report that the government has just received from him, he stated that he had surrounded Savannah and that he did not doubt the early capture of that town.

The loss of Savannah will be a heavy blow to the Confederates.

In the West, General Thomas, who was besieged at Nashville by the Confederates under General Flood, after receiving reinforcements attacked his enemy and forced him to withdraw, capturing several thousand prisoners and thirty to forty cannons. The Confederate general will be compelled to abandon Tennessee again.

However, the people of the South do not seem to be discouraged. Mr. Geoiffroy, the French Chargé d'Affaires, showed me a letter from his Consul in Richmond dated the day before yesterday. He said that the Confederates are prepared to defend themselves to the last. He spoke also of their intention of arming the Negroes, and added that the South is under no illusions about the impossibility of maintaining slavery. Their only goal is to separate from the North.[2]

At Christmas, General Sherman presented Lincoln with the city of Savannah "as a Christmas gift." But there was great disappointment in the failure to take Wilmington as well. In his last report for the year 1864, Stoeckl wrote:

According to the plan of operations drawn up by the federal military leaders, the port of Wilmington was to be attacked and taken at the same time as that of Savannah. They were all the more sure of success since the preparations for this expedition have been made on a gigantic scale. But the results have not been what the government expected.

The port of Wilmington on the coast of North Carolina is of great importance to the South. Ships can enter it from all sides and for that reason it is difficult to blockade. It is to Wilmington that the blockade-runners made in England have been going. It is estimated that eight out of ten of these ships succeed in evading the vigilance of the federal cruisers and enter the port.

The expedition for the attack on Wilmington was composed of forty-eight armor-plated warships and forty transports, carrying 12,000 to 15,000 men. The land and sea forces simultaneously attacked the fortifications, which defended the entry to the port, but they met unexpected resistance. After a battle of two days the fleet retired and the land troops were forced to re-embark. Admiral Porter, commander of the fleet, and General Butler, leader of the land troops, are accusing each other and are trying to shift the responsibility for this disaster to each other. The fleet has suffered little damage but the land troops have had considerable losses. Of the five or six thousand men who tried to capture the main Confederate fort, scarcely half succeeded in reaching the ships. General Butler has already returned to Fort Monroe.

The expedition was accompanied by an infernal machine or torpedo of tremendous proportions. It was a ship loaded with 300 tons of powder. This invention which they believed would be a new means of attack against the land fortifications, had been discussed for a long time in a secret committee of technicians. Some among them held that at a distance of 400 meters the shock produced by the explosion of this machine would destroy the fort, and even blow up its powder magazines. The ship was hauled onto the beach at a distance of less than 400 meters. Nevertheless the explosion produced no effect. The Americans who had been so enthusiastic about the new invention were more upset by the failure of their monster torpedo than by the lack of success of the expedition.[3]

It had become crystal clear to Lincoln that the issue between the North and the South "could only be tried by war and decided by victory." But there were well-meaning advocates of peace conferences who still insisted that the issue could be settled by mediation. They begged Lincoln to be permitted to negotiate with commissioners of the South.

Stoeckl observed, "We must believe that Mr. Lincoln is conscientiously willing to make peace."[4] He overlooked no opportunity to hasten the day of peace. Therefore, it was no surprise to the Russian Minister to learn that

Mr. Lincoln has invited former President Pierce to Washington and entrusted him with a mission of peace. I met Mr. Pierce in New York two years ago and had a long conversation with him on the affairs of the nation. He was then opposed to force and told me that even the dissolution of the Union was preferable to civil war.

The high office which Mr. Pierce once occupied and his moderate opinions made him most suitable to fulfill a mission of peace between the two sections. Mr. Pierce has already been closely associated with Jefferson Davis who, during the Pierce administration, occupied the post of Secretary of War.[5]

Another would-be peacemaker was Francis P. Blair, a restless politician from Maryland, and father of Lincoln's Postmaster General. He persuaded the President to grant him a permit "to go south and return." In Richmond he held a confidential interview with Jefferson Davis. Stoeckl reported to his government that he had learned from a "sure source" that "Mr. Blair gave Jefferson Davis the assurance that if he sent commissioners instructed to negotiate, Lincoln would receive them officially."[6]

Naïvely Blair proposed to the Confederate President that the Union and Confederate armies cease fighting each other and unite to drive the French out of Mexico. The rebel leader expressed willingness to appoint and send, or to receive, agents "with a view to secure peace to the two countries." Lincoln replied to Blair that he was ready to receive any Southern agent who should be informally sent to him "with the view of securing peace to the people of our one common country." Continuing his report to the Czar, Stoeckl wrote:

> Following this step, three Confederate delegates presented themselves under a flag of truce at the outposts of the federal army before Richmond and asked for permission to come to Washington. These delegates were Alexander H. Stephens, R. M. T. Hunter and John A. Campbell. All three had taken an active and important part in public affairs. The first two served in Congress for twelve and fifteen years, respectively, and the third was a Judge of the Supreme Court of the United States.
>
> The President did not grant them permission to come to Washington, but ordered them to stop at Fort Monroe where he promised to go and meet them. He did, in fact, go with the Secretary of State, and on February 3, had a conference with the commissioners of the South which lasted several hours. [It was held at Hampton Roads, on board the *River Queen*.]
>
> The Secretary of State told me that the interview was one of extreme cordiality; that they avoided making the least suggestion which might offend, but they were unable to reach an agreement, and the conference therefore came to nothing.
>
> I managed to get some details from a senator, an intimate friend of the President. He told me that the commissioners had first asked for an armistice and for negotiations to be opened on the various

issues between the North and the South. Mr. Lincoln refused the armistice, declaring that he could only deal on the basis of the submission of the South and the reconstruction of the Union. The commissioners did not accept his terms and they departed.

Another individual who also enjoys the confidence of the President assured me that the last word has not yet been spoken on the subject, and that Lincoln continues to communicate with the Confederate authorities through General Grant and without the knowledge of the Secretary of State. An article published yesterday in the *New York Tribune* seems to confirm this assertion. It states that it is absurd to believe that the President went in person to Fortress Monroe simply to tell the insurgents that they had to lay down their arms; that if nothing was settled, it was because the question was too serious to be settled definitely by the commissioners and even by the President, chief of the state though he may be, without consultation with their associates in power, and that the conference might well be the prelude to an approaching peace.

I enclose the *Tribune* article. What makes it important is that the *Tribune* is the leading newspaper of the Republican Party, and that Mr. Greeley, its editor, has almost an unlimited influence over the President.

It is possible that the President and some people of his immediate circle may be sincere in the peaceful intentions which are imputed to them, but I must admit that I find it hard to believe. So far I do not see anything in these negotiations except the desire on the part of the government to fix the responsibility of the continuation of the war on its enemies, and to make the people bear with greater patience and resignation the burden of taxes and of conscription. I have no doubt at all that the secessionist leaders of Richmond are acting with the same motives.[7] . . .

The South could not accept Mr. Lincoln's terms which were tantamount to unconditional surrender.[8]

With Jefferson Davis speaking of "the two countries," and unwilling to accept anything less than the acknowledged independence of the Confederacy; and with Lincoln reiterating the phrase, "our one common country," and insisting that there could be but one basis of negotiation—Union and Emancipation—all attempts at peaceful mediation failed. He had exhausted all honorable means to secure peace. There was nothing to do but to continue to fight it out. Sorrowfully Stoeckl wrote,

> The conference, which gave rise to so much hope, only went to prove that the two sides were further apart than ever from reaching an agreement and that a reconciliation was impossible. The war will continue, and on both sides they are preparing for the coming campaign which will be more bitter than ever.[9]

Notwithstanding Lincoln's firm attitude, his unprecedented trip to Fortress Monroe to negotiate with the commissioners of the Confederacy gave rise to sensational rumors both in Washington and in London. Blair's naïve overture to Jefferson Davis, that the North and South reconcile their domestic troubles through a restored Union and uniting to fight the common enemies of America, caused gloomy forebodings in London. A number of British leaders took it for granted that England was the chosen enemy for this proposed foreign war. Lincoln, so ran the rumors, was prepared to send armies into Mexico and Canada. Stoeckl commented that today such a policy would be very popular in the North, but that "Lincoln might change his mind tomorrow."

On the other hand, the rumors which were afloat in Washington were to the effect that Lincoln was prepared to be "soft" with the South.

> These reports produced real panic among the radicals who were preparing to attack the President if he made the least concession to the South. There already exists a marked coldness between the President and the "ultras" of his Party who fear that Mr. Lincoln, now that he is re-elected, will try to free himself from their influence. Recently I had the opportunity of discussing this with one of them. He said to me: "We did not re-elect Mr. Lincoln for his ability, but only because he obeys the Party orders to the letter. He must accept our views, whatever they may be, or we will find the means to ruin him." In outlining these views, he said to me: "We wish to subjugate the South completely and to reduce it to a territory governed by the authority of the North."
>
> Some of these radicals go even further. They wish to exile all the inhabitants of the South and to populate its vast territory with immigrants from the North.
>
> These dissensions, threatening discord in the ruling Party, and

creating serious financial troubles despite the vast resources of the North, are not very favorable indications. The conquest of the South, which may probably be achieved, could temporarily stop the bloodshed, but it will not stop the progress of this revolution which is undermining the foundations of the political and social structure of the United States. The more I follow the conflicting views the more the result seems to me uncertain and distant.[10]

The Russian Minister continued to express doubt as to the outcome of the Civil War even while Sherman was marching irresistibly through the Southland, and Grant's iron hand lay heavily on the ramparts of Richmond. Clearly the Confederacy was crumbling. Its days were numbered. The Russian Minister apprised St. Petersburg of the North's capture of Fort Fisher and the closing of Wilmington to Confederate blockade-runners:

> It is evident that the seceded States are almost exhausted, which is hardly unexpected after such a long and bitter struggle. They are short of men. The armies of the North, reinforced by the last two conscriptions, must be at least up to 700,000 men. The Confederates have scarcely 200,000 to send against them.
>
> But what is more serious for the South is that discord seems to have broken out among the heads of the Confederation. It appears that they are divided into two factions. One, led by Jefferson Davis, wishes the immediate abolition of slavery and the continuation of the war. They hope that by freeing their slaves, they will win the favor of the foreign powers, especially France and England, and will obtain, if not material aid, at least their moral support. The other faction wants slavery to continue and seems disposed to return to the Union only on condition that the North will permit them to retain a portion of their Negroes at least temporarily. The federal government will follow a wise course if it takes these differences of opinion into consideration when it endeavors to reconstruct the Union. The goal of restoration of the Union would thus be more easily achieved in this way than by conquest. Subjugation is not yet complete. When it does come about, the North will find greater difficulties in winning obeisance of the people of the South than it had in conquering them.[11]

In the meanwhile Secretary Seward thought the time had come to propose to the nations of Europe to withdraw their recognition of

Southern belligerent rights. In March, he suggested to Stoeckl that Russia should take the lead in proposing this measure to England and France. But the Russian Minister advised Prince Gortchakov not to undertake this effort. In his opinion it would not meet with success.[12]

Prince Gortchakov, ever eager for reconciliation between North and South, favored a plan of mediation prepared by Constantine Catacazy, affiliated with the Foreign Office. Catacazy, who had resided for a number of years in the United States as Secretary of the Russian legation and who in 1869 was to succeed Stoeckl as the Czar's Ambassador to Washington, felt that the time was most opportune to mediate the conflict. Russia, he believed, as the warm friend of both the North and the South, was the proper medium to bring the two together. Gortchakov was inclined to agree with Catacazy's suggestion. But he would leave it wholly to Stoeckl's judgment and discretion to act upon the proposal. But the Russian Minister declared that no mediation, friendly or otherwise, could now end the bloodshed. The peace would have to be achieved by the generals on the battlefields.

The second inauguration of Lincoln took place on March 4, 1865. It was a raw and dismal day in the early hours, but it turned bright and clear later when the sun burst through the clouds. The ceremonies were held on a platform erected in front of the Capitol. Stoeckl sat in a section reserved for the foreign diplomats, directly behind the seats of the Supreme Court Justices.

As Lincoln stepped forward to take the oath of office, Stoeckl observed how greatly the President had changed in appearance since his first inaugural. Four years before he had appeared as a physical giant from the prairies of Illinois. But four years of war, bloodshed, worry and sleepless nights had taken their toll. Now he appeared haggard. His shoulders stooped. The furrows on his face had deepened. His cheeks were sunken. Great rings were under his eyes.

Then he spoke. Standing bareheaded under the March sky now suffused with warm sunlight, he delivered his Second Inaugural Address. It was a brief message—only a few noble, beautiful sentences spoken in a clear, resolute voice. He spoke from the depths of his heart. His message was a benediction and a plea—like the words of a prophet bidding the people to complete the task God Almighty had put before them, and to expiate their sins in humility. The closing words were like a sacred poem, lofty in tone, majestic in grandeur:

Fondly do we hope—fervently do we pray—that this mighty scourge of war may speedily pass away. Yet, if God wills it that it continue until all the wealth piled by the bondsman's two hundred and fifty years of unrequited toil shall be sunk, and until every drop of blood drawn with the lash shall be paid by another drawn with the sword, as was said three thousand years ago, so still it must be said, "The judgments of the Lord are true and righteous altogether."

With malice toward none; with charity for all; with firmness in the right, as God gives us to see the right, let us strive on to finish the work we are in; to bind up the nation's wounds; to care for him who shall have borne the battle, and for his widow, and his orphan—to do all which may achieve and cherish a just and lasting peace among ourselves, and with all nations.

Following the inauguration Stoeckl observed:

Military operations have recently taken on extraordinary activity and everything seems to indicate that we are on the eve of great events. The federal government has changed tactics. Instead of scattering its troops on a wide front in Confederate territory, it has massed them all on the Atlantic coast. The fall of the ports of Savannah, Charleston and of Wilmington has facilitated the transportation of provisions and munitions by sea.

The principal objective of the campaign is Richmond. General in Chief Grant, convinced of the impossibility of successfully assaulting the fortifications which surround this city, has planned to encircle it with all the forces at his command.

This plan of campaign has been put into execution by the different divisions of the army. General Sherman, after resting his troops in Savannah, left that city at the beginning of February with a force of 70,000 men headed straight for Richmond. Another company of 30,000 to 35,000 men went to Newburn in North Carolina, and is also rushing towards Richmond. Finally, a third column of about 20,000 men under General Sheridan crossed West Virginia and is advancing on Richmond from the west. General Grant is awaiting the arrival of his lieutenants in the hope of capturing Richmond and the whole Confederate army. These various army corps combined total 250,000 to 275,000 men, including the troops under Grant, who are presently besieging Richmond.

We have no accurate information as to the strength of the Confederate forces. They are estimated at approximately 130,000 to 150,000 men, of whom 70,000, commanded by General Lee, are defending Richmond, and an almost equal number under General Johnston are attempting to stop the march of Sherman.

Everything depends on this general. If the Confederates do not succeed in stopping him, the government and what remains of the army of the South will be forced to abandon Richmond and to withdraw to the interior. The secessionists may be able to continue the struggle by waging a defensive action in the region of the Blue Ridge Mountains. But the loss of Richmond will be a serious blow to the cause of the South, whose people are already utterly demoralized by the defeats which they have recently suffered, especially by the loss of their ports which prevents them from receiving aid from outside sources.[13]

With Grant crushing Lee from the east, and Sheridan sweeping down from the west and carrying everything before him, Richmond fell on April 3. Within a few hours Stoeckl was writing a detailed report of this great Northern victory to his superiors in St. Petersburg:

The fall of Richmond is one of the most important events of the entire war. It has completely disorganized the military and civil systems of the South. Jefferson Davis' government is in flight. The armies of Confederate Generals Lee and Johnston may combine and withdraw into the Blue Ridge Mountains of Virginia. But it is unlikely that these troops will be able to resist the force of 300,-000 men who will soon be surrounding them. In any event the lack of provisions and arms will soon force them to give up. It is rather improbable that the demoralized army, lacking food and arms, can continue the resistance much longer.[14] . . .

The only region where the federals might still meet resistance is in Texas. This State of tremendous size and bordering Mexico is easier to defend than Virginia, and all attempts made by the armies of the North to invade it have failed. In any event, this will only be a sectional struggle.

The war to all intents and purposes may be considered at an end.[15]

In the midst of composing this dispatch Stoeckl received the news
that "the Confederate army under Lee has surrendered to General
Grant." Lee, finding himself at Appomattox Court House, some seventy
miles west of Petersburg, surrounded and without hope of escape,
yielded to Grant's courteous invitation to surrender and spare further
slaughter.

> Grant has given them the most honorable conditions. The
> officers and soldiers, without exception, will be permitted to re-
> turn home without trouble. The officers will be permitted to retain
> their swords and personal belongings. General Grant acted with
> commendable moderation. We hope it will set an example to the
> politicians.[16]

Stoeckl subsequently apprised St. Petersburg of General Johnston's
capitulation to General Sherman "on the same terms as General Lee":

> This capitulation includes all the Confederate troops in all the
> Southern States east of the Mississippi. Texas and a small part of
> Arkansas are, therefore, all that remain of the Confederation. But
> the federal officers stationed in the West are negotiating with Gen-
> eral Kirby Smith, commander of the Confederate troops, and are
> trying to persuade him to lay down his arms by offering him the
> same conditions which were granted to the armies of the East.
> The federal government considers the war definitely over and
> has already taken measures to reduce the army to a strength of
> 100,000 or 150,000 men.[17]

Now with the conflict ended, "the government is faced with the
tremendous problems of reconstruction."[18] The sudden climax took the
Russian Minister completely by surprise. It "has given the lie to all
predictions," he told Prince Gortchakov. He had predicted that the
war would continue until both North and South would drop from
sheer exhaustion:

> Hardly three weeks ago, the President himself told me he was
> hopeful that the war would be over by the end of the year. An
> indication how little the government expected this turn of events
> is the fact that they are still recruiting 300,000 men in the North,
> who are due to replace the soldiers whose terms expire next
> autumn. The fact is that the South was weaker than supposed. Four
> years of all-out war has completely exhausted it. There were no

more men to fill the gaps in the army caused by casualties and sickness. The capture of the ports of Savannah, Charleston and Wilmington deprived the Confederates of arms, provisions and many other necessities which, despite the blockade, had reached them in great abundance from England. To this must be added the conflicts of opinion which broke out among the Southern States. Some Governors, dissatisfied with Jefferson Davis, refused to supply troops from their States. The Virginians, who supplied the main body of troops which defended Richmond, seeing the indifference of the other Southern States, were reluctant to go on fighting and General Lee, a Virginian himself, had great difficulty in persuading them to follow him after the fall of Richmond.[19]

With the South "put down," Stoeckl again predicted that the "problems of governing a conquered people would be great and difficult."[20]

Democracy Has Stood the Test

WITH THE end of the Civil War, critics and enemies of democracy throughout the world became cognizant of an amazing fact: American democracy had undergone the convulsions of four years of the bitterest, bloodiest and costliest of civil wars and had weathered the storm without much serious damage. Amid the exigencies of war, a free national election, with all its incidental strife, had been held according to schedule. Though stern necessity had compelled Lincoln to assume dictatorial powers unparalleled in the nation's history, the people had been free to vote him out of office altogether. Faith in republican institutions not only remained intact but had actually grown stronger. The Constitution of the United States, stretched and strained by the exigencies of the war, immediately, with the ending of the national crisis, could once more be invoked to protect the rights and liberties of the citizen.

Stoeckl, in common with many other European observers, had believed democracy to be tottering and had predicted its certain fall. America's rapidly developing power was in no way due to democracy, he had believed. The source of her strength and prosperity lay in confederation, but the old Union was gone forever. The breach between the North and South was irreparable, he had said.

He had constantly criticized the "inept leadership" of Lincoln, his "vacillation," and his "lack of moral courage." How explain the triumph of the federal government in the absence of strong leadership?

The Russian shrugged his shoulders and remarked that nothing is impossible for this extraordinary American people. Nothing is too difficult for them. If they lack strong leadership, they get along without it. "All predictions fail when one has to do with a people Providence has taken under his special protection."[1]

Stoeckl had predicted that the inevitable failure of democracy in the United States where it "operated under uniquely favorable conditions," would contribute to its failure everywhere. Now he was ready to admit that the triumph of democracy in the United States was a triumph for democratic institutions everywhere.

All these things Baron de Stoeckl observed as he set about to answer for the benefit of autocratic Russia the question: Has democracy stood the test? Never an admirer of democracy, he nevertheless answered honestly in the affirmative. Writing to Prince Gortchakov on that fateful April 14, 1865, Stoeckl summarized the amazing outcome of the American Civil War as follows:

> The Civil War has been a succession of events which, like everything that has happened to this exceptional people, has given the lie to all predictions and calculations.
>
> At the beginning, the rebellion of the Southern States caused only slight anxiety. We could not imagine that a people of 4,000,000 could resist the 20,000,000 of the North. But we were surprised later to see an army of 300,000 men not only capable of defending the seceded States, but strong enough to threaten the very borders of the North.
>
> As late as last summer they were still fighting on the territory of Pennsylvania and we were besieged in Washington. At that time the public debt was rising above a billion dollars and the paper money was only worth one-third of its normal value. We despaired of reconstructing the Union, when suddenly and without our being able to understand the reason, confidence began to rise again. Bonds rose in value. The government recovered its credit and raised enough money to meet the expenses of war which were rising to two or three million dollars per day. Hundreds of thousands of men flocked to reinforce the federal armies, and the government became stronger day by day.
>
> Finally, the climax surprised everyone. It came suddenly—an unexpected event. Richmond fell. General Lee, with the main

army of Virginia, was going down to defeat at the very moment when the administration was making preparations to continue the war through the next autumn. The Confederation was collapsing from sheer exhaustion three weeks after the conference of the commissioners of the South with Mr. Lincoln, who must have been still rather uncertain about the final victory of his armies since he was even then discussing the reconstruction of the Union on the basis of a compromise.

I must say here that the war could have been ended sooner if the government had been more skilful in using the vast resources that it possessed. I shall not refer again to the intrigues of the men in power, to their quarrels and their jealousies towards the generals. I have mentioned that more than once in my reports. But if the government was incompetent, the people proved themselves great. Thanks to the sacrifices they were prepared to undergo, the insurrection was put down not by the skill of the men in authority, but by an irresistible strength of the nation at large.

The struggle is over but it has created a new situation for the institutions and even the everyday life of this country. "States rights" have always been one of the foundations of the American Constitution. Before the rebellion each State governed itself, but during the last four years the federal government and Congress have gradually extended their power and have managed to exercise complete control over the internal affairs of the States. The people have at all times been opposed to centralization in which they saw peril to their liberties. They have yielded to it of late as a necessity imposed by the war. But they will seek to regain these rights, and it is to be feared that serious conflicts may result between the federal government and the States.

Deciding the future of the emancipated Negroes will be a difficult problem to solve. What is to be done with the 4,000,000 colored people in the midst of a population which in the North just as much as in the South considers them an inferior race? Several plans have been suggested to colonize them outside the country or to resettle them in the West, but without any success. Now they have suggested another plan. They want to force the Negroes to enter contracts with the landed proprietors to work for a certain number of years at wages. This plan may be good in theory, but it is too similar to the system of the coolies which is in practice in some colonies. The substitution of the work of the coolies by that of the Negroes in tropical countries has been a favorite topic for radical philanthropists. But they have not shown any practical results. Several hundred thousand Chinese and Italians have been taken to Cuba. Nine-tenths have succumbed to the climate, to hard labor and bad treatment on the part of the planters. Mortality among the coolies is three or four times higher than among slaves. That is quite natural, for the planter takes an interest in his slaves, but masters do not bother about laborers hired only for a brief time.

The same thing will happen in America if the system which they want to try is adopted. Slavery has been a problem for the United States. The presence of freed Negroes will be troublesome for them. The Negro will be tolerated only as long as he is useful to the Americans who, like all Anglo-Saxons, are always ready to speak piously about the rights of humanity, but are slow to put them into practice. It is to be feared that the black race may suffer the lot of the several million aborigines who formerly populated the North American continent and of whom only a slight trace remains.

The Civil War has thoroughly upset the financial system of the United States. When Mr. Lincoln came into power, the federal debt was gradually raised to $70,000,000, that is to say, $4,000,000 annual interest. Today it is officially up to two and one half billion, but according to the information I have, a host of unforeseen items will increase this figure to three and a half billion dollars, which represents approximately $200,000,000 annual interest. Income includes $75,000,000 produced by customs and $250,000,000 coming from taxes. Deducting therefrom the annual interest, there scarcely remains $125,000,000 to supply the needs of the government. Now the army alone, if it is reduced to 100,000 men, and that is the minimum, will absorb this sum, for here the upkeep of a soldier is estimated at more than $1,000 per year. The taxes which they have imposed until now are already so heavy that it will be impossible to increase them. It will, therefore, be necessary to reorganize the financial system entirely.

But the most difficult trace of the rebellion to eradicate will be the animosity of the South. This problem is worrying the people more and more. We hope that common interests will gradually cause the hatreds to disappear and persuade the people of the South to form a new attachment for the Union. It is rather improbable. These same interests existed before the uprising, yet they did not prevent the rebellion from breaking out.

All the confederations which have existed have been based on fragile foundations. This truism is particularly applicable to a confederation like that of the United States which extends over such a vast territory. The people of the North and those of the South have grown increasingly apart in their customs and in their habits. The same is true about California. That State remained only half loyal to the Union. It made only small financial contributions but did not supply a single man during the entire war.

The animosities and jealousies of the various sections of the Union do not date from the present. The uprising would have broken out twenty years ago but for the skill and the moderation of the men who then governed the country. Unfortunately, men of that caliber are no longer found among the people whom universal suffrage, as practiced in the United States, has placed in charge of affairs. In 1861 the uprising might have been prevented if there had been in the administration and in Congress leaders like Clay, Webster, Calhoun and so many others who have been the glory of the American people.

The dangers which I indicate here for the nation loom for the more or less distant future. Right now the American people must recover their equilibrium. They have passed through one of the greatest revolutions of a century replete with political convulsions, and they have come out of it with their resources unexhausted, their energy renewed through surmounting a thousand differences, and the prestige of their power greater than ever.[2]

Although American democracy had successfully passed the severe test imposed by a cataclysmic civil war, Stoeckl's summary continued, it had yet to face another political revolution—reconstruction. This new formidable test would be met successfully, he predicted, only if the United States would reform its political institutions. This meant limiting the suffrage, keeping the demagogues out of power, and inducing honest and conservative men to hold office.

He hoped that "the American people would demonstrate to the world that democracy could be kept from developing into radicalism and anarchy—a political phenomenon rare in the annals of republics."

He realized that the American ship of state, so badly battered by the storms of civil war, would have no easy sailing through the rocks and shoals of reconstruction. The bitterness and hatreds engendered by decades of sectional strife and the bloodshed of four years of fratricidal conflict could not be quickly forgotten.

Notwithstanding this opinion of the Czar's Minister to Washington, the St. Petersburg *Journal* in the fall of 1865 made this observation on behalf of Russian officialdom:

> The work of pacification goes on with that rapidity, that energy, that practical good sense which the Americans ever bring to all their undertakings. In both the North and South the people have cast aside all bitterness, all desire for revenge and think only of repairing the calamitous consequences of a fratricidal struggle.[3]

Whereupon Stoeckl shrugged his shoulders and conceded that however stormy the revolution of reconstruction threatened to be, the American people would not succumb to it any more than they had to the Civil War.[4] For as he had said before, "One of the characteristics of this nation is its confidence in itself, in its destiny, and in its belief that 'the best government that God ever saw will last forever.' "[5]

Russian Tributes to Lincoln

WITH A deep feeling of thankfulness that the Civil War with its bloodshed and hardships was over, Abraham Lincoln turned to the task of reconstructing the nation. But he was not destined to carry out his plans. On the evening of April 15, 1865, in his box at Ford's Theater, he met his death at the hands of the half-crazed actor, John Wilkes Booth.

The dreadful news of the assassination of the Emancipator winged its way across the country and throughout the world. It was received in the North with incredulity and paralyzing shock which quickly turned to rage and hysterical cries of vengeance. From all over the world came expressions of sympathy and indignation. Mourning was genuine among the masses of England, who had always opposed recognition of the Confederacy. Both Houses of Parliament expressed "sorrow and indignation." The French Senate and Chamber of Deputies, imperialists and republicans alike, voted a joint resolution of sympathy, and Emperor Napoleon sent a personal message of condolence to Mrs. Lincoln. From Germany, Sweden, Norway—even from China, Japan and Siam—came expressions of grief over the abhorred act of the assassin.

In St. Petersburg, Czar Alexander II was in mourning over the death of his twelve-year-old son and heir to the throne, the Czarevitch Nicholas, which occurred on April 24. But a note from Prince Gortchakov expressed the condolences of the Emperor and his imperial Cabinet:

Scarcely has my August Master returned to his dominions, when he orders me to testify to you his grief at this painful event. Tried himself by a woeful loss which is also a cause of national mourning for Russia, the Emperor joins me in the unanimous regrets which encircle the memory of the eminent statesman, snatched away so suddenly and in so terrible a manner from his noble career.

Stoeckl, despite his criticism of Lincoln as a statesman, had had nothing but good will towards him as an individual. The President's death, therefore, affected him deeply. Shortly afterwards, the Russian Minister was advising his government that when Lincoln died some Americans acted as though the world was coming to an end. But with the new President—Andrew Johnson—at the helm, the American ship of state was sailing on in proper order.

The curious parallelism that marked the history of Russia and the United States during the mid-nineteenth century—their common fear of England; each with a domestic insurrection to suppress; the liberation of the serfs in Russia and the emancipation of the slaves in the United States—was further extended by the strange coincidence that Alexander the Liberator, like Lincoln the Emancipator, was destined to meet death by assassination.

Just one year after the brutal murder of the American Emancipator, the first of many subsequent attempts was made on the life of the Russian Czar Liberator. On April 16, 1866, as the Emperor was about to enter his carriage in the Letny Gardens in St. Petersburg, a student named Dimitri Karakozov raised his pistol to fire. This youth, member of a band of nihilist fanatics, had been waiting long for this opportunity. But the shot was deflected by a liberated peasant, Ossip Komissarov, who providentially chanced to be passing by and had stopped to view his liberator, whom he had never seen before. As the would-be assassin pulled the trigger, Komissarov lunged at him and struck the pistol from his uplifted arm, causing the shot to go wild.

Karakozov was seized by the police and would have been lynched by the infuriated crowd which quickly gathered, but for the remonstrance of the Emperor. "Why did you try to kill me?" the monarch asked the nihilist. "Because you have deceived us and given us an illusory liberty and emancipation without land," was the sullen reply.[1]

Komissarov, a journeyman capmaker by trade, became the hero of the hour. The Czar pronounced him a noble. Honors and decorations were showered on him by different sovereigns. Grateful countrymen presented him with lands, houses, money and the freedom of their cities. Karakozov, the twenty-four-year-old would-be assassin, was quickly condemned to death by hanging. His sentence was carried out a little more than a year after Mrs. Mary Surratt, George Atzerodt, David Herold, and Lewis Powell—Booth's fellow conspirators—died on the gallows for their participation in the conspiracy which took the life of Abraham Lincoln.

At the news of Czar Alexander II's providential escape from assassination, so soon after Lincoln's murder, U. S. Minister Clay hastened to express to the Emperor the warm congratulations of the United States government, and to assure him of the sincere respect, affection and friendship of the American people. The Russian monarch replied that he was deeply touched by this manifestation of friendship. "I trust under Providence," he said, "that our mutual calamities will strengthen our friendly relations and render them permanent."[2]

In the meantime, the leaders of the Republican Party in Congress concluded that something more solemn and tangible than a mere expression of congratulations was due to a nation that had been so sympathetic to our cause during the dark hours of the Civil War. Accordingly both Houses of Congress joined in a resolution authorizing the sending of a special envoy in a naval vessel to Russia to convey in person to His Imperial Majesty America's good will and congratulations to "the twenty millions of serfs upon the providential escape from danger of the Sovereign to whose head and heart they owe the blessings of their freedom."

Gustavus Vasa Fox, the Assistant Secretary of the Navy, was selected to head this delicate mission. The naval ironclad monitor *Miantonomoh* was assigned to carry him and his party to Kronstadt. It was to be accompanied by the side-wheel steamer *Augusta*.[3] It was a mission unique in American history.

The *Miantonomoh* started from Newfoundland on June 5, 1866, and arrived at Queenstown, Ireland, on June 16. Stops were also made in England, France, Denmark and Finland. Everywhere the Americans were cordially received. Great curiosity was manifested over the ironclad, "a strange vessel, with a strange figure and still stranger name."

In France, Fox had a private audience at the Tuileries with Emperor Napoleon III. The conversation turned to his Mexican adventure. "Mexico was in anarchy," the Emperor explained. "I desired only to establish a stable government, and thus prevent further expeditions; and, now I am about to withdraw, I presume it will be overrun by your people."

Fox assured the French Emperor that this was not the intention of the United States. "We have an immense and valuable country that will not be crowded until a hundred millions of people have settled in it. . . . The war has developed our resources to such a degree that we feel no anxiety in regard to it."[4]

Later Fox had an interview with Prince Napoleon in the presence of U. S. Minister John Bigelow. In the course of the conversation the Prince admonished, "Do not be too friendly with Russia." To which the navy official replied, "Russia and America have no rival interests. Russia has always been friendly to America, and we reciprocate the feeling."

"But you can stand alone," said the Prince. "You do not want friends."

Fox answered, "When it was doubtful whether we should ever stand again, at a time when the most powerful nations menaced us, Russia felt and expressed her sympathy for us, and America will never forget it."

"Russia is for herself alone," the French prince retorted. When Fox remained silent, the subject was changed.[5]

When the United States vessels finally came to anchor in the port of Kronstadt in August, the Americans were warmly greeted by Rear Admiral Lisovski. In the name of the Emperor he welcomed the mission to Russia.

On August 8 Fox, accompanied by Minister Clay, formally presented the Resolution of Congress to Czar Alexander II in Peterhof Palace. Prince Gortchakov, Minister of Foreign Affairs, who had also become Chancellor of the Empire, stood at the Emperor's right. After the formal introductions, Fox read the following address in the English language:

"Sire: The Resolution which I have the honor of presenting to Your Imperial Majesty is the voice of a people whose millions of lips speak from a single heart.

The many ties which have long bound together the great Empire of the East, and the great Republic of the West, have been multiplied and strengthened by the unwavering fidelity of the imperial government to our own, throughout its recent period of convulsion.

The words of sympathy and friendship then addressed to the government at Washington, by command of Your Imperial Majesty, are fixed in the eternal remembrance of a grateful country. As one of the wide family of nations, we yield our willing homage to that act of humanity which is especially referred to in the Resolution of Congress. The peaceful edict of an enlightened sovereign has consummated a triumph over an inherited barbarism, which our western republic has only reached through long years of bloodshed.

It is, therefore, with profound emotion that I offer to Your Imperial Majesty, to the emancipated subjects, and to all the people of this vast realm, our heartfelt congratulations upon the providential escape from danger, which led to this spontaneous expression of regret for the attempt, and thankfulness for its merciful arrest and failure.

The story of the peril from which a kind Providence has delivered Your Imperial Majesty brings with it the remembrance of the mighty sorrow which so lately filled every loyal heart in our own land at the sudden loss of our chief, our guide, our father.

We thank God that a grief like this was spared to our friends and allies—the Russian people.

May the Father of all nations and all rulers protect, prolong, and bless the life which He has so signally preserved, for the service of the people to which it belongs, for the good of mankind, and for the glory of His holy name!"

At the close, Mr. Fox handed to His Imperial Majesty the Joint Resolution of Congress. Accepting it, the Emperor replied to Mr. Fox's address in Russian. His words were translated by Prince Gortchakov into English, substantially as follows:

His Majesty said that he rejoices at the friendly relations existing between Russia and the United States, and he is pleased to see that those relations are so well appreciated in America. He is convinced that the national fraternity will be perpetual, and he, for his part, will contribute all his efforts to sustain it, and to strengthen the bonds. He is deeply sensible of the proofs of the personal sympathy and affection of the American people, conveyed in the Resolution of Congress, and he is grateful for them. He desires to thank those who have come so great a distance to bear these proofs to him, and he assures them of a warm welcome to the soil of Russia.

His Majesty adds that the cordial reception given to his squadron in the United States will never be effaced from his memory.[6]

Later the Czar sent a formal note to President Johnson expressing the appreciation of all Russia as well as of himself personally for the testimonials of friendship conveyed by Mr. Fox. In addition, Gortchakov requested Stoeckl to say to the President that he regards the mutual sympathy between the two countries to be

> a consolatory fact in the face of the recent complications which have just awakened in old Europe sentiments of hate, ambition, rivalry, bloody struggles, appeals to force, so little in harmony with the progress of humanity. . . . The seeds of mutual good will and friendship sown between two great peoples, almost between two continents, will bear fruit, become traditional, and inaugurate between them relations founded on a real spirit of Christian civilization.[7]

These effusive declarations revived conjectures, both in Europe and America, as to the existence or imminence of a full-dress Russian-American alliance.

Before leaving Peterhof Palace, Fox paid his respects to Komissarov, the liberated peasant who had saved the Czar's life. "I congratulate you, in the name of the people of the United States, in having been chosen by Divine Providence to save a life dear not only to Russia, but to the civilized world," the American envoy told the hero of Russia. Later the Americans were the Emperor's guests at the review of the Imperial Guard.

The days and weeks that followed during the months of August and September were crowded with an endless series of receptions, banquets and balls given in honor of the American mission. A number of the affairs were graced by the presence of the Emperor, the Empress and the most important dignitaries of the imperial government.

There were exchange visits between the officers of the American vessels and the Russian fleet. There were visits to the Kremlin in Moscow, to palaces, cathedrals and historic places. There were entertainments, parades, fireworks and demonstrations in the streets nearly everywhere that the Americans went. And everywhere they were received with enthusiastic shouts and cheers. The banquet halls, streets and public buildings were decorated with shields bearing the portraits of Washington, Lincoln and Johnson as well as of Czar Alexander II, and the Stars and Stripes waved alongside of the Russian national emblem.

In Moscow, Fox, seeing the Russian and American flags flying side by side, said: "If the hearts of the Americans present could be uncovered, there would be found what I now behold, the flags of Russia and of America intertwined. May these two flags in peaceful embrace be thus united forever."[8]

The cities of St. Petersburg, Moscow, Kronstadt and others bestowed honorary citizenship on Mr. Fox in elaborate and beautiful ceremonies. Merchants' associations and naval clubs bestowed honorary memberships upon the American officers.

The invitations to the grand dinner given by the Kronstadt Naval Club stated that the Russian officers desired "to express the sentiments of friendship they bear toward the citizens of the United States, as well as to show their appreciation of the warmth and heartiness of the reception accorded to the Russian fleets in the cities of New York, Washington, Boston and San Francisco."[9]

Among the distinguished Russian naval officers who sang the praises of the American mission at this affair were Vice Admiral Krabbe, Minister of the Navy, and Rear Admirals Lisovski and Popov, commanders of the Russian fleets which had visited America's Atlantic and Pacific ports in 1863.

The Naval Club's desire "to show their appreciation of the warmth and heartiness of the reception accorded to the Russian fleets in the cities of New York, Washington, Boston and San Francisco," was significant.

At all the receptions and banquets there were speeches by Russian dignitaries. Not once did anyone claim that the purpose of the voyage of the Russian naval squadrons to the harbors of the United States had been to aid Lincoln's government against possible intervention by England and France. Not once was there a reference to "sealed orders." On the contrary the Czar himself and his spokesmen voiced only "appreciation" and "gratitude" on their part for what the government and the people of the United States had done on Russia's behalf.

Thus Vice Admiral Krabbe, who as chief of the Czar's Imperial
Navy had ordered Rear Admirals Lisovski and Popov to take their
fleets to New York and San Francisco Harbors, said at a farewell dinner in honor of the Fox American mission: "You remember, gentlemen, with what attention and enthusiasm we followed the news of the
reception in America of Admirals Lisovski and Popov. At last Heaven
has allowed us to thank our dear guests personally for their hospitality."[10]

At the merchants' dinner at the Great Fair in Nizhni Novgorod on
the banks of the Volga, Mr. Schipov, president of the Fair, declared:

> I thank our dear American visitors for the kind reception their
> country gave our Russian naval officers. When Russia was ex-
> periencing a dark hour, America showed her sympathy in unmis-
> takable signs, and Kronstadt, St. Petersburg and Moscow have
> been trying to return similar evidences of friendship. The friend-
> ship of America has transformed more than one of the old enemies
> of Russia into friends. The appearances alone of sympathy be-
> tween Russia and America have sufficed to bring about such a re-
> sult.[11]

And at a grand banquet given by Prince Dolgoruki, the Governor
General of Moscow, the Russian official said in his address of welcome
to Fox and his associates: "The brilliant reception given by the United
States to the Russian squadron in 1863 and 1864 has left in Russian
hearts an ineffaceable remembrance of gratitude, and has drawn together still more closely, if possible, the ties of love and of sympathy
which unite the two nations."[12]

If there was any truth at all to the legend which had grown up in
the United States that the Russian fleets had come to New York and
San Francisco Harbors with "sealed orders" to help the United States,
it received no substantiation whatsoever from Russia's own spokesmen.
At the numerous receptions and banquets, when words flowed in tor-
rents, the hosts could speak only of Russia's debt of gratitude to the
United States.

Addressing the guests at a banquet given by the aristocratic English
Club of St. Petersburg in honor of the United States deputation, Admiral Lisovski said:

> Allow me to tell you why success attended us when we were in
> America. We found there a brilliant and friendly welcome pre-

pared for us. That welcome we owe to the words of Prince Gortchakov, who, as you all know, had refused at that time, in the most
unmistakable terms, to intervene in the Civil War in America,
leaving entirely to the glory, the strength, and the wisdom of the
United States government the care of ending the struggle as it
thought best. Such is the reason of the success, or of the foundation of the success, which our expedition met with. In every citizen we saw a friend, made by the words of Prince Gortchakov.[13]

Notwithstanding the utter absence of any Russian claims of altruistic
motives for sending their fleet to the United States during the dark
hours of the Civil War, members of the American mission persisted in
alluding to the aid and comfort which came to the North from the
visit. At one dinner Fox read a lengthy poem which Oliver Wendell
Holmes had written especially for the occasion. Typical of the ten
verses of the poem were these three:

> Though watery deserts hold apart
> The worlds of East and West,
> Still beats the self-same human heart
> In each proud nation's breast.
>
> When darkness hid the stormy skies
> In war's long winter night,
> One ray still cheered our straining eyes,
> The far-off Northern light.
>
> A nation's love in tears and smiles
> We bear across the sea;
> O Neva of the hundred isles,
> We moor our hearts in thee![14]

In a later poem Holmes added to the myth of Russo-American friendship by singing panegyrically of the nation "who was our friend when
the world was our foe."

At all the affairs the Russian hosts were profuse in their praise of
Abraham Lincoln, the American martyr. Prince Gortchakov concluded
an address with "a few words of respect to the memory of President
Lincoln—that great citizen who sacrificed his life in the performance
of his duty."[15] At the great municipal banquet in Moscow, Prince

Stcherbatov, Mayor of Russia's ancient Capital, spoke eloquently of Lincoln, the "untiring warrior for a sacred cause." He said:

> With a loving interest do we follow each other's successes, with mutual sympathy do we sustain each other in the hour of danger, and we unite to praise the glorious names of the great men whom Providence in mercy sends in the times of the great nations' trials. The name of Lincoln is one of those illustrious names. Untiring warrior for a sacred cause, he pressed forward, never losing sight of his guiding star; and his death was the last tribute of his loyal service to his country and to humanity. But the great immortal idea did not perish with his life. Lincoln bequeathed the accomplishment of his work to his people, to his successor, and his last will is now nearly fulfilled.
>
> May God Almighty help you to reap the harvest of your glorious labors and endeavors. May He strengthen the ties of the revived Union of your great nation; may the American people, blessed by peace, advance steadily onward to the realization of its glorious historical calling, with its chosen leader at its head.[16]

An elaborate and scholarly tribute to the memory of Abraham Lincoln was read at the Moscow banquet by Basile Kokorev, a rich banker. Following Prince Stcherbatov as a speaker at a Moscow banquet, this influential Russian bracketed Lincoln with Columbus and Washington as the three men who had had the most powerful impact upon the New World:

> Columbus discovered the New World, Washington founded its civilization, and Lincoln gave equal rights to his countrymen by abolishing slavery. Sentiments of thankfulness and gratitude at the name of Lincoln, for what he did for the good of mankind, are felt as a duty by every Russian. All the actions of Lincoln, as our Mayor, Prince Stcherbatov, has observed, sprang from the force of his character, from his steadfast aspiration toward the proposed aim, in spite of every obstacle. When a youth in poor circumstances, in New Salem, Lincoln used to say: "Failures ought not to deprive us of courage; on the contrary, they are the means of exciting the activity of the brain."

After a most laudatory recital of Lincoln's rise to the presidency and his conduct of the war, the Russian speaker concluded:

At the end of four years Lincoln was again elected President. We may easily imagine the triumph of his people on this occasion, when even in Russia there was an outbreak of universal jubilation at the news. We all saw in this re-election the pledge of the triumph of the Northern over the Southern States.

Rumors of threats, and of attempts made against the life of Lincoln, produced the greatest sorrow in Russia. We feared for a life not only indispensable for the New World, but precious for all mankind. The gloomy apprehensions were not dispelled, when our whole country was astounded by the shocking news that on April 15, 1865 the traitorous hand of a murderer cut short the life of him who called up to an independent life millions of slaves, who during the whole war traveled without any guard, who received everyone without announcement, who could have been killed at any moment, but who was guarded by Providence for the fulfilment of His decrees. But when the great deed of Lincoln's was done, and mankind stretched out its hands to put the laurels of merited glory upon his head, the Most High called him up to Him, to receive a higher, heavenly reward. Men are not able to reward the deeds of a life which was entirely devoted to acts of philanthropy and of truth. Only He who was crucified for the benefit of mankind, the Almighty Son of God, can reward such deeds.

Then with the profoundest reverence let us lift our hands to Heaven, and express our sincere gratitude, and the wish of an eternal memory to the name of the friend of mankind, and the defender of truth—Abraham Lincoln![17]

But of all of the Russian tributes to Abraham Lincoln, none was more eloquent and sincere than the one voiced by Count Leo Tolstoi, the social philosopher and great man of letters of czarist Russia, who, though born in the higher circles of Muscovite aristocracy, spent a lifetime battling for the rights of the peasants and the oppressed. It was Tolstoi who in 1881 was to plead with Alexander III for mercy for the assassins of the young Emperor's father, urging that they be exiled to "some place in America."

Author of such great works as *Anna Karenina, Kreutzer Sonata, Resurrection*, and *War and Peace*, this onetime aristocrat and crusader for human rights believed Harriet Beecher Stowe's *Uncle Tom's Cabin* to be one of the world's great books because it represented art "issuing from love to God and man." He regarded William Lloyd Garrison as "not only the liberator of slaves in America, but also the great prophet of humanity."[18]

To a newspaperman who interviewed him at his estate in Yasnaya, Tolstoi related an amazing experience which revealed how the fame of Lincoln had spread even among the primitive peoples of Asia. With intense feeling he spoke of Lincoln's ever-deepening influence upon mankind, exclaiming, "Of all the great national heroes and statesmen of history, Lincoln is the only real giant." Yes, there were Alexander, Frederick the Great, Caesar, Napoleon, Gladstone and Washington—all outstanding figures in mankind's story. But "in greatness of character, in depth of feeling and in a certain moral power," they "stand far behind Lincoln."

> Lincoln was a man of whom a nation has a right to be proud; he was a Christ in miniature, a saint of humanity, whose name will live thousands of years in the legends of future generations. We are still too near to his greatness, and so can hardly appreciate his divine power; but after a few centuries more our posterity will find him considerably bigger than we do. His genius is still too strong and too powerful for the common understanding, just as the sun is too hot when its light beams directly on us.
>
> If one would know the greatness of Lincoln one should listen to the stories which are told about him in other parts of the world. I have been in wild places, where one hears the name of America uttered with such mystery as if it were some heaven or hell. I have heard various tribes of barbarians discussing the New World, but I heard this only in connection with the name of Lincoln. Lincoln as the wonderful hero of America is known by the most primitive nations of Asia. This may be illustrated through the following incident:
>
> Once while traveling in the Caucasus I happened to be the guest of a Caucasian chief of the Circassians, who, living far away from civilized life in the mountains, had but a fragmentary and childish comprehension of the world and its history. The fingers of civilization had never reached him nor his tribe, and all life beyond his native valleys was a dark mystery. Being a Mussulman he was naturally opposed to all ideas of progress and education.
>
> I was received with the usual Oriental hospitality and after our

meal was asked by my host to tell him something of my life. Yielding to his request, I began to tell him of my profession, of the development of our industries and inventions and of the schools. He listened to everything with indifference, but when I began to tell about the great statesmen and great generals of the world he seemed at once to become very much interested.

"Wait a moment," he interrupted, after I had talked a few minutes. "I want all my neighbors and my sons to listen to you. I will call them immediately."

He soon returned with a score of wild-looking riders and asked me politely to continue. It was indeed a solemn moment when those sons of the wilderness sat around me on the floor and gazed at me as if hungering for knowledge. I spoke at first of our Czars and of their victories; then I spoke of the foreign rulers and of some of the greatest military leaders. My talk seemed to impress them deeply. The story of Napoleon was so interesting to them that I had to tell them every detail, as, for instance, how his hands looked, how tall he was, who made his guns and pistols and the color of his horse. It was very difficult to satisfy them and to meet their point of view, but I did my best. When I declared that I had finished my talk, my host, a gray-bearded, tall rider, rose, lifted his hand and said very gravely:

"But you have not told us a syllable about the greatest general and greatest ruler of the world. We want to know something about him. He was a hero. He spoke with a voice of thunder; he laughed like the sunrise and his deeds were strong as the rock and as sweet as the fragrance of roses. The angels appeared to his mother and predicted that the son whom she would conceive would become the greatest the stars had ever seen. He was so great that he even forgave the crimes of his greatest enemies and shook brotherly hands with those who had plotted against his life. His name was Lincoln and the country in which he lived is called America, which is so far away that if a youth should journey to reach it he would be an old man when he arrived. Tell us of that man."

"Tell us, please, and we will present you with the best horse of our stock," shouted the others.

I looked at them and saw their faces all aglow, while their eyes were burning. I saw that those rude barbarians were really interested in a man whose name and deeds had already become a legend. I told them of Lincoln and his wisdom, of his home life and youth. They asked me ten questions to one which I was able to answer. They wanted to know all about his habits, his influence upon the people and his physical strength. But they were very astonished to hear that Lincoln made a sorry figure on a horse and that he lived such a simple life.

"Tell us why he was killed," one of them said.

I had to tell everything. After all my knowledge of Lincoln was exhausted they seemed to be satisfied. I can hardly forget the great enthusiasm which they expressed in their wild thanks and the desire to get a picture of the great American hero. I said that I probably could secure one from my friend in the nearest town, and this seemed to give them great pleasure.

The next morning when I left the chief a wonderful Arabian horse was brought me as a present for my marvelous story, and our farewell was very impressive.

One of the riders agreed to accompany me to the town, and get the promised picture, which I was now bound to secure at any price. I was successful in getting a large photograph from my friend, and I handed it to the man with my greetings to his associates. It was interesting to witness the gravity of his face and the trembling of his hands when he received my present. He gazed for several minutes silently, like one in a reverent prayer; his eyes filled with tears. He was deeply touched and I asked him why he became so sad. After pondering my question for a few moments he replied:

"I am sad because I feel sorry that he had to die by the hand of a villain. Don't you find, judging from his picture, that his eyes are full of tears and that his lips are sad with a secret sorrow?"

Like all Orientals, he spoke in a poetical way and left me with many deep bows.

This little incident proves how largely the name of Lincoln is worshipped throughout the world and how legendary his personality has become.

Now, why was Lincoln so great that he overshadows all other national heroes? He really was not a great general like Napoleon or Washington; he was not such a skilful statesman as Gladstone or Frederick the Great; but his supremacy expresses itself altogether in his peculiar moral power and in the greatness of his character. He had come through many hardships and much experience to the realization that the greatest human achievement is love. He was what Beethoven was in music, Dante in poetry, Raphael in painting, and Christ in the philosophy of life. He aspired to be divine—and he was.

It is natural that before he reached his goal he had to walk the highway of mistakes. But we find him, nevertheless, in every tendency true to one main motive, and that was to benefit mankind. He was one who wanted to be great through his smallness. If he had failed to become President, he would be, no doubt, just as great as he is now, but only God could appreciate it. The judgment of the world was right from the start. Sooner or later Lincoln would have been seen to be a great man, even though he had never been an American President. But it would have taken a great generation to place him where he belongs.

Lincoln died prematurely by the hand of the assassin, and naturally we condemn the criminal from our viewpoint of justice. But the question is, was his death not predestined by a divine wisdom, and was it not better for the nation and for his greatness that he died just in that way and at that particular moment? We know so little about that divine law which we call fate that no one can answer. Christ had a presentiment of His death, and there are indications that Lincoln also had strange dreams and presentiments of something tragic. If that was really the fact, can we conceive that human will could have prevented the outcome of the universal or divine will? I doubt it. I doubt also that Lincoln could have done more to prove his greatness than he did. I am convinced that we are but instruments in the hands of an unknown power and that we have to follow its bidding to the end. We have a certain apparent independence, according to our moral character, wherein we may benefit our fellows, but in all eternal and universal questions we follow blindly a divine predestination. According to that eternal law the greatest of national heroes had to die, but an immortal glory still shines on his deeds.

However, the highest heroism is that which is based on humanity, truth, justice and pity; all other forms are doomed to forgetfulness. The greatness of Aristotle or Kant is insignificant compared with the greatness of Buddha, Moses and Christ. The greatness of

Napoleon, Caesar or Washington is only moonlight by the sun of Lincoln. His example is universal and will last thousands of years. Washington was a typical American, Napoleon was a typical Frenchman, but Lincoln was a humanitarian as broad as the world. He was bigger than his country—bigger than all the Presidents together. Why? Because he loved his enemies as himself and because he was a universal individualist who wanted to see himself in the world—not the world in himself. He was great through his simplicity and was noble through his charity.

Lincoln is a strong type of those who make for truth and justice, for brotherhood and freedom. Love is the foundation of his life. That is what makes him immortal and that is the quality of a giant. I hope that his centenary birthday will create an impulse toward righteousness among the nations. Lincoln lived and died a hero, and as a great character he will live as long as the world lives. May his life long bless humanity![19]

The Mystery of the Alaska Purchase

A FEW months after the triumphant return to the United States of Fox's mission to Russia, the long-pending negotiations for the sale of Alaska came to a sudden climax.

At a strange midnight conference, the two incredible international bedfellows, Russia and the United States, became close territorial neighbors. How close, no one was to realize until the dawn of the air age.

A world accustomed to seeing Russia add more and more land to her domain until today she controls one-fifth of the earth's surface, may well wonder at the motive which induced her to transfer to the United States nearly 600,000 square miles of her territory for a trifling sum of money.

In the sale of Alaska—immensely rich in timber, fisheries, furs and unsuspected mineral resources—Russia for the first and only time in her history consented to the alienation of a vast area of her territory by a peaceful cession. Why?

Minister Clay reported that the general feeling among Russians regarding the sale of Alaska to the United States was, "Well, we have sold to you cheaply, but it's all in the family." In other words, it was felt that the imperial government's unprecedented action was motivated by altruistic friendship for this nation. This was largely a myth.

Equally unwarranted was the popular belief in the United States that we purchased that "dreary waste of glaciers, icebergs, white bears and

walrus fit only for Esquimaux," because we were under some obligation
to Russia for her friendship during the Civil War.

True, the amity between the Great Autocracy and the Great Democracy was partially responsible for the Alaskan deal. For example, Senator Charles Sumner, Chairman of the Committee on Foreign Affairs
of the Senate, concluded his speech urging the ratification of the treaty
with this declaration: "Even if you doubt the value of these possessions,
the treaty is a sign of amity. It is a new expression of that *entente
cordiale* between the two powers which is a phenomenon of history."

But chiefly the transaction was actuated by other more compelling
reasons. Russia was anxious to get rid of her distant American possession because it had become valueless to her and difficult to admin-
ister. She was in constant fear that Alaska might fall into the hands of
her hated enemy, Great Britain. She believed it advisable to strip for
the inevitable contest. So, inspired by hostility to England and amity
for the United States, plus $7,200,000 in gold, the imperial government
consented to sell the vast territory to the United States.

The Alaskan deal was an item of unfinished business inherited by
the Lincoln-Johnson administrations from their predecessors. As has
already been pointed out, during the Crimean War, when the Russians
were daily expecting the British Pacific fleet to seize Alaska, the Czar's
representatives attempted to forestall this anticipated seizure through a
fictitious sale of the territory to an American company. In case of a
British attack, the claim could then be made that American rather than
Russian territory was involved. The United States government refused
to become a party to this scheme.[1]

During the Buchanan administration, Russian Minister Stoeckl was
sounded out on the possibility of his government ceding Alaska to the
United States. Senator William M. Gwin of California told the Czar's
envoy that Russia was too far away ever to do anything with this
territory. On the other hand the inhabitants of California and Washington Territory were vitally interested in Alaska's fisheries and fur
seals. The Senator thought that the United States government would
pay $5,000,000 for the possession. Later, Assistant Secretary of State
Appleton informed Stoeckl that the President was convinced that the
acquisition of Alaska would be advantageous to the people of our
Pacific coast, and that he was prepared to negotiate for its purchase.
From St. Petersburg, Prince Gortchakov replied that the offer was not
as high as his government might expect but that it merited consider-

ation. The Prince, therefore, instructed the Minister of Finance to conduct an investigation and report back to him as a basis of action.[2]

The report when finally submitted favored the sale of Alaska to the United States. But by that time, Abraham Lincoln had become President, the nation was embroiled in a civil war, and action on Alaska necessarily had to be deferred. However, in 1861, Russia and the United States agreed to cooperate in establishing cable connections between St. Petersburg and San Francisco by way of the Bering Sea and Siberia. In his third annual message to Congress, Lincoln pointed out that "Satisfactory arrangements have been made with the Emperor of Russia, which, it is believed, will result in effecting a continuous line of telegraph through that empire from our Pacific coast." This new manifestation of amity between the two nations prompted our Minister, Clay, to urge the Russian authorities to transfer to American interests the privileges which the Russian-American Company had sublet to the Hudson Bay Company.

On a steamer trip over the Atlantic in 1863, Clay met Robert J. Walker, who had become a financial agent to Europe after serving as Secretary of the Treasury in the Cabinet of President Polk. Walker had acquired a reputation as "a life-long annexationist in favor of annexation in any quarter." More than twenty years before the final successful negotiations for the sale of Alaska to the United States, Walker had suggested the acquisition of Russian America in a letter to President Polk. On this trans-Atlantic trip in 1863, Walker told Clay that Czar Nicholas had expressed willingness to give up Russian America to the United States if we would move up our Pacific coast possessions to 54° 40' and thus take steps to shut British America from the Pacific.[3]

"I impressed upon Walker the importance of the ownership of the western coast of the Pacific in connection with the vast trade which was springing up with China, Japan and the western islands," Clay reported to Secretary Seward.

Walker became a most enthusiastic propagandist for the purchase of Alaska. It was, therefore, not surprising that Stoeckl eventually hired him as counsel for the Russian government to aid in "facilitating" the transaction.

But the most influential of the proponents of the acquisition of Alaska was Secretary Seward, "the greatest of all American expansionists." As early as 1846, Seward declared that America's population was destined "to roll its resistless waves to the icy barriers of the North, and to encounter oriental civilization on the shores of the Pacific." This zealous believer in America's manifest destiny declared in a speech at St. Paul in 1860 that the outposts which Russia was building would yet be the outposts of America. He saw in the acquisition of Alaska a means of strengthening American influence in British Columbia and of hastening political union of Canada and the United States. With extraordinary foresight he predicted, "The Pacific Ocean with its coasts and islands is destined to become in the future the great theater of the world's affairs."

Seward found a strong ally in Senator Sumner, who also favored acquiring Alaska, but not so much in a desire for territory as for "amity with Russia" and a desire to "dismiss another European sovereign from our continent."[4]

Seward, Sumner and other American statesmen were watching with deep concern the rapid progress of the British movement for the consolidation of the eastern provinces of British America. In March 1867, the House of Representatives, without a dissenting vote, approved a resolution from the Committee on Foreign Affairs expressing the solicitude of the United States concerning the proposed confederation of the British-American provinces, and stating that such a measure would probably increase the embarrassment already existing between the United States and Great Britain. Some members of Congress declared that a British confederation in Canada would inevitably drive the United States into closer cooperation with Russia.

In the meantime inhabitants of Washington Territory had memorialized the United States government to survey the fishing grounds in the Bering Strait region and to use its best efforts to induce Russia to permit American citizens to enter the ports and harbors of Alaska for fuel, water and provisions, and to cure fish and repair vessels. In addition, Senator Cole of California presented a request of some California citizens for a franchise to take the place of the Hudson Bay Company to Russia's Minister in Washington.

Late in the autumn of 1866, when Stoeckl returned to St. Petersburg on a visit, he presented all these matters to Prince Gortchakov. Stoeckl had long considered Alaska to be a "breeder of trouble" with the United States, and had thought that the sooner it was disposed of, the better.[5] As far back as 1857, he had concluded that by ceding Alaska to the United States a serious blow could be inflicted against Great Britain. He declared, "if the United States becomes master of our possessions, British Oregon (Columbia) will be cut off by the Americans on the north and the south, and will escape with difficulty their aggressions."

Gortchakov agreed with Stoeckl that it was extremely difficult to govern the distant American possession. Then why not take a step toward the expulsion from the Pacific of the British nation, whose powers in the East Russia justly feared—especially when such a step would secure the perpetual friendship of the powerful re-united American Republic?

Accordingly, Stoeckl was empowered, on his return to the United States, to launch negotiations for a sale of Russian America.

Arriving in Washington in March 1867, the Russian Minister at once informed Secretary Seward that the imperial government was ready to sell Alaska. Seward was ready to buy. Stoeckl said the price would be $10,000,000. Seward offered $5,000,000. A cable outlining this offer was sent to St. Petersburg on March 15. Four days later came Prince Gortchakov's reply to Stoeckl. The Russian Minister called on Secretary Seward at his residence on the evening of March 29, 1867, just two days after the adoption of the House of Representatives resolution voicing concern over the British-American confederation, and advised him that his government was prepared to compromise. The Secretary of State decided to forego his whist game, and insisted that they get down to business. A compromise figure of $7,200,000 was quickly agreed upon—$7,000,000 for the cession, with the additional payment of $200,000 to satisfy the claims of the Russian-American Company, a trading concern.

The Russian Minister suggested that the formal treaty be prepared the next day. But Seward exclaimed, "Why wait until tomorrow? Let us make the treaty tonight."

Senator Sumner was quickly summoned. State Department clerks were rounded up from their homes. Seward and Stoeckl worked all night on the wording of the treaty. By 4 o'clock of the morning of March 30, 1867 the document was ready. So only twelve hours after the commencement of these final negotiations, the convention for the transfer of Alaska and the Aleutian Islands from Russia to the United States was duly signed and sealed. For the comparatively trifling sum of $7,200,000 the United States was to add nearly 600,000 square miles of territory to her possessions—369,529,600 acres, to be exact, at about two cents per acre.

Hardly was the ink on the treaty dry when it was presented to an astonished Senate for approval. Spurred on by the persuasive Chairman Sumner of the Committee on Foreign Affairs, who made the principal address for ratification, the Senate promptly approved the convention by a vote of 37 to 2.

But there was a different reaction when the House began the consideration of the bill for the appropriation of the funds necessary to enable the President to fulfill the terms of the treaty. Some Congressmen, bitterly hostile to President Johnson, refused to do anything that would bring credit to his administration.

But in the main the opposition arose from a sincere belief that it was inexpedient to appropriate money to purchase a territory that was worthless, and from a conviction that the United States should not seek the right to govern a horde of savages in a climate unfit for habitation by civilized men.[6]

Seward was ridiculed for attempting to purchase a God-forsaken wasteland of "polar bear gardens, perpetual icebergs, eternally cannonading volcanoes and destructive hurricanes." Wits delighted in referring to the region as "Seward's Folly" and "Walrussia."

Objections were also voiced because of the secrecy and mystery which surrounded the transaction. Even Clay, our Minister at St. Petersburg, and a zealous advocate of our acquiring Alaska, wrote to Seward that the "secrecy took me with a most agreeable surprise." However, Clay congratulated the Secretary of State "upon this brilliant achievement, which adds so vast a territory to the Union. . . . I regard it as worth at least $50,000,000, and hereafter the wonder will be that we got it at all."[7]

It was intimated that we were under friendly obligations to Russia for having offered us her fleet during the Civil War; and a story was current that at least part of the purchase price for the "worthless" Russian-American territory was in reality repayment to the Czar's government for expenses incurred in sending the fleet to American waters. This caused Benjamin F. Butler, who opposed annexation of noncontiguous territory, to declare:

> If we are to pay for Russia's friendship this amount, I desire to give her the $7,200,000 and let her keep Alaska. I have no doubt that at any time within the last twenty years we could have had

Alaska for the asking, provided we would have taken it as a gift; but no man, except one insane enough to buy the earthquakes of St. Thomas and the icefields of Greenland, could be found to agree on any terms for its acquisition to this country.[8]

Manifest destiny was not to be silenced. One of its eloquent spokesmen, Chairman Nathan P. Banks of the House Committee on Foreign Affairs, pointed to the Aleutian Islands on the map and predicted that the Aleutians would become "the drawbridge between America and Asia," over which we could carry our institutions and laws to the East as well as to the islands of the Pacific.[9]

While Congress thus argued and wrangled, President Johnson, with the consent of the Russian government, took possession of Alaska. The formal transfer took place on October 18, 1867 at Sitka, where appropriate ceremonies were held. United States troops, 250 in number, and the Russian garrison were drawn up side by side facing a flagpole and the open sea. "Present arms," sounded simultaneously in English and Russian. The double-eagle emblem of Muscovy was lowered, and up went the Stars and Stripes. Salutes were fired by both batteries, and Alaska was formally a part of the United States of America.

Congress, convening in 1868, was confronted with a *fait accompli*. The House of Representatives now had little choice. On July 14, 1868 it reluctantly approved the bill appropriating the funds due Russia under the purchase agreement. Few if any of the congressmen and senators felt that the United States was getting an amazing bargain. "I doubt," said Seward, "if there was any member of either house of Congress who supposed the government had any other motive in the purchase of Alaska than to recognize its obligation to the Czar."[10]

From St. Petersburg, Clay wrote that Russians were expressing the hope that the cession would lead ultimately to the expulsion of England from the Pacific.[11] American advocates of manifest destiny, on their part, saw in the acquisition of Alaska the first step in the occupation of the whole North American continent. It was an entering wedge toward the peaceful absorption of Canada. In fact, some now expected Great Britain to tender her North American colonies to the United States. What actually happened as a consequence of the acquisition of Alaska by the United States was a stimulation of the determined Anglo-Canadian policy of completing the scheme for the confederation of the British colonies from sea to sea. The union of the provinces of Quebec,

Ontario, Nova Scotia and New Brunswick was the beginning of the era of expansion and consolidation. From it sprang the great Dominion of Canada of today.

Not all of the $7,200,000 Alaskan purchase price reached St. Petersburg. A portion was deposited in the Riggs Bank in Washington to the credit of Baron de Stoeckl.[12] Rumors still persisted that part of the purchase price was in reality a repayment by the United States of expenses incurred by Russia in sending her fleet here.

Thus Charles Glover, President of the Riggs National Bank, remembered that as a young employee of the bank in 1868, he was handed two warrants upon the United States Treasury, with instructions to place them in the bank safe. His recollection years later was that one warrant was for $1,400,000, and the other for $5,800,000, and that the warrants remained in the safe of the bank for a week, after which they were sent to New York. The Glover account of the affair, in a conversation with Franklin K. Lane long after the event, was at considerable variance with other reports and only adds to the confusion which marks the whole episode:

These warrants were the payment to Russia for the Territory of Alaska. Why were there two warrants? I never knew until some years later, when I learned the story from Senator Dawes, who said that prior to the war, there had been some negotiations between the United States and Russia for the purchase of Alaska, and the price of $1,400,000 was agreed upon. In fact, this was the amount that Russia asked for this great territory, which was regarded as nothing more than a barren field of ice.

During the war the matter lay dormant. We had more territory than we could take care of. When England, however, began to manifest her friendly disposition toward the Confederacy, and we learned from Europe that England and France were carrying on negotiations for the recognition of the Southern States, and possibly of some manifestation by their fleets against the blockade which we had instituted (and which they claimed was not effective and merely a paper blockade), we looked about for a friend, and Russia was the only European country upon whose friendship we could rely. Thereupon Secretary Seward secured from Russia a demonstration, in American ports, of Russian friendship. Her ships of war sailed to both of our coasts, the Atlantic and the

Pacific, with the understanding that the expense of this demonstration should be met by the United States, out of the contingent fund. It was to be a secret matter.

The war came to a close, and immediately thereafter Lincoln was assassinated and the administration changed. It was no longer possible to pay for the demonstration, secretly, under the excuse of war, but a way was found for paying Russia through the purchase of Alaska. The warrant for $1,400,000 was the warrant for the purchase of Alaska, the warrant for $5,800,000 was for Russia's expenses in her naval demonstration in our behalf, but history only knows the fact that the United States paid $7,200,000 for this territory, which is now demonstrated to be one of the richest portions of the earth in mineral deposits.[13]

Had Lincoln and Seward actually made a secret arrangement to repay the Czar's government as soon as convenient, for sending the Russian fleet? Was the purchase of Alaska the manner in which Seward undertook to fulfill America's obligation? Speculation regarding these questions continued for many years. But the matter was never completely cleared up—least of all by statements like that of Glover which consisted chiefly of boyhood recollections and hearsay.

But more ugly were the persistent rumors and charges that a part of the Alaska purchase money was used by the Russian Minister in bribing members of Congress to vote for the appropriation.[14] The *Worcester Spy* published charges that Robert J. Walker and government officials had received large sums from the appropriation. Reports reached Washington that while the sum paid Russia was $7,200,000, the draft transmitted abroad and cleared through London was only $5,000,000. Speculation immediately arose as to what happened to the remainder of $2,200,000. Nearly everyone connected in one manner or another with the advocacy of the transaction or with facilitating the passage of the appropriation bill, was suspect. Rumor put down Secretary of State Seward with having received no less than $250,000. General Nathan P. Banks, Chairman of the House Foreign Affairs Committee, who had zealously championed the bill, was credited with the same amount. A number of other congressmen were on the list for various sums.[15]

Goaded on by the widespread publication of these scandalous reports, the House of Representatives ordered a thorough investigation of the ugly charges of corruption. At the hearing before the House committee on expenditures, Walker testified that he and his associate counsel, Frederick P. Stanton, had received fees totaling $26,000 for services as lobbyists for the Russian Minister, in promoting the passage of the legislation. He also admitted that he had conferred with Senator Sumner and Representatives Banks and Thaddeus Stevens about the matter, and had written newspaper articles to accelerate public opinion in favor of the appropriation.[16]

The Russian Minister, he testified, had retained him early in May 1868, when hostility to the appropriation became evident in the House. Stoeckl was fearful lest Congress adjourn without voting any appropriation. Not only was there powerful opposition from congressmen motivated by partisan hostility toward President Johnson and from those who believed Alaska to be a worthless wasteland, but there was also an unexpected serious threat to block action on the bill by a group who had become interested in the so-called Perkins claim.[17]

Benjamin Perkins, a merchant of Boston, claimed that during the Crimean War the Russian government had retained him through a member of its Washington legation to procure one hundred fifty tons of gunpowder and thirty-five thousand stands of arms for the Czar's army. It was a verbal agreement, he asserted. After the end of the war, when Russia refused to pay Perkins for his services, he filed suit in the State courts of New York. The case was dismissed. Although Perkins accepted $200 from the legation, he did not drop his claim for damages. The amount he asked was $300,000. His counsel offered to compromise for $130,000. But the imperial government refused to acknowledge any obligation whatsoever. Perkins then petitioned Secretary of State Cass and later Secretary Seward to intercede on his behalf. But since pressing the claim against "a proud and impatient autocracy" would involve the "impeachment, either of the veracity or the memory of a minister accredited to this government, and whose relations to it have always been of the most considerate and friendly character," they refused to support the claim.

Perkins died. The matter was all but forgotten, when, years later, the heirs of Perkins appeared before the congressional committees dealing with the Alaska purchase measure, and appealed for justice. The claim skyrocketed to the sum of $800,000. A stock company was organized and interests in the claim were distributed to senators, congressmen, lawyers, lobbyists and newspaper editors who enlisted in the agitation to force the Russian government to pay. The Perkins lobbyists first attempted to persuade the Senate to order $800,000 to be withheld from the purchase price before the treaty was ratified. Failing there, they turned to the House of Representatives, where they hoped to block the appropriation bill until Russia would buy them off.

Thaddeus Stevens, powerful majority leader of the House and Chairman of the Committee on Appropriations, was among the first to champion the Perkins claim in the House of Representatives. This ruthless and vindictive assailant of President Johnson paused long enough in his efforts to drive the President from the White House to insist that the Czar's government do justice to the widow of Benjamin Perkins by paying the claim that had nearly tripled in amount since the deceased claimant had first presented it to Stoeckl. However, Seward and Stoeckl conferred with Stevens and succeeded in inducing him to disassociate himself from the case.

But Benjamin F. Butler presented an amendment to the appropriation bill providing that $500,000 be withheld from the $7,200,000 Alaska purchase price to satisfy obligations due from the Russian government.[18] Stoeckl was greatly worried. He wrote to St. Petersburg that Butler was interested in the Perkins matter to the extent of $30,000; and that other influential leaders were also financially motivated. He asked for additional instructions. St. Petersburg replied that he should insist on the full $7,200,000 payment. The two governments could then in due course take up the Perkins claim.[19] Walker, Stoeckl's Washington lobbyist, thought the time would come when it would be necessary "to manipulate some members of the committee."[20]

On July 14, 1868 the bill carrying the appropriation was finally passed. From St. Petersburg, U. S. Minister Clay wrote that he thought that Stoeckl "had been roughly handled by the parties to the [Perkins] claim."[21]

Had congressmen been paid for their favorable votes? The investigating committee could find no direct and conclusive evidence to warrant taking action against any individual. Walker, though admitting receipt of fees from Stoeckl to himself and associate counsel, emphatically denied ever offering money to any member of Congress, or having any personal knowledge of payment to any public official.

Secretary Seward appeared before the committee and declared that he had no knowledge whatever of the use the Russian Minister made of the $7,200,000.[22] Stoeckl was tendered an invitation to send a repre-

sentative of the Russian legation to make a statement concerning the
subject. But to the committee's regret and disappointment, the Czar's
envoy declined the invitation.[23]

The committee learned that of the $7,200,000 paid by the U. S.
Treasury to Stoeckl, $7,035,000 was sent abroad. The remainder of
$165,000 was deposited in the Riggs National Bank to the credit of the
Russian Minister. Of these funds, $26,000 was admittedly paid to
Walker and his associate counsel. The balance of $139,000 was with-
drawn in various amounts between August 1 and September 16, 1868.
A payment of $3,000 was traced to the brother of John W. Forney,
Secretary of the U. S. Senate till June 4, 1868, who was also publisher
of the *Washington Chronicle* and the *Philadelphia Press*, which gave
steady and strong editorial support for the acquisition of Russian
America. Another $1,000 payment was traced to a California news-
paperman. But what Stoeckl did with the balance of $135,000, the in-
vestigating committee was unable to ascertain.[24]

The committee admitted in its report that the results of the investigation were far from satisfactory. But nothing could be done without
proper evidence.

Years later, there was found among the papers left by President
Johnson, a strange memorandum in his own handwriting, which cast
an ominous light upon the mysterious Alaska affair. Less than four
months after the termination of his gruelling impeachment trial, President Johnson went out for a carriage ride with Secretary Seward.
They stopped under a grove of trees for "refreshments." While par-
taking of the cup that cheers, Seward began to go over the recent dead-
lock in the House of Representatives over the Alaska appropriation
bill and the suspicious actions of some of the congressmen. Russian
Minister Stoeckl, whose relations with the Secretary of State were very
intimate, had given him some sensational information of bribery con-
nected with the transaction. Amid the refreshments imbibed under the
shady trees on that early September day of 1868, Seward confided to
Johnson what Stoeckl had told him. On his return to the White House
the embittered President made a permanent record of this conversation
by pencilling the following memorandum on a sheet of note paper,
reproduced here verbatim:

> On the 6th of Sept Sundy 1868 Mr. Seward and myself rode
> out some seven or eight miles on the Road leading to Malsboro

Md—near place called old fields, we drove out into a shady grove of oak trees—While there taking some refreshment, in the current of conversation on various subjects, the Secretary asked the question if it had ever occurred to me how few members there were in congress whose actions were entirely above and beyond pecuniary influence. I replied that I had never attempted to reduce it to an accurate calculation, but regretted to confess that there was a much smaller number exempt than at one period of life I had supposed them to be—He then stated you remember that the appropriation of the seven $ million for the payment of Alaska to the Russia Govnt was hung up or brought to a dead lock in the H of Reps—While the appropriation was thus delayed the Russian minister stated to me that John W. Forney stated to him that he needed $30,000 that he had lost $40,000, by a faithless friend and that he wanted the $30,000 in gold—That there was no chance of the appropriation passing the House of Reps without certain influence was brought to bear in its favor—The 30,000 was paid hence the advocacy of the appropriation in the Chronicle—He also stated that $20,000 was paid to R. J. Walker and F. P. Stanton for their services—N. P. Banks chairman of the committee on foreign relations $8000, and that the incorruptable Thaddeous Stevens received as his "sop" the moderate sum of $10,000—All these sums were paid by the Russian minister directly and indirectly to the respective parties to secure appropriation of money the Govnt had stiputed to pay the Russian Govnt in solemn treaty which had been ratified by both Govmts.—

Banks and Stevens was understood to be the counsel for a claim against the Russian Govnt for Arms which had been furnished by some of our citizens—known as the Perkins Claim—Hence a fee for their influence in favor of the appropriation &c—Banks was chairman of the Committee on foreign retions—[25]

The "incorruptable Thaddeous" Stevens was a sick old man when the appropriation bill was under consideration. He died on August 11, a few days after Stoeckl began to withdraw the funds he had on deposit in the Riggs Bank. Even if he were on the Russian's "pay-off" list, as intimated, it was unlikely that he ever got his share.[26]

President Johnson's memorandum of Seward's statement of suspected recipients of Stoeckl's bounty is, of course, no proof that either Stevens or Banks actually received a bribe from the Russian Minister. On the other hand, if Seward was not certain of the facts, why did he make the statement to President Johnson, and why did the latter make a permanent record of it among his papers? These must remain among the many unanswered questions involving the mystery of the Alaska purchase.

Czar Alexander II was very pleased with Stoeckl's $7,200,000 deal, and ordered Prince Gortchakov to reward the Minister to Washington with a gift of 25,000 rubles. Stoeckl was disappointed. He felt that his government should have been more liberal, considering that he obtained $2,000,000 more for the cession than had been expected.[27]

Trained in Russian diplomacy, which had few scruples against using bribery as a means of achieving its ends, Stoeckl was nevertheless disgusted over the corruption, shady dealing and dirty work that had to be resorted to in order to get the bill approved. With his discreet bribes he had contributed liberally to the fetid, unsavory atmosphere he complained about. Nevertheless, as soon as the transaction was completed he requested the Russian Foreign Office to take him away from Washington and send him to "any other post" in the world—anywhere that he could forget the rough handling he had received from congressmen, lobbyists, "mercenary editors" and others in connection with the Alaskan transaction.[28]

Stoeckl's wish was granted. In October 1868, he was replaced in Washington by Constantine Catacazy, a wily, meddlesome intriguer who was poorly balanced for diplomatic service. He quickly proved himself offensive to the United States government, and his forced recall began the rupture of the Russo-American *entente cordiale* of Civil War days.

After a sojourn in the United States of more than a quarter of a century, Edouard de Stoeckl who loved to be called "Baron" although he possessed no title of nobility,[29] had failed utterly to gain a genuine understanding of the American people and their democratic institutions. Trained in the autocratic philosophy of Nicholas I, it was next to impossible for him to understand those who believed in the ideals of Lincoln. With the termination of his mission to Washington, he was free to return to his beloved Russia, where—in the words of Lincoln—"they make no pretense of loving liberty . . . where despotism can be taken pure, and without the base alloy of hypocrisy."

CHAPTER NOTES

All references identified by "S" refer to Edouard de Stoeckl's diplomatic dispatches to the Russian Foreign Office. They are known as "Central Archive, Moscow, Russia, Foreign Affairs, 49" and will be found in the Division of Manuscripts in the Library of Congress, Washington, D. C.

All dates are according to the Western (New Style) calendar. During the period covered by this book, the Russian (Old Style) calendar was twelve days behind that of the West; thus their July 2 would be equivalent to our July 14.

CHAPTER I

1. *The Illinois Journal*, Sept. 7, 1849 (original in Illinois State Historical Society, Springfield, Ill.); Nicolay and Hay, *Complete Works of Abraham Lincoln* (12 vols.), Vol. 2, pp. 127-28.
2. H. M. Flint, *Life of Stephen A. Douglas*, p. 49.
3. *The Illinois Journal*, Jan. 12, 1852.
4. Paul M. Angle, *New Letters and Papers of Lincoln* (1930), pp. 81-83.
5. Carl Sandburg, *Abraham Lincoln, The Prairie Years*, Vol. 2, p. 71.
6. Letter to Joshua Speed, Aug. 24, 1855. Nicolay and Hay, Vol. 2, p. 287.
7. Frank A. Golder, Russian-American Relations during the Crimean War. *American Historical Review*, Vol. 31 (1925-26), p. 464.
8. Golder, p. 465.
9. Archives of the Russian Foreign Office, Washington, No. 544, Nov. 4, 1854; second date not given. From Golder, p. 467.
10. Frank A. Golder, The Purchase of Alaska. *American Historical Review*, Vol. 25 (1919-20), p. 411. James Morton Callahan, The Alaska Purchase. *West Virginia University Studies in American History*, Series I, Nos. 1 and 2 (1908), p. 8.
11. Resolution favoring mediation, by Thomas L. Clingman in the House of Representatives, Dec. 11, 1854. *Congressional Globe*, Vol. 30, p. 76. Resolution of Charles Sumner in the Senate, Dec. 21, 1854. *Senate Journal*, 33rd Congress, 2nd Session, p. 63.
12. Archives of the Russian Foreign Office, Washington, Nos. 1370 and 1779, July 14, 1855. From Golder, Russian-American Relations, p. 472.

CHAPTER 2

1. S., No. 60, Dec. 23, 1860.
2. S., No. 60, Dec. 23, 1860.
3. S., No. 146, Jan. 4, 1861. From Frank A Golder, The American Civil War Through the Eyes of a Russian Diplomat. *American Historical Review*, Vol. 26, (1920-21), p. 456.
4. S., No. 1681, Aug. 27, 1856. From Golder, p. 455.
5. S., No. 60, Dec. 23, 1860.
6. S., No. 60, Dec. 23, 1860.
7. S., No. 60, Dec. 23, 1860.
8. S., No. 61, Dec. 31, 1860.
9. S., No. 61, Dec. 31, 1860.
10. S., No. 1, Jan. 15, 1861.
11. S., No. 2, Jan. 21, 1861.
12. S., No. 2, Jan. 21, 1861.
13. S., No. 2, Jan. 21, 1861.
14. S., No. 2, Jan. 21, 1861.
15. S., No. 62, Jan. 7, 1861.
16. S., No. 62, Jan. 7, 1861.
17. Gilbert A. Tracy, *Uncollected Letters of Abraham Lincoln*, p. 171.
18. Nicolay and Hay, Vol. 6, pp. 78-79.
19. S., No. 5, Feb. 2, 1861.
20. S., No. 7, Feb. 12, 1861.
21. S., No. 10, Feb. 18, 1861.
22. S., No. 11, Feb. 28, 1861.

CHAPTER 3

1. S., No. 3, Jan. 21, 1861.
2. S., No. 11, Feb. 25, 1861.
3. S., No. 10, Feb. 18, 1861.
4. S., No. 11, Feb. 25, 1861.
5. E. D. Adams, *Great Britain and the American Civil War* (2 vols., 1925), Vol. 1, pp. 115-7.

6. S., No. 11, Feb. 25, 1861.
7. S., No. 11, Feb. 25, 1861.
8. S., No. 15, March 12, 1861.
9. S., No. 15, March 12, 1861.
10. S., No. 15, March 12, 1861.
11. S., No. 15, March 12, 1861.
12. S., No. 18, March 25, 1861.
13. S., No. 20, April 9, 1861.
14. Frederick Bancroft, *William H. Seward*, Vol. 2, p. 117.
15. S., No. 810, April 7, 1861; Adams, Vol. 1, p. 54, note 1.
16. S., No. 20, April 9, 1861.
17. S., No. 22, April 14, 1861.
18. S., No. 26, April 15, 1861.
19. Bancroft, Vol. 2, p. 135.
20. S., No. 35, May 23, 1861.
21. S., No. 24, April 14, 1861.
22. Nicolay and Hay, *Abraham Lincoln, A History*, Vol. 3, pp. 445-47. Frederick Bancroft, Seward's Proposition of April 1, 1861 for a Foreign War and a Dictatorship. *Harper's Monthly*, Vol. 99 (1899), pp. 781-91.
23. Nicolay and Hay, *Works*, Vol. 5, p. 280.
24. Bancroft, *William H. Seward*, Vol. 2, p. 135.

CHAPTER 4

1. S., No. 27, April 27, 1861.
2. S., No. 27, April 27, 1861.
3. S., No. 30, May 6, 1861.
4. S., No. 30, May 6, 1861.
5. S., No. 32, May 13, 1861.
6. S., No. 33, May 13, 1861.
7. S., No. 35, May 23, 1861.
8. S., No. 39, June 3, 1861.
9. S., No. 46, July 3, 1861.
10. Richardson, *Messages and Papers of the Presidents*, Vol. 6, pp. 15-16, 18, 19.
11. On Battle of Bull Run and its effect upon the North, S., No. 50, July 21, 1861; No. 51, July 21, 1861; No. 52, July 26, 1861; No. 53, Aug. 4, 1861.
12. The Confederate loss was: killed, 387; wounded, 1,582; missing, 13; total, 1,982.
13. S., No. 52, July 26, 1861.
14. S., No. 53, Aug. 4, 1861.

15. S., No. 55, Aug. 13, 1861; No. 57, Sept. 9, 1861; No. 62, Oct. 6, 1861; No. 63, Oct. 21, 1861; No. 67, Nov. 5, 1861; No. 71, Dec. 3, 1861.
16. S., No. 55, Aug. 13, 1861.
17. S., No. 63, Oct. 21, 1861.
18. S., No. 68, Nov. 18, 1861.
19. S., No. 71, Dec. 3, 1861.
20. S., No. 57, Sept. 9, 1861.
21. S., No. 57, Sept. 9, 1861.

CHAPTER 5

1. S., No. 6, Jan. 4, 1860.
2. S., April 14, 1861 (no number); No. 24, April 14, 1861; No. 38, June 3, 1861.
3. S., No. 23, April 14, 1861.
4. S., No. 23, April 14, 1861
5. S., No. 35, May 23, 1861.
6. S., No. 42, June 17, 1861.
7. S., No. 37, June 3, 1861.
8. S., No. 37, June 3, 1861.
9. S., No. 35, May 23, 1861.
10. S., No. 40, June 10, 1861.
11. S., No. 68, Nov. 18, 1861.
12. S., No. 68, Nov. 18, 1861.
13. Titian J. Coffee, *Reminiscences of Abraham Lincoln* (edited by Allen Thorndike Rice), p. 245.
14. French Foreign Office, Vol. 126, No. 80, Jan. 14, 1862. Cited in F. L. Owsley, *King Cotton Diplomacy*, pp. 217-23.
15. Adams, *Great Britain and the American Civil War*, Vol. 1, pp. 281-3.
16. S., No. 34, May 5, 1862.
17. S., No. 1776, Sept. 28, 1862.
18. S., No. 79, Nov. 17, 1862.
19. S., No. 2, Jan. 26, 1863.
20. S., No. 2, Jan. 26, 1863.
21. S., No. 4, Feb. 10, 1863.
22. Seward to Dayton, Feb. 6, 1863, in Edward McPherson, *The Political History of the United States During the Great Rebellion*, pp. 345-346.
23. S., No. 10, Feb. 24, 1863.
24. John T. Morse, Jr., *Charles Sumner* (American Statesmen Series), p. 250-51. The details of Sumner's resolutions will be found in the *Congressional Globe*, March 3, 1863, pp. 1497-1541.

25. S., No. 12, March 2, 1863.
26. S., No. 17, March 10, 1863.
27. S., No. 14, March 2, 1863.

CHAPTER 6

1. Lincoln Papers (Library of Congress): Telegram, Blair to Clay, March 27, 1861; Mearns, Vol. 2, p. 493.
2. Lincoln Papers: Letter, Clay to Lincoln, March 28, 1861; Mearns, Vol. 2, p. 495.
3. Rice, ed., *Reminiscences of Abraham Lincoln*, pp. 299-300.
4. Henry Adams, *Letters of Henry Adams*, p. 92.
5. Lincoln Papers: Clay to Lincoln, May 11, 1861.
6. Lincoln Papers: No. 10024-5, Clay to Seward, from Paris, May 22, 1861; Mearns, Vol. 2, pp. 612-3.
7. Owsley, *King Cotton Diplomacy*, p. 208.
8. Lincoln Papers: Clay to Seward, May 22, 1861.
9. James R. Robertson, *A Kentuckian at the Court of the Tsars*, p. 46.
10. Diplomatic Correspondence of the U.S. in the Archives of the Department of State, June 21, 1861.
11. Lincoln Papers: No. 12084-5, Clay to Lincoln, from St. Petersburg, Sept. 27, 1861.
12. Lincoln Papers: No. 10880-4, Clay to Lincoln, private, July 25, 1861.

CHAPTER 7

1. Lincoln Papers: No. 14755-7, Clay to Lincoln, from St. Petersburg, March 1, 1862.
Robertson, p. 104.
2. Nicolay and Hay, *Complete Works*, Vol. 7, p. 79.
3. Nicolay and Hay, pp. 79-80.
4. Nicolay and Hay, pp. 80-81.
5. A. K. McClure, *Abraham Lincoln and Men of War Times*, pp. 164, 165.
6. *New York Herald*, Jan. 17, 1862.
7. Clay to Seward, Dispatches, Russia, Vol. 19, No. 22, April 13, 1862, in U.S. Dept. of State Manuscripts, 1860-1869. Washington.

8. Lincoln Papers: No. 16526-7, Clay to Lincoln, June 17, 1862.
9. James M. Callahan, Russo-American Relations during the Civil War. *West Virginia University Studies in American History*, Series I, No. 1.
F. W. Seward, *Life and Letters of William H. Seward*, Vol. 3, p. 49.
10. John Bigelow, *Retrospections of an Active Life*, Vol. 1, pp. 499-500.
11. Cameron to Seward, June 26, 1862, Dispatches, Russia, in U.S. Dept. of State Manuscripts, 1860-1869. Washington.
12. Lincoln Papers: No. 17632-3, Clay to Lincoln, from Washington, Aug. 13, 1862.
13. Lincoln Papers: No. 18303-4, Clay to Lincoln, from Washington, Sept. 9, 1862.
14. Quoted by Charles A. de Arnaud, *The Union and Its Ally Russia*, p. 25, *Cincinnati Gazette*, Aug. 19, 1862; Thomas, p. 129.
15. Rice, *Reminiscences*, pp. 302-4.
16. Lincoln Papers: No. 18735-6, Clay to Lincoln, from Washington, Sept. 29, 1862.
17. Lincoln Papers: Nos. 18733-4 and 19122, Clay to Lincoln, from Washington, Sept. 29, 1862 and Oct. 21, 1862.
18. Lincoln Papers: No. 19122, Clay to Lincoln, from Washington, Oct. 21, 1862.
19. Lincoln Papers: Nos. 21987-8 and 21989-91, Clay to Lincoln, from Washington, Feb. 26, 1863.
20. Lincoln Papers: No. 22521-2, Clay to Lincoln, from New York, March 19, 1863.
21. Lincoln Papers: No. 22780-3, Clay to Lincoln, private, from New York, April 2, 1863.

CHAPTER 8

1. Susan Dallas (ed.), *George Mifflin Dallas Diary*, p. 209.
2. *Journal of St. Petersburg*, Aug. 6, 1862.
Benjamin P. Thomas, Russo-American

Relations, 1815-1867. *Johns Hopkins Studies*, Series 48 (1930), pp. 130-31.
3. S., No. 57, Sept. 9, 1861.
4. S., No. 57, Sept. 9, 1861.
5. Notes, Russia, Vol. 5, Gortchakov to Stoeckl, Jan. 4, 1862; Thomas, p. 126.
6. S., No. 76, Feb. 24, 1862.
7. MS. Dispatches, Russia, Vol. 19, No. 16, Oct. 29, 1862. See Benjamin P. Thomas, *Russo-American Relations, 1815-67* (Johns Hopkins Studies, Ser. 48, 1930, p. 133).
8. Nicolay and Hay, *Abraham Lincoln, A History*, Vol. 6, pp. 66-67.
9. Russian Archives, Foreign Office to Stoeckl, Oct. 27, 1862 (Old Style); E. D. Adams, *Great Britain and the American Civil War*, Vol. 2, pp. 60, 63.
10. Palmerston MS., Russell to Palmerston, Oct. 20, 1862; Adams, Vol. 2, p. 54.
11. Taylor to Seward, Nov. 15, 1863. *Diplomatic Correspondence* (1863-64), Vol. 2, pp. 844-46, in U.S. Dept. of State Manuscripts, 1860-1869. Washington.
12. James M. Callahan, *The Diplomatic History of the Southern Confederacy*, p. 95. (See McPherson) Dispatches from U. S. Legation, Russia: Bayard Taylor to Seward, No. 30, March 3, 1863 (encloses intercepted communication of Judah P. Benjamin to Lamar); 14 Instr. Russia, Seward to Clay, No. 2, March 31, 1863.
13. S., No. 81, Dec. 1, 1862.
14. S., No. 82, Dec. 1, 1862.
15. S., No. 79, Nov. 17, 1862.
16. S., No. 81, Dec. 1, 1862.
17. S., No. 29, April 26, 1863.
18. S., No. 10, Feb. 24, 1863.
19. S., No. 10, Feb. 24, 1863.
20. Nicolay and Hay, *Abraham Lincoln, A History*, Vol. 6, pp. 68-76.
21. MS. Instructions, Russia, Vol. 14, No. 10, Dec. 23, 1862; Marie Hansen Taylor and Horace E. Scudder (eds.), *Life and Letters of Bayard Taylor*, Vol. 1, pp. 399-401; Diplomatic Correspondence (1863-64), Vol. 2, pp. 851-52.
22. S., No. 10, Feb. 24, 1863.
23. Taylor, Vol. 1, pp. 401-3.

CHAPTER 9
1. *Diary of Gideon Welles* (3 vols., 1911), Vol. 1, p. 443.
2. *Harper's Weekly*, Vol. 7 (Nov. 21, 1863), p. 746.
3. Same.
4. Same.
5. *Harper's Weekly*, Vol. 7 (Oct. 17, 1863), pp. 661-62.
6. Same, p. 662.
7. Same, p. 661.
8. *Harper's New Monthly Magazine*, Vol. 27 (1863), p. 848.
9. Welles, *Diary*, Vol. 1, pp. 480-81.
10. Tyler Dennett (ed.), *John Hay Diaries; Lincoln and the Civil War* (1939), p. 134.
11. Dennett, p. 128.
12. Earl S. Pomeroy, The Visit of the Russian Fleet in 1863. *New York State Historical Assn.*, Vol. 24 (1943), pp. 512-7.
13. Benjamin F. Gilbert, Welcome to the Czar's Fleet. *California Historical Society Quarterly*, San Francisco (March 1947), pp. 13-19.
14. Frank A. Golder, The Russian Fleet and the American Civil War. *American Historical Review*, Vol. 20 (1914-15), pp. 801-12.
15. Dennett, p. 137.
16. Schleiden MS; see G. B. Adams, *Great Britain and the American Civil War*, Vol. 1, p. 171.
17. *Harper's Weekly*, Vol. 7 (Oct. 17, 1863), p. 658.
18. *Life of Thurlow Weed, Including his Autobiography* (2 vols., 1883-84), Vol. 2, p. 346. Horace Cutter, Russia and America. *Overland Monthly*, 2d Ser., Vol. 20 (1892), pp. 311-3.
19. Weed, Vol. 2, p. 347.
20. Thomas L. Harris, *The Trent Affair* (1896), pp. 208-10.
21. Thomas W. Balch, *The Alabama Arbitration*, pp. 28-31. What We Owe to Russia. *New York Evening Express*, Sept. 1, 1874.

Chapter Notes

Chapter Notes

CHAPTER 10

1. Paul M. Angle, *New Letters and Papers of Lincoln*, pp. 81-82.
2. Nicolay and Hay, *Complete Works*, Vol. 6, p. 315.
3. Seward to Dayton, May 11, 1863, Messages and Documents, 38 Congress, 1 Session, Washington, 1864, pt. II, pp. 738-739, cited in Harold E. Blinn, Seward and the Polish Rebellion of 1863. *American Historical Review*, Vol. 17, (1939-40), pp. 828-33.
4. W. Read West, Contemporary French Opinion on the American Civil War. *Johns Hopkins Univ. Studies in Hist. and Polit. Sci.*, 1924. Quotation from *La Patrie*, Jan. 12, 1864.
5. James R. Robertson, *A Kentuckian at the Court of the Tsars*, pp. 149-50.
6. E. A. Adamov, Russia and the United States at the Time of the Civil War. *Journal of Modern History*, Vol. 2 (1930), pp. 586-611, esp. 603-7.
7. Frank A. Golder, The Russian Fleet and the American Civil War. *American Historical Review*, Vol. 20 (1914-15), pp. 803-4.
8. Adamov, pp. 603-7.
9. Adamov, p. 597.
10. John T. Morse, Jr., *Charles Sumner* (American Statesmen Series), p. 247.
11. MS Archives, Department of State: Foreign Relations, 1863.
12. John Bigelow, *Retrospections of an Active Life*, Vol. 1, p. 500, note 1. Jordan and Pratt, *Europe and the American Civil War*, p. 272.
13. Henry Clews, England and Russia in our Civil War. *North American Review*, Vol. 178 (1904), pp. 812-9.
14. Oscar S. Strauss, United States and Russia. *North American Review*, Vol. 181 (1905), p. 243.
15. Golder, p. 812.

CHAPTER 11

1. Professor A. D. White, The Development and Overthrow of the Russian Serf System. *Atlantic Monthly*, Vol. 10 (1862), pp. 538-52.
2. According to the statistics of the Russian Ministry of the Interior, there were 22,558,748 serfs in Russia on January 1, 1861, out of a total population of 60,143,478. These included 21,976,232 who were the personal property of the landowners, 541,962 who belonged to proprietors of factories and shops, and 40,554 who belonged to various other establishments.
3. Nathan Appleton, *Russian Life and Society*, ps. 184, 195, 200; *Atlantic Monthly* 8, pp. 39-57, July 1861; *Atlantic Monthly* 10, pp. 538-552, November 1862.
4. S., No. 28, April 22, 1862.
5. Nicolay and Hay, *Complete Works*, Vol. 8, p. 15.

CHAPTER 12

1. S., No. 2171, Dec. 1, 1862.
2. S., No. 69, Sept. 25, 1862.
3. Andrew D. White, *Autobiography*, Vol. 2, pp. 28-29. Also White, The Development and Overthrow of the Russian Serf System. *Atlantic Monthly*, Vol. 10 (1862), pp. 538-52.
4. Wharton Barker, The Secret of Russian Friendship. *The Independent*, Vol. 56 (March 24, 1904), 645-9.
5. Mr. Barker has written that during this memorable audience with Czar Alexander II on Aug. 17, 1879, the Russian Emperor also said to him:

In the autumn of 1862, the governments of France and Great Britain proposed to Russia, in a formal, but not in an official way, the joint recognition by European powers of the independence of the Confederate States of America. My immediate answer was: "I will not cooperate in such action; and I will not acquiesce. On the contrary, I shall accept the recognition of the independence of the Confederate States by France and Great Britain as a casus belli for Russia. And, in order that the governments of France and Great Britain may understand that this is no idle threat, I will send a Pacific fleet to

San Francisco and an Atlantic fleet to New York." *Sealed orders to both Admirals were given. My fleets arrived at the American ports; there was no recognition of the independence of the Confederate States by Great Britain and France. The American rebellion was put down, and the great American Republic continues. All this I did because of love for my own dear Russia, rather than for love of the American Republic. I acted thus because I understood that Russia would have a more serious task to perform if the American Republic, with advanced industrial development, were broken up and Great Britain should be left in control of most branches of modern industrial development.* The Independent, *Vol. 56 (1904), p. 648.*

CHAPTER 13

1. William Roscoe Thayer, *Life and Letters of John Hay* (2 vols., 1915), Vol. 1, pp. 196-7.
2. S., No. 55, July 22, 1862.
3. S., No. 57, Aug. 8, 1862.
4. S., No. 9, Feb. 24, 1862.
5. S., No. 9, Feb. 24, 1862; No. 15, March 11, 1862; No. 18, March 17, 1862; No. 19, March 28, 1862; No. 35, May 12, 1862.
6. S., No. 24, April 13, 1862.
7. S., No. 28, April 22, 1862.
8. S., No. 32, May 5, 1862.
9. S., No. 39, May 26, 1862.
10. S., No. 42, June 2, 1862.
11. S., No. 48, June 23, 1862.
12. S., No. 48, June 23, 1862.
13. S., No. 50, July 1, 1862.
14. S., No. 54, July 3, 1862.
15. S., No. 56, July 22, 1862.
16. S., No. 59, Aug. 8, 1862.
17. S., No. 63, Sept. 5, 1862; No. 64, Sept. 9, 1862.
18. S., No. 65, Sept. 9, 1862.
19. S., No. 64, Sept. 9, 1862.
20. S., No. 70, Sept. 25, 1862.
21. S., No. 75, Nov. 4, 1862.

22. S., No. 88, Dec. 16, 1862; No. 92, Dec. 22, 1862.
23. S., No. 97, Jan. 5, 1863.
24. S., No. 3, Jan. 26, 1863.
25. S., No. 100, Jan. 12, 1863.
26. S., No. 1, Jan. 26, 1863.
27. S., No. 8, Feb. 16, 1863.
28. S., No. 18, March 10, 1863.
29. S., No. 13, March 2, 1863.
30. S., No. 19, March 24, 1863.
31. S., No. 18, March 10, 1863.
32. S., No. 5, Feb. 10, 1863.
33. S., No. 9, Feb. 24, 1863.
34. S., No. 19, March 24, 1863.
35. S., No. 23, April 7, 1863.
36. S., No. 27, April 13, 1863.
37. S., No. 31, April 26, 1863.
38. S., No. 27, April 13, 1863.
39. S., No. 31, April 26, 1863.
40. S., No. 33, May 4, 1863.
41. As officially reported, the Union loss at Chancellorsville was 1,082 killed, 6,849 wounded, and 4,214 missing. Including the losses at Fredericksburg, Marye's Heights and Salem Church the Union loss in the entire campaign, April 27 to May 5, was 1,606 killed, 9,762 wounded, and 5,919 missing, an aggregate of 17,287. The Confederate loss during the campaign was 1,665 killed, 9,081 wounded, and 2,018 captured, an aggregate of 12,764.
42. S., No. 35, May 11, 1863.
43. S., No. 43, June 2, 1863. Confederate General Pemberton, defending Vicksburg, surrendered to Grant on July 4, 1863. Grant's losses in his entire Vicksburg campaign from April 30, including Sherman's siege of Jackson, were 1,243 killed, 7,095 wounded, and 535 missing. The exact Confederate losses are not known but have been estimated at 40,-000 men killed, wounded and captured.
44. Actually the force was under the command of General Jackson, whose army of 6,000 men was joined by Ewell with 8,000 and Edward Johnson with 3,000 men. Ballard, *The Military Genius of Abraham Lincoln*, pp. 85-86.
45. S., No. 44, June 16, 1863.
46. S., No. 48, June 22, 1863.

47. S., No. 51, July 6, 1863. As officially reported, the Union loss at Gettysburg was 3,072 killed, 14,497 wounded, and 5,434 missing, an aggregate of 23,003. The Confederate loss was 2,592 killed, 12,709 wounded, and 5,150 missing, an aggregate of 20,451.
48. S., No. 53, July 14, 1863.
49. S., No. 53, July 14, 1863.
50. S., No. 55, July 14, 1863.
51. S., No. 54, July 14, 1863.
52. S., No. 58, Aug. 2, 1863.
53. S., No. 61, Sept. 23, 1863.
54. S., No. 64, Sept. 23, 1863.
55. S., No. 66, Nov. 7, 1863.

CHAPTER 14
1. S., No. 74, Dec. 4, 1863.
2. Frank A. Golder, The American Civil War through the Eyes of a Russian Diplomat. *American Historical Review*, Vol. 26 (1920-21), 457.
3. S., Feb. 12, 1862 (no number).
4. S., No. 74, Dec. 4, 1863.
5. S., No. 81, Dec. 31, 1863.
6. S., No. 9, Feb. 19, 1864.
7. S., No. 66, Nov. 7, 1863.

CHAPTER 15
1. S., No. 1900, Dec. 11, 1864.
2. S., No. 16, March 28, 1864.
3. Channing, *History of the United States*, Vol. 6, p. 595.
4. S., No. 12, March 7, 1864.
5. S., No. 16, March 28, 1864.
6. S., No. 25, May 3, 1864.
7. S., No. 27, May 13, 1864.
8. Colin R. Ballard, *The Military Genius of Abraham Lincoln* (1952), p. 237.
W. E. Woodward, *Meet General Grant* (1928), pp. 202, 203.
T. Harry Williams, *Lincoln and his Generals* (1952), p. 312.
U. S. Grant, *Personal Memoirs* (World, 1952), see "Strategy" in the index to this edition.
9. S., No. 29, May 23, 1864.
10. S., No. 35, June 13, 1864.
11. S., No. 41, July 12, 1864.
12. S., No. 44, July 14, 1864.

13. S., No. 45, July 18, 1864.
14. S., No. 56, Oct. 17, 1864.
15. S., No. 59, Nov. 6, 1864.
16. S., No. 59, Nov. 6, 1864.

CHAPTER 16
1. S., No. 65, Dec. 5, 1864.
2. S., No. 70, Dec. 19, 1864.
3. S., No. 76, Dec. 31, 1864.
4. S., No. 6, Jan. 24, 1865.
5. S., No. 6, Jan. 24, 1865.
6. S., No. 7, Feb. 7, 1865.
7. S., No. 7, Feb. 7, 1865.
8. S., No. 8, Feb. 13, 1865.
9. S., No. 8, Feb. 13, 1865.
10. S., No. 8, Feb. 13, 1865.
11. S., No. 3, Jan. 24, 1865.
12. S., No. 523, March 13, 1865.
13. S., No. 19, March 21, 1865.
14. S., No. 21, April 4, 1865.
15. S., No. 23, April 10, 1865.
16. S., No. 23, April 10, 1865.
17. S., No. 32, May 2, 1865.
18. S., No. 21, April 4, 1865.
19. S., No. 23, April 10, 1865.
20. S., No. 6, Jan. 24, 1865.

CHAPTER 17
1. S., Aug. 15, 1867 (no number given); Frank A. Golder, The American Civil War through the Eyes of a Russian Diplomat. *American Historical Review*, Vol. 26 (1920-21), p. 461.
2. S., No. 24, April 14, 1865.
3. Robertson, *A Kentuckian at the Court of the Tsars*, p. 262.
4. S., No. 9, Feb. 28, 1866.
5. S., Jan. 24, 1865 (no number given); Golder, p. 461.

CHAPTER 18
1. J. F. Loubat (ed. by John D. Champlin, Jr.), *Fox's Mission to Russia*, p. 11.
2. Robertson, *A Kentuckian at the Court of the Tsars*, p. 194.
3. Loubat, pp. 10-21.
4. Same, pp. 44-45.
5. Same, pp. 46-47.
6. Same, pp. 88-90.

7. Same, pp. 302-5.
8. Same, p. 233.
9. Same, p. 101.
10. Same, p. 378.
11. Same, p. 292.
12. Same, p. 233.
13. Same, pp. 356-57.
14. Same, pp. 180-81.
15. Same, p. 345.
16. Same, pp. 243-44.
17. Same, pp. 254-58.
18. Albert Parry, Tolstoi Looks at America. *Asia Magazine*, Vol. 30 (1930), pp. 772-77.
19. Tolstoi Holds Lincoln World's Greatest Hero. Interview by Count S. Stakelberg, *New York World*, Feb. 7, 1909.

CHAPTER 19

1. Frank A. Golder, The Purchase of Alaska. *American Historical Review*, Vol. 25 (1919-20), p. 412.
2. James M. Callahan, The Alaska Purchase. *West Virginia University Studies in American History*, Series I, Nos. 1 and 2, p. 8.
3. Golder, pp. 415, 416.
4. Moorefield Storey, *Charles Sumner*, p. 339.
5. Golder, pp. 413, 418.
6. Callahan, p. 23.
7. Russian Dispatches, Clay to Seward, May 10, 1867; Callahan, p. 21.
8. Callahan, p. 23.

9. *Congressional Globe*, Vols. 40-42, Appendix, pp. 386-88.
10. John Bigelow, in *New York Sun*, Jan. 5, 1902.
11. Callahan, p. 21.
12. Robertson, p. 236.
13. *Letters of Franklin Lane* (Anne W. Lane and Louise H. Wall, eds.), pp. 260-61.
14. William A. Dunning, Paying for Alaska. *Political Science Quarterly*, Vol. 27 (1912), pp. 385-398.
15. Dunning, p. 392.
16. H. R. Rep. Fortieth Congress, Third Session, No. 35, pp. 40-43; Dunning, p. 393.
17. For accounts of the Perkins claim, see Robertson, Chapter 17; Golder, pp. 422-23; Dunning, pp. 390-91.
18. Dunning, p. 391.
19. Golder, p. 423.
20. Golder, p. 423.
21. Robertson, p. 207.
22. Dunning, pp. 395-96.
23. Dunning, p. 392.
24. Dunning, pp. 392-95.
25. Dunning, pp. 385-86.
26. Dunning, pp. 397-98.
27. Golder, p. 421.
28. Golder, p. 424.
29. In 1864 Stoeckl was made a privy counselor but was granted no title of nobility. See Hunter Miller, Russian Opinion of the Cession of Alaska. *American Historical Review*, Vol. 48 (1942-43), p. 521.

BIBLIOGRAPHY

ADAMOV, E. A. *Russia and the United States at the Time of the Civil War*, Journal of Modern History (1930) II, 586-602.

ADAMS, CHARLES FRANCIS (son). *Charles Francis Adams*. Boston: Houghton Mifflin Co., 1900.

ADAMS, EPHRAIM DOUGLASS. *Great Britain and the American Civil War*. Longmans, Green & Co., 1925.

ADAMS, HENRY. *Letters of Henry Adams*, (1858-1891), Worthington C. Ford, ed. Boston: Houghton Mifflin Co., 1930.

ANGLE, PAUL MCCLELLAND, ed. *New Letters and Papers of Lincoln*. Boston: Houghton Mifflin Co., 1930.

APPLETON, NATHAN. *Russian Life and Society*. Boston: Appleton-Century Co., 1904.

DE ARNAUD, CHARLES A. *The Union and its Ally Russia*. Washington: Gibson Bros., 1890.

Atlantic Monthly, Vol. VIII, July 1861, No. XLV, pp. 39-57; Vol. X, Nov. 1862, pp. 538-552.

BAILEY, THOMAS A. *America Faces Russia*. Ithaca, N. Y.: Cornell University Press, 1950.

BALCH, THOMAS W. *The Alabama Arbitration*. Philadelphia: Allen, Lane & Scott, 1900.

BALLARD, BRIG. GEN. COLIN R. *The Military Genius of Abraham Lincoln*. Cleveland and New York: The World Publishing Co., 1952.

BANCROFT, FREDERIC. *The Life of William H. Seward*, 2 vols. New York: Harper & Bros., 1900.

BARINGER, WILLIAM. *Lincoln's Rise to Power*. Boston: Little, Brown & Co., 1937.

BARINGER, WILLIAM E. *A House Dividing*. Abraham Lincoln Assn., 1945.

BARKER, WHARTON. *The Secret of Russian Friendship*, in the Independent LVI, March 24, 1904.

BARNES, THURLOW WEED. *Memoir of Thurlow Weed*, by his grandson. Boston: Houghton Mifflin Co., 1884. Vol. I is the Autobiography of Thurlow Weed.

BEMIS, SAMUEL F., ed. *American Secretaries of State*. New York: Alfred A. Knopf, 1927-1929, 10 vols.

BIGELOW, JOHN. *Retrospections of an Active Life*, 5 vols. New York: Baker & Taylor Co., 1909-1913.

BIGELOW, JOHN. *Retrospections of an Active Life*. New York: Baker & Taylor Co., 1909.

BLINN, HAROLD E. *Seward and the Polish Revolution of 1863*, American Historical Review, (Richmond) July 1940, vol. 45, p. 828-833.

BRIGHT, JOHN. *The Diaries of John Bright*, R. A. J. Walling ed. London, 1932.

BUCHANAN, JAMES. Mr. Buchanan's Administration on the Eve of the Rebellion. New York: D. Appleton & Co., 1866.

BUEL, CLARENCE C. and JOHNSON, ROBERT U. *Battles and Leaders of the Civil War*, 4 vols., New York: The Century Company, 1887.

CALLAHAN, JAMES MORTON. *Russo-American Relations During the American Civil War*. Morgantown: West Virginia University Studies in American History, 1908, Series I, Diplomatic History, No. 1.

———. *Diplomatic History of the Southern Confederacy*. Johns Hopkins University Studies, 1901.

Central Archive, Moscow, Russia, Foreign Affairs, 49 (Library of Congress, Washington).

CHARNWOOD, LORD. *Abraham Lincoln*. London: Constable & Co., Ltd., 1916.

CLAY, CASSIUS MARCELLUS. *The Life of Cassius Marcellus Clay, Memoirs, Writings and Speeches*. Cincinnati, J. F. Brennan & Co., 1886.

CLEWS, HENRY. *England and Russia in Our Civil War*, North American Review, vol. 178, June 1904.

CURTIS, GEORGE T. *Life of James Buchanan*. New York: Harper and Bros., 1883, 2 vols.

CUTTER, HORACE F. *Russia and America*, Overland Monthly, 2nd ser., vol. 20, July-Dec. 1892.

DALLAS, GEORGE MIFFLIN. Diary, ed. by Susan Dallas. Philadelphia: John Lippincott, 1892.

DANA, CHARLES A. *Lincoln and His Cabinet*. Cleveland and New York: Devine Press, 1890.

DAVIS, JEFFERSON. *The Rise and Fall of the Confederacy*, 2 vols. New York: Appleton and Co., 1881.

DE ARNAUD, CHARLES A. *The Union and Its Ally Russia*. Washington: Gibson Bros., 1890.

DENNETT, TYLER, ed. *Lincoln and the Civil War in the Diaries and Letters of John Hay*. New York: Dodd, Mead & Co., 1939.

Department of State Records, Washington, D. C.

Diplomatic Correspondence, National Archives, Washington, D. C.

DUNIWAY, CLYDE AUGUSTUS. *Maximilian of Mexico* (Reasons for the Withdrawal of the French from Mexico) in American Historical Assn. Annual Report, Washington, 1902.

DUNNING, WILLIAM A. *Paying for Alaska*, Political Science Quarterly XXVII, No. 3, Sept. 1912.

FLINT, HENRY MARTYN. *Life of Stephen A. Douglas*. Philadelphia: Potter, 1863.

FOSTER, JOHN W. *A Century of American Diplomacy*. New York: Houghton Mifflin Co., 1901.

GILBERT, BENJAMIN F. *Welcome to the Czar's Fleet*, California Historical Society Quarterly (San Francisco), March 1947, p. 13-19.

GOLDER, FRANK ALFRED. *The American Civil War Through the Eyes of a Russian Diplomat*, American Historical Review (1921) XXVI, No. 3, 454-463.

———. *Bering's Voyages*. New York: American Geographical Society, 1922.

———. *History of Russia*, by Sergiei Fedorovich Planotov, translated by E. Aronsberg, edited by F. A. Golder. New York: The Macmillan Co., 1925.

———. *Guide to Materials for American History in Russian Archives*, vol. II (Washington, Carnegie Institution, 1937).

———. *The Purchase of Alaska*, American Historical Review XXV, 411-425.

———. *Russian Expansion on the Pacific*, 1641-1850. Cleveland: The Arthur H. Clark Co., 1914.

———. *The Russian Fleet and the Civil War*, American Historical Review (1915) XX, No. 4, 801-812.

GRAHAM, STEPHEN. *Tsar of Freedom*. New Haven: Yale University, 1935.

GRANT, ULYSSES SIMPSON. *Personal Memoirs*. New York: C. L. Webster & Co., 1885-1886; Cleveland and New York: The World Publishing Co., 1952.

Harper's Weekly, (New York) 1861-1865.

HARRIS, THOMAS LEGRAND. *The Trent Affair*. Indianapolis & Kansas City: The Bowen-Merrill Co., 1896.

HART, ALBERT BUSHNELL. *Salmon Portland Chase*. Boston and New York: Houghton Mifflin Co., 1899.

HAWKINS, GENERAL RUSH CHRISTOPHER. *The Coming of the Russian Ships in 1863*. North American Review, 1903, vol. 178, p. 539-544.

HENDRICK, BURTON J. *Lincoln's War Cabinet*. Boston: Little, Brown & Co., 1946.

HENRY, ROBERT S. *The Story of the Confederacy*. Indianapolis: The Bobbs-Merrill Co., 1936.

HERTZ, EMANUEL. *Abraham Lincoln, A New Portrait*, 2 vols., New York, Horace Liveright, Inc., 1931.

HILDT, JOHN C. *Early Diplomatic Negotiations of the United States with Russia*, Johns Hopkins University Studies in History and Political Science, 1906, Ser. 24, Nos. 5-6.

HOLMES, OLIVER WENDELL. *Poetical Works*. Boston: Houghton Mifflin Co., 1887.

JOHNSON, ROBERT U. and BUEL, CLARENCE C. *Battles and Leaders of the Civil War*, 4 vols., New York: The Century Company, 1887.

JORDAN, DONALDSON and PRATT, EDWIN J. *Europe and the American Civil War*. Boston: Houghton Mifflin Co., 1931.

KARPOVICH, MICHAEL and VERNADSKI, GEORGI V. *A History of Russia*. New Haven: Yale University Press, 1943.

KOHLER, PHYLLIS PENN, ed. and translator from the French. *The Journals of the Marquis Astolphe de Custine*. New York: Pellegrini & Cudahy, 1951.

KRASNYI, ARKHIV. (Red Archives). Vol. 38, *The Role Russia Played During the American Civil War, 1861-65*; vol. 52, *The Sale of Alaska*; vol. 94, *The Visit of the Russian Fleet to the United States*; vols. 4, 7, 22, 40, 57, 61, *The Polish Uprisings of 1863*.

Lane, Frank. *Letters,* edited by Anne W. Lane and Louise H. Wall. Boston and New York: Houghton Mifflin Co., 1922.

Laserson, Max M. *The American Impact on Russia.* New York: The Macmillan Co., 1950.

Latane, John Holladay. *A History of American Foreign Policy.* New York: Doubleday, Page & Co., 1927.

Leech, Margaret. *Reveille in Washington, 1860-1865.* New York: Harper & Bros., 1941.

Lester, C. Edwards. *The Life and Public Services of Charles Sumner.* New York: United States Publishing Co., 1874.

Lewis, Lloyd. *Sherman, Fighting Prophet.* New York: Harcourt, Brace & Co., 1932.

Lincoln Papers, Robert Todd Lincoln collection, Library of Congress, Washington, opened to public, 1947.

Loubat, Joseph Florimond. *The Fox Mission to Russia in 1866,* ed. by John D. Champlin, Jr. New York: D. Appleton & Co., 1879.

Martin, Percy F. *Maximilian in Mexico.* New York: Charles Scribner's Sons, 1914.

McClure, Alexander K. *Abraham Lincoln and Men of War-Times.* Philadelphia: The Times Publishing Co., 1892.

McMaster, John B. *History of the People of the United States during Lincoln's Administration,* New York: Appleton & Co., 1927.

McPherson, Edward. *The Political History of the United States during the Great Rebellion.* Washington: Philip & Solomons, 1882.

Mearns, David D. *The Lincoln Papers,* The Story of the Collection with Selections to July 4, 1861, 2 vols. New York: Doubleday & Co., Inc., 1948.

Monaghan, Jay. *Diplomat in Carpet Slippers.* Indianapolis: The Bobbs-Merrill Co., 1945.

Moore, John Bassett, ed. *Works and Papers of James Buchanan.* Philadelphia and London: J. P. Lippincott Co., 1908.

Morse, John T., Jr. *Abraham Lincoln,* 2 vols. Boston and New York: Houghton Mifflin Co., 1893.

Nevins, Allan. *Ordeal of the Union,* 2 vols. New York: Charles Scribner's Sons, 1947.

———. *The Emergence of Lincoln,* 2 vols. New York: Charles Scribner's Sons, 1950.

Nicolay, John G. and Hay, John. *Abraham Lincoln: A History.* New York: The Century Co., 1890.

———, eds. *Complete Works of Abraham Lincoln.* New York: Francis D. Tandy Co., 1905.

Official Records of the Union and Confederate Armies, published by the United States in 130 volumes, with 138,579 pages of text and 1,006 maps and charts.

Owsley, Frank Lawrence. *King Cotton Diplomacy.* Chicago: University of Chicago Press, 1931.

PARKES, HENRY B. *History of Mexico.* Boston: Houghton Mifflin Co., 1938.

PARRY, ALBERT. *Cassius Clay's Glimpse into the Future,* Russian Review, New York 1943, vols. 2, No. 2, pp. 52-67.

POMEROY, EARL S. *The Visit of the Russian Fleet in 1863,* New York State Historical Association, October 1943, XXIV, 512-517.

POORE, BENJAMIN PERLEY. *Perley's Reminiscences of Sixty Years in the National Metropolis,* 2 vols. Philadelphia: Hubbard Brothers, 1886.

RANDALL, J. G. *Lincoln the President,* 2 vols. New York: Dodd, Mead & Co., 1945.

RHODES, JAMES FORD. *History of the United States from the Compromise of 1850,* 8 vols.; New York: Harper & Bros. and The Macmillan Co., 1893-1919.

RICE, ALLEN THORNDIKE, ed. *Reminiscences of Abraham Lincoln by Distinguished Men of His Time.* New York: North American Publishing Co., 1886.

RICHARDSON *Messages and Papers of the Presidents of the United States,* 20 vols., New York: Bureau of National Literature, Inc., 1897.

ROBERTSON, JAMES ROOD. *A Kentuckian at the Court of the Tsars.* Berea, Ky.: Berea College Press, 1935.

RUBINCHEK, LEONID, ed. and translator, Krasnyi Arkhiv (Red Archives). *The American Slavic and East European Review* VI, No. 18-19, Columbia University Press.

SANDBURG, CARL. *Abraham Lincoln: The War Years.* New York: Harcourt, Brace & Co., 1939.

SCHURZ, CARL. *Speeches, Correspondence and Political Papers of Carl Schurz,* 6 vols., Frederic Bancroft, ed. New York: G. P. Putnam's sons, 1913.

——. *Reminiscences of Carl Schurz,* 2 vols. New York: The McClure Co., 1907-1908.

SEWARD, FREDERICK W. *Seward at Washington, as Senator and Secretary of State,* 2 vols., New York, 1891.

——. *Reminiscences of a War-Time Statesman and Diplomat,* 1830-1915. New York: G. P. Putnam's Sons, 1916.

SEWARD, WILLIAM HENRY. *Speech in the Senate of the U.S., March 9, 1852, Against the Armed Intervention of Russia in the Hungarian Revolution.* Washington: Buell & Blanchard, 1852, 28, 3rd ed.

SHAW, ALBERT. *Abraham Lincoln: His Path to the Presidency.* New York: Review of Reviews Corp., 1929.

——. *Abraham Lincoln: The Year of His Election.* New York: Review of Reviews Corp., 1929.

SHEAHAN, JAMES W. *The Life of Stephen A. Douglas.* New York: Harper & Bros., 1860.

SHERIDAN, P. H. *Personal Memoirs,* 2 vols. New York: Charles L. Webster & Co., 1891.

SOROKIN, PITRIM A. *Russia and the United States.* New York: Literary Classics, E. P. Dutton & Co., 1944.

Sparks, Edwin E., ed. *The Lincoln-Douglas Debates of 1858.* Springfield: Illinois State Historical Library, 1908.

Storey, Moorefield. *Charles Sumner,* Standard Library edition. Boston and New York: Houghton Mifflin Co., 1900.

Strauss, Oscar S. *United States and Russia,* North American Review, vol. 181 (August 1905), pp. 237-250.

Sumner, Charles. *The Works of Charles Sumner.* Boston: Lee and Shepard, 1870-1883, 15 vols.

Taylor, Bayard. *Life and Letters,* ed. by Marie Hansen Taylor and Horace E. Scudder. Boston: Houghton Mifflin Co., 1884.

Thayer, William Roscoe. *Life and Letters of John Hay,* 2 vols. Boston: Houghton Mifflin Co., 1915.

Thomas, Benjamin Platt. *Russo-American Relations,* 1815-1867. Johns Hopkins University Studies (1930) Series XLVIII, No. 2.

———. *A Russian Estimate of Lincoln,* Abraham Lincoln Association, Bulletin No. 23, 3-6 (1931).

Tocqueville, Alexis de. *Democracy in America,* the Henry Reeve text as revised by Francis Bowen, and further corrected and edited with introduction, etc., by Phillips Bradley. New York: Alfred A. Knopf, 1945.

Tracy, Gilbert A., ed. *Uncollected Letters of Abraham Lincoln.* Boston: Houghton Mifflin Co., 1917.

Vernadski, Georgi V. and Michael Karpovich. *A History of Russia.* New Haven: Yale University Press, 1943.

Vernadski, Georgi V. *Political and Diplomatic History of Russia.* Boston: Little, Brown & Co., 1936.

Weed, Harriet A. and Barnes, Thurlow Weed, editors. *Thurlow Weed,* 2 vols., 1883-1884. Boston: Houghton Mifflin Co.
Vol. II of this set is *Memoir of Thurlow Weed* by his Grandson.

Welles, Gideon. *Diary of Gideon Welles,* ed. by John T. Morse, 3 vols. Boston: Houghton Mifflin Co., 1911.

West, W. Read. *Contemporary French Opinion on the American Civil War.* Johns Hopkins University Studies in Historical and Political Science, LXII, No. 1, 1924.

White, Andrew D. *Autobiography of Andrew Dickson White.* New York: The Century Co., 1905, 2 vols.

Williams, T. Harry. *Lincoln and His Generals,* Alfred A. Knopf, 1952.

Woldman, Albert A. *Lawyer Lincoln.* Boston: Houghton Mifflin Co., 1936.

Woodward, W. E. *Meet General Grant.* New York: Horace Liveright, 1928.

INDEX

143, 144; illness prevents (President from) entertaining Russians, 146, 147; 153; attitude on Polish question, 158-159, 161; on secession, 159; 164; *Harper's Weekly* cartoon, 165; 167; and emancipation, 172-179; reply to Greeley's *Prayer of Twenty Millions* editorial, 174-175; and Thirteenth Amendment, 178-179; Emancipation, 179, 181; criticized by Stoeckl, 182-185; "Lincoln's war," 190-191; call for troops, 194; and conscription, 196; 197-198; and battle of Chancellorsville, 204; differences among advisors, 211-212; Stoeckl on Lincoln, McDowell and McClellan, 219; re-election opposed, 226-227; renomination, 234; re-election doubted, 239; reply to Greeley, 239; confident, 241; re-elected, 242-243; and peace negotiations, 245-246; refuses armistice, 247-248; threat of ruin, 248; second inauguration, 250; appearance, 250; address, 251; reported uncertain of final victory, 253; 257; assassination, 261; Stoeckl's comments, 262; 267; tribute by Prince Stcherbatov, 270; tribute by Basile Kokorev, 270-271; tribute by Count Leo Tolstoi, 271-276; and Russian telegraph line, 279; 285; on Russian despotism, 290
Lincoln, Mary Todd, 147
Lisboa, Senhor de, 46
Lisovski, Rear Admiral, 141, 142, 149, 161, 163, 267, 268
London *Times*, 107, 110, 191
Longstreet, General James, 214
Louisiana secedes, 27, 33
Lyons, Richard Bickerton Pemell, Lord, 50-51, 56, 86, 87, 95, 96, 102

McClellan, Captain George B., observer in Crimean War, 11; General, replaces McDowell, 74-75; fails to attack, 77-78; defeat in Peninsular campaign, 95
McDowell, General Irvin, 71, 72, 219
McLean, Justice John, 21
Manassas Gap, 72

Marcy, William L., Secretary of State, 11, 12, 13
Marshall, Samuel S., 6
Marx, Karl, *Communist Manifesto*, 3
Maryland, 38, 59, 60, 63, 74
Massachusetts, 58
Maximilian, Emperor of Mexico, 86
Mazzini, Giuseppe, 8
Meade, General George Gordon, 209-211
Mercier, Henri, French Minister, 56, 86, 87, 90, 94, 96, 97-98, 99, 102, 158
Merrimac and *Monitor*, 192-193
Mexico, 102, 263
Miantonomoh, 263
Mississippi convention, on slavery, 168
Missouri Compromise, 18
Missouri *Republic*, 160
Mobile, Alabama, 224, 228
Moscow, 267, 268

Napoleon III, Emperor Louis, of France, 11, 86, 90, 91, 94; presses for European coalition to recognize Confederate States, 95, 97, 99, 101, 102, 125; plan for armistice, 132; solo attempt at mediation, 137, 138; attitude on Polish affair, 157-158, 263
New Orleans, 211
New York, City of, 267, 268
New York *Herald*, 116, 135
New York *Tribune*, 18, 62, 247
New York *World*, 143
Nicholas I, Czar of Russia, 3, 4, 13, 109, 125, 170, 279, 290
Nicolay, John G., 132, 153, 190
Nizhni Novgorod Fair, 268

Palmerston, Henry John Temple, Viscount, British Prime Minister, 95, 107, 112, 133
Patterson, General Robert, 71, 72
Peck, Ebenezer, 6
Pensacola, Florida, 34
Perkins, Benjamin, claim, 286, 287, 289
Peter the Great, Emperor, 143, 169
Petersburg, Virginia, 239
Philadelphia *Press*, 288
Pickens, Francis W., 25